SOCIO-ECONOMIC SURVEYS
of Three Villages in Andhra Pradesh

A STUDY OF AGRARIAN RELATIONS

Edited by

V. K. Ramachandran   Vikas Rawal   Madhura Swaminathan

Research and Writing

Madhura Swaminathan   Vikas Rawal   R. Ramakumar
Niladri Sekhar Dhar   Pallavi Chavan   Biplab Sarkar
Shamsher Singh   Aparajita Bakshi   Paramita Ghosh
Navpreet Kaur   Meghna Dutta   V. K. Ramachandran

FOUNDATION for
AGRARIAN
STUDIES

Tulika Books

Published by

Tulika Books

35 A/1 (third floor), Shahpur Jat, New Delhi 110 049

in association with

Foundation for Agrarian Studies

www.agrarianstudies.org

First published in India 2010

ISBN: 978-81-89487-67-6

Printed in Delhi

SOCIO-ECONOMIC SURVEYS
of Three Villages in Andhra Pradesh

A STUDY OF AGRARIAN RELATIONS

Foreword

The study of agrarian relations is still a neglected subject. Mainstream academics often ignore the importance of the radical transformation of agrarian structure as a necessary condition for the further development of the economy and of society. The research wings of international organisations such as the World Bank make grudging references to obsolete agrarian relations, but push for corporate commercial agriculture as the means to overcome this impediment. That is why the vast body of research promoted by these organisations hardly takes up the study of agrarian relations. That task is left to the few individual academics and institutions that are conscious of the importance of the study of agrarian relations in transforming our country into a modern, progressive nation. One such institution, the Foundation for Agrarian Studies, has undertaken the difficult task of studying emerging changes in agrarian relations in various states as part of its seven-year Project on Agrarian Relations in India. Andhra Pradesh was the first state to be selected for study.

Because of their preoccupation with the day-to-day work of organisation and agitation, activists of mass organisations of kisans and agricultural labour are unable to study agrarian relations systematically. Close collaboration is needed between academics and activists in order to combine theoretical insights, scientific methods and empirical experience to arrive at an understanding that is, in turn, useful for mass mobilisation. I believe that the present collaboration between the All-India Kisan Sabha and the Foundation for Agrarian Studies is a good example for emulation by others.

The study of agrarian relations in Andhra Pradesh has been sporadic. Although many village studies have been conducted, the study of agrarian relations *per se* has received less attention. P. Sundarayya's surveys in 1974 of Ananthavaram and

Kaza villages in Guntur district were pioneering studies in this field. In my opinion, the present study is, to a certain extent, carrying forward that effort and may indeed spur further studies. This study will help organisations and activists who are working among the rural masses to understand the issues facing the peasantry and rural workers, and to fine-tune their strategies of mobilisation.

The present book is a result of the huge efforts of the team of scholars, investigators and technical staff who worked for this project. I congratulate them on their valuable work.

Hyderabad   B.V. Raghavulu
29 December 2009

Preface

This volume is a field report on surveys of three villages in Andhra Pradesh. The surveys were conducted in December 2005 and May–June 2006 by scholars and field investigators of the Foundation for Agrarian Studies, as a part of the Foundation's Project on Agrarian Relations in India (PARI).

Andhra Pradesh was the first state from which villages were selected for study as a part of PARI. The study villages were Ananthavaram village in Kollur mandal, Guntur district; Bukkacherla village in Raptadu mandal, Anantapur district; and Kothapalle village in Thimmapur L.M.D. mandal, Karimnagar district. The selection of Ananthavaram as the first village to be studied also had special analytical and symbolic significance for the organisers: it was one of two villages surveyed by P. Sundarayya and others in 1974.

The surveys were conducted in Andhra Pradesh in two rounds: the first round in December 2005 and the second in May–June 2006. The December 2005 surveys (Andhra Pradesh Round 1) were census-type surveys that covered all households in each village. The May–June 2006 surveys, which focussed on household and individual incomes and employment, were stratified random sample surveys. Some of the estimates from the 2005 and 2006 surveys are therefore not strictly comparable.

This volume is called a "survey report" because it reports results from the analysis of statistical data collected through the village surveys. We have not analysed, for instance, the history of the study areas, or government policies or documents, in order to place our findings in historical or policy context, nor have we reviewed the extensive scholarly literature on the economy and society in Andhra Pradesh. We do believe, however, that this report can be read and used as an independent document. We have analysed data by socio-economic class and by social group, and hope that the report contributes information, statistical data and analysis to the discussion on agrarian relations, livelihoods and economic distress in contemporary rural Andhra Pradesh and India.

A very large part of the data that we have collected remains to be analysed. Two areas that come to mind immediately and are, we find, of substantial contemporary relevance, are land transfers and the impact of the land market on agrarian relations, and migration from and between rural areas.

In this volume, we have presented material separately for socio-economic classes, and for Dalit, Adivasi, Backward Class and Muslim households.[1] A more detailed analysis of the caste-wise data, and of the dominant castes of different villages, must also await later study, as must a more detailed, including qualitative, analysis of issues of wage labour and employment. The chapters that are presented here have been written to a deadline, and the members of the writing team plan to write more detailed papers on these and related subjects in the future.

The report draws on the work of field investigators, data entry assistants, data analysts and social scientists. Special contributions were made to the writing of individual chapters in this volume by R. Ramakumar and Pallavi Chavan (on indebtedness and credit markets), R. Ramakumar (on agricultural conditions in Andhra Pradesh), Niladri Sekhar Dhar (employment), Paramita Ghosh (literacy and education), Biplab Sarkar (crop incomes), Shamsher Singh (household amenities), and the editors.

The surveys and this report were made possible by the effort, support, advice and knowledge of many organisations and individuals. They include the PARI field investigators and technical data-entry staff, the Andhra Pradesh Committees of the All-India Kisan Sabha and All-India Agricultural Workers' Union, Venkatesh Athreya, V. Anila, J. Baburao, Indira Chandrasekhar, Geyanand, J. Jayaram, Jayshree Kewalramani, S. Mahendra Dev, Surjya Kanta Mishra, K. Nagaraj, R. Kuppa Naidu, S. Ramachandran Pillai, V. Rambhupal, D. Rama Devi, P. Narasimha Rao, N. Venugopala Rao, S. Malla Reddy, B. Sambi Reddy, Abhijit Sen, Sri Rama Rural High School in Chilumuru, Sundarayya Vijnana Kendra, V. Surjit, B. Tulasidas, K. Tulasi Vishnu Prasad, the staff of Tulika Books, K. Varadha Rajan, G. Vijaya Krishna and John Wesley.

---

[1] In all the chapters, the category "Other Castes" refers to Hindus who are not from Scheduled Caste (Dalit), Scheduled Tribe (Adivasi) or Backward Class households.

V.K. Ramachandran and Madhura Swaminathan are grateful for support from the Indian Statistical Institute, Kolkata. Vikas Rawal thanks the Centre for Economic Studies and Planning, Jawaharlal Nehru University, New Delhi.

We owe a special debt of gratitude to B.V. Raghavulu, secretary of the Andhra Pradesh State Committee of the CPI(M), and long-time student of agrarian relations in the state, who facilitated the research and urged us to write this report — and to do so with no further delay, and to an alarmingly tight deadline.

Kolkata
30 December 2009

V.K. Ramachandran
Vikas Rawal
Madhura Swaminathan

Contents

Tables

CHAPTER 5

CHAPTER 10

1

The Project on Agrarian Relations and the Three Study Villages: An Introduction

Since 2005, the Foundation for Agrarian Studies has been engaged in a Project on Agrarian Relations in India (PARI). The Project was designed and is conducted in consultation with the All India Kisan Sabha, the All India Agricultural Workers' Union, and the All India Democratic Women's Association.

The objectives of PARI are to study and analyse:

- village-level production, production systems and livelihoods, and the socio-economic characteristics of different strata of the rural population;
- sectional deprivation in rural India, particularly with regard to the Dalit and Scheduled Tribe populations, women, specific minorities and the income-poor; and
- the state of basic village amenities and the access of rural people to the facilities of modern life.

The study is being conducted over a period of about seven years. In every selected state, our practice is to survey two or three villages in different agro-ecological and socio-economic regions. The villages studied will ultimately represent a wide range of regions in the country.

Our team conducts a census-type survey that covers every household and individual in each village. A village-level questionnaire is also canvassed in each village. In addition, a village profile, based on existing sources of secondary data, is constructed. Our archive also includes photographs of the surveyed villages.

The information collected in the census questionnaire covers the following:

- Demographic data
- Education levels

Features of the Economy of Rural Andhra Pradesh

The state of Andhra Pradesh was formed on 1 November 1956, bringing together the regions of coastal Andhra, Rayalaseema and Telangana. At the time of its formation, the state was predominantly an agrarian society. In 1960–61, about 59 per cent of the state's domestic product came from the agricultural sector. According to data from the Census of India 1961, about 80 per cent of male workers and 85 per cent of female workers in rural Andhra Pradesh were either cultivators or agricultural labourers (Unni 1989). Even when rural and urban areas are considered together, 71 per cent of male workers and 82 per cent of female workers were either cultivators or agricultural labourers.

In 1961, within workers in agriculture in rural areas, 47 per cent of male workers and 41 per cent of female workers were classified as cultivators. Similarly, 26 per cent of male workers and 43 per cent of female workers were classified as agricultural labourers. In 1961, the proportion of workers in Andhra who were cultivators was lower, and the proportion of workers who were agricultural labourers higher, than the corresponding share of workers in India as a whole. Data from the Agricultural Labour Enquiry of 1956–57 show that 36 per cent of all rural households in Andhra Pradesh earned the major share of their income from agricultural labour. In rural India as a whole, the corresponding share was 25 per cent (Unni 1989).

Big landowners were a major feature of Andhra Pradesh's agrarian economy in the 1950s. In 1953–54, the bottom 50 per cent of rural households in the state owned just 1 per cent of the total owned area (Sharma 1994). At the other extreme, the top 20 per cent of rural households owned 83 per cent of the total owned land. In 1953–54, the Gini coefficient for the distribution of ownership holdings (which measures the extent of concentration of ownership) in Andhra Pradesh was 0.80, which was higher than the Gini coefficient for India, 0.75 (Sharma 1994).

Much later, when P. Sundarayya organised his village surveys in 1974, the situation was largely similar. He wrote about Ananthavaram village that,

> A study of the distribution of land according to the various categories of holdings shows a tremendous concentration of land in

Ananthavaram village . . . While 412 families accounting for 50.3 per cent of the total number in the village had no land at all, 40 families, owning over 10 acres each and constituting five per cent of the total, hold 53.2 per cent of all the land. (Sundarayya 1977: 54).

At the time of the formation of Andhra Pradesh, the major crops grown in the state were paddy and other cereals. In the period 1962–65, paddy was cultivated in 28 per cent of gross cropped area in the state (Bhalla and Singh 2001). About 38 per cent of gross cropped area was cultivated with other cereals (including millets). Pulses were cultivated in about 12 per cent of gross cropped area. In all, food grain was culti-vated on about 78 per cent of gross cropped area in 1962–65. The major non-food crops cultivated were oilseeds and cotton. Oilseeds were cultivated in about 13 per cent of the gross cropped area, and cotton occupied about 3 per cent of the gross cropped area.

There were major regional variations in the development of the agrar-ian economy in the 1950s and 1960s. One important indicator of these variations is the disparity in the spread of irrigation. Right from the days of state formation, Rayalaseema and the southern parts of Telangana were dry regions, backward in irrigation development and prone to fre-quent drought. In 1956–57, only 16 per cent of the net area sown in Rayalaseema and only 19 per cent of the net area sown in Telangana was irrigated. On the other hand, Coastal Andhra was the most prosper-ous region in Andhra Pradesh, benefiting particularly from the irrigation projects of the colonial period that harnessed the Krishna and Godavari rivers. In 1956–57, about 43 per cent of the net area sown in Coastal Andhra was irrigated.

The regional variations in the conditions of agriculture were described by P. Sundarayya thus:

While the Circar districts were comparatively more developed eco-nomically, socially and politically, with a number of projects and other irrigation facilities, the Rayalaseema districts are backward in all re-spects, with a backward agriculture, no big projects and more domi-nation of feudal relations and oppression. There were hardly any big industries except in Vizagapatam district, where the shipbuilding yard owned by the Scindias and the two jute mills owned by Europeans were situated. The rest of the working class was mostly dependent for its livelihood on petty industries such as tobacco, mica mines, foundries, rice and oil mills, etc. (Sundarayya 2006: 102).

* * *

Between the 1950s and 2000s, while important changes have taken place in the structure and growth of Andhra Pradesh's rural economy, some of its basic historical features have remained largely unaltered. These broad features of change may be summarised as below.

First, the implementation of land reforms in Andhra Pradesh has been a major failure. While early reforms did succeed in weakening the old intermediaries, erstwhile landlords have continued to hold on to large tracts of land under different guises. Land reform has not yet provided security of tenure for tenants in the state. Estimates by various studies show that about 30 per cent of the total cultivated land is under informal or concealed tenancy. Rents continue to be very high under tenancy contracts. Confiscation and redistribution of ceiling surplus land has been slow. Data put together in the Andhra Pradesh Human Development Report show that "against an estimated surplus land of 20 lakh acres, only 7.9 lakh acres were declared surplus, of which 6.47 lakh acres were taken possession by the government and 5.82 lakh acres were distributed" (CESS 2008: 65). The area of land actually distributed formed only 4 per cent of net sown area in the state.

Data from the landholding surveys of the NSSO show that even in 2003, about 3 per cent of the households in rural areas of the state owned about 37 per cent of the total land owned. In other words, while subdivision of holdings among the upper-caste landlord families has reduced the average size of land owned, land concentration on the one hand and landlessness on the other continue to be features of contemporary rural life in Andhra Pradesh. In 2003, about 53 per cent of all households, about 65 per cent of Dalit households and about 49 per cent of Adivasi households in rural Andhra Pradesh did not own any land other than homesteads (Bakshi 2008a). If we consider *absolute* landlessness, 14 per cent of rural households in the state were landless in 2003, while the corresponding share for rural India was 10 per cent.

Secondly, while the share of persons dependent on agriculture for livelihood has not fallen significantly over the years, the share of the state's income from agriculture has fallen sharply. According to the 2001

Census, cultivators accounted for 23 per cent of the work force, while agricultural labourers accounted for another 40 per cent of the work force. In other words, although 63 per cent of the work force continued to depend on agriculture for their livelihood, agriculture and allied sectors contributed only 25 per cent to the state's domestic product (at constant prices) in 2006–07, as compared to 59 per cent in 1960–61. The falling share of income from agriculture, unaccompanied by a concomitant fall in the share of the work force dependent on agriculture, has led to increased pressure on land and water resources.

Thirdly, the cropping pattern in the state has undergone changes over the years. The share of food grain in the gross cropped area fell sharply, from 78 per cent in the period 1962–65 to 54 per cent in the period 1997–2000 (Kubo 2005). The major reason for the fall in the area cultivated with food grain was the fall in the area cultivated with coarse cereals. The share of area under coarse cereals in gross cropped area fell from 38 per cent in 1962–65 to 11 per cent in 1997–2000. Paddy continues to be the most important food grain, occupying about 31 per cent of gross cropped area in 1997–2000.

The area cultivated with non-food grain crops increased from 22 per cent of gross cropped area in the period 1962–65 to 46 per cent of gross cropped area in the period 1997–2000. Within non-food grain crops, the major growth in area was in oilseeds, whose share in the gross cropped area increased from 13 per cent in 1962–65 to 20 per cent in 1997–2000. Within oilseeds, it was the area under groundnut that grew most sharply. The other major non-food grain crop whose cultivation increased between the 1960s and 1990s was cotton. As a share of gross cropped area, the area cultivated with cotton grew from 3 per cent in 1962–65 to 8 per cent in 1997–2000.

In 2006-07, the share in gross cropped area of the major crops cultivated in the state were as follows: food grain (57 per cent), paddy (31 per cent), pulses (15 per cent), oilseeds (18 per cent), cotton (8 per cent).

Fourthly, the nature of irrigation development changed greatly in the state between the 1950s and 2000s. In 1956–57, about 27 per cent of the gross cropped area was irrigated. In 2006–07, about 47 per cent of the gross cropped area was irrigated (DES 2007). However, data from the Agricultural Census show that much of the recent increase in irrigated area was the result of an increase in area "partly irrigated" (and

not area "wholly irrigated"). Of the total area wholly and partly irrigated, the share of wholly irrigated area actually fell in the 1980s and
1990s.

Public investment in irrigation in Andhra Pradesh has fallen in recent
decades, and this fall has affected the development of irrigation ad-
versely. The annual growth rate of public gross fixed capital formation
in agriculture fell from 7.6 per cent in the 1980s to 3.9 per cent in the
1990s (CESS 2008). The growth rate of private gross fixed capital formation also fell from 5.2 per cent in the 1990s to (–)1.7 per cent in the
1990s — an absolute fall in capital formation. One of the consequences
of poor investment in irrigation was the decline in irrigated area itself.
Official data show that the total net irrigated area in Andhra Pradesh fell
from 44 lakh hectares in 1990–91 to 37 lakh hectares in 2004–05 — a
throwback to the levels of 1980–81 (CESS 2008).

The sources of irrigation have also undergone major changes. In
1970, 49 per cent of the net irrigated area in the state was irrigated by
canals, while 30 per cent was irrigated by tanks and 17 per cent with
groundwater (CESS 2008). In 2006–07, canals irrigated only 36 per
cent and tanks only 14 per cent of the net irrigated area. The major
share of net irrigated area (47 per cent) was irrigated by groundwater.
The most important new source of groundwater was tube wells, which
irrigated 32 per cent of the net irrigated area in 2006–07; other dug
wells accounted for the remaining 15 per cent share.

The sharpest growth in the area cultivated with tube-well irrigation in
Andhra Pradesh took place after 1987. In the 1990s, while there was
continuing growth, albeit slow, in the area cultivated with tube wells, the
area cultivated with canal and tank irrigation actually declined.

A phenomenal growth of tube wells in the state took place in
Telangana, followed by Rayalaseema, where the development of surface irrigation has historically been poor. Data from the Agricultural
Census show that in 1980–81, there was only one district in the state
(West Godavari) where more than 10 per cent of the holdings was
irrigated with tube wells. However, by 1995–96, there were eleven districts (West Godavari, East Godavari, Adilabad, Medak, Rangareddy,
Mahbubnagar, Kurnool, Anantapur, Cuddapah, Nellore and Chittoor)
where more than 10 per cent of the holdings was irrigated with tube
wells. Out of these eleven districts, there were five districts (Medak,
Rangareddy, Mahbubnagar, Anantapur and Cuddapah) where more than

one-third of the irrigated holdings was irrigated with tube wells in 1995–96.

Falling investment in surface irrigation and the poor recharge of wells have, over the years, contributed to the overexploitation of groundwater in the state. In Rayalaseema and Telangana, where dependence on groundwater is the highest, heavy investments incurred in the installation of tube wells have rendered the economics of cultivation fragile. In the 1990s and 2000s, loans taken for installing tube wells have been an important reason for the rising burdens of debt on poor and marginal peasants.

* * *

The agrarian economy of Andhra Pradesh has been characterised as having entered "an advanced state of crisis" from 1991–92, when neoliberal policies began to be implemented in India, (GoAP 2005: 1). The role of imperialism in the formulation of these new policies has introduced new dimensions to the contradictions of the earlier regime — that is, the failure of the Indian state to resolve the agrarian question.

Economic reforms after 1991 weakened the institutional support structures for agriculture in India. The protection offered to agriculture from imports was removed, resulting in a fall in prices of many commodities. As part of fiscal reform, major input subsidies were brought down relative to the size of the agricultural economy. Public capital formation in agriculture continued to fall, and the growth of public expenditure on research and extension slowed down. The policy of social and development banking ceased to be official policy. Policies on land use underwent significant changes. Regulated markets came to be treated as obstacles to efficient marketing. Land reform was, in practice, taken off the official agenda.

An important aspect of this "advanced state of crisis" in Andhra Pradesh was stagnation in the growth of agricultural output in the 1990s and beyond. Between 1980–81 and 1991–92, the aggregate value of crop output increased by 2.7 per cent per annum. However, the growth rate declined significantly, to 0.4 per cent per annum, between 1991–92 and 2004–05 (CESS 2008). In particular, the growth rate in output of paddy, oilseeds and cotton fell after 1991–92. There were two phases after 1991–92: a period of mild deceleration of output growth between 1991–92 and 2001–02, and a period of sharp deceleration of output growth after 2001–02. Different aspects of the impact of liberalization, for example, on the costs of cultivation, household incomes and credit markets, have been discussed and analysed in the chapters that follow.

It was in the dry regions of Rayalaseema and Telengana that deceleration of growth was the sharpest after 1991–92 (GoAP 2005). Stagnation affected small and marginal farmers, tenant farmers and rural labourers disproportionately (GoAP 2005).

The most visible manifestation of the agricultural stagnation and crisis after 1991–92 was the large number of suicides by farmers in the state. According to data compiled by the Andhra Pradesh Rythu Sangam, there were 4,403 suicides by farmers between 1998 and 2006. The largest number of suicides were reported from the Telangana region (2,927), followed by Rayalaseema (931) and Coastal Andhra (545).

- Schooling, reasons for absence from school, and dropping out (data are for 6 to 14-year-olds)
- Occupation and work status
- Ownership and operational landholding of assets
- Tenurial status
- Cropping pattern and crop production
- Ownership of assets
- Participation in government schemes
- Household electricity, sanitation and water facilities
- Housing
- Incomes and earnings
- Patterns and levels of employment
- Indebtedness

The following rounds have thus far been completed under PARI:

Andhra Pradesh Rounds 1 and 2, December 2005 and May 2006
Uttar Pradesh Round, July 2006
Rajasthan Round, May–June 2007
Maharashtra Round, May–June 2007
Madhya Pradesh Round, May–June 2008
Karnataka Round, May–June 2009

ANDHRA PRADESH ROUNDS

Village Selection

Andhra Pradesh was the first state from which villages were chosen for study. As is well known, the state of Andhra Pradesh is conventionally divided into five agro-ecological zones.[1] They are:

1. North Coastal Andhra (Srikakulam, Visakhapatnam and Vijayanagaram districts);
2. South Coastal Andhra (West Godavari, East Godavari, Krishna, Guntur, Prakasam and Nellore districts);
3. North Telangana (Adilabad, Warangal, Nizamabad, Khammam and Karimnagar districts);
4. South Telangana (Mahbubnagar, Medak, Rangareddy, Nalgonda and Hyderabad districts); and
5. Rayalaseema (Chittoor, Cuddapah, Kurnool and Anantapur districts).

After consultations with the leaders of the agrarian movement in Andhra Pradesh, we decided to conduct our survey in one village of each of the following three regions:

South Coastal Andhra. We selected Guntur district, which is a typically paddy-dominated area.

North Telengana. We decided to select an agricultural economy where irrigation is from borewells and the cropping pattern is a combination of food grain and other crops. The districts most typical of such agriculture are Karimnagar and Nizamabad in North Telangana. We selected Karimnagar district for the second village survey.

Rayalaseema. We decided to choose a village from Anantapur district, which is India's most drought-prone district after Jaisalmer in Rajasthan.

Within each of the selected districts, we prepared a shortlist of villages (using a set of criteria that included population size, index of irrigation and type of irrigation). From the first region, we decided purposively to resurvey Ananthavaram, a

---

[1] For detailed studies on the characteristics of each of these zones and contrasts between them, including disparities in agricultural development, see Rao and Mahendra Dev (2003) and Rao and Subrahmanyam (2002).

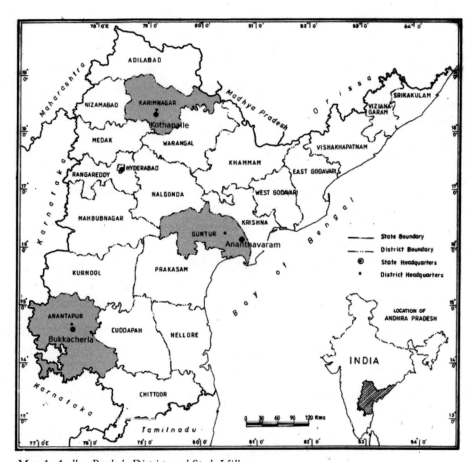

Map 1 *Andhra Pradesh: Districts and Study Villages*

village surveyed by P. Sundarayya in 1974. For the second region, we prepared a shortlist of villages based on three census data-based criteria (population in the modal size class of 500–900 households, an irrigation index of 45 to 65, and a village with the share of groundwater-irrigated area to total area between 40 and 90 per cent). From this shortlist, after visits and discussions with local persons, Kothapalle P.N. of Thimmapur LMD mandal was selected.

For the third region, a shortlist of villages was prepared using three similar criteria (population between 250 to 650 households, irrigation index between 7 and 16 per cent, and share of groundwater in total irrigation between 70 and 85 per cent), and after preliminary inquiries, Bukkacherla village in Raptadu mandal was selected.

Survey Method

In each of the three villages, a census-type survey of households was conducted in December 2005.

In order to collect detailed data on employment and incomes, a second-round sample survey was conducted in May 2006 in the three villages. The sampling methodology used for the follow-up survey is described below.

In each village, households were divided into different strata on the basis of the extent of landownership. Sampling proportions for each stratum were chosen to ensure that households in the stratum were adequately represented in the sample. Within each stratum, households were sorted by caste and the actual size of ownership holding. Then a circular systematic sample with a random start was drawn. The sample sizes in Ananthavaram, Bukkacherla and Kothapalle were 153, 99 and 102 households respectively (see Annexure).

Ananthavaram

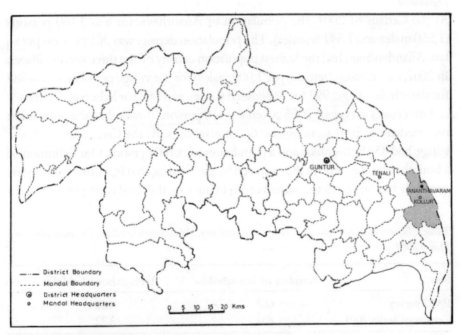

Map 2 *Ananthavaram village, Kollur mandal, Guntur district*

Location

Ananthavaram village is in Kollur mandal, Guntur district. The nearest town and railway station are at Tenali, which is 17 km away. The mandal headquarters, Kollur, is 8 km away. The village has a concrete all-weather road passing through it. It is on a regular bus route, with a bus available at least every 45 minutes. There are two bus stops in the village. Other means of regular transport for people and goods are transport autorickshaws, jeeps and small motor-vans.

There is a post office in the village, a ration shop, a branch of the Andhra Bank, a medical store and two public telephone booths. There is, however, no public health care facility, although two private medical practitioners have consultation rooms in the village. The nearest Primary Health Centre is at Kollur, and the nearest sub-divisional hospital and private hospitals are at Tenali.

The area of the village, according to the Census of 2001, is 1,029 hectares or 2,543 acres.

Population

At the Census of 2001, the population of Ananthavaram was 3,100 persons (1,550 males and 1,541 females). The population density was 301 persons per sq km. Ananthavaram had the highest population density of the three survey villages. In 2001, the sex ratio (females per 1,000 males) for the village population was 988 for the whole village, 993 for Scheduled Castes and 982 for Scheduled Tribes.

Our census survey of 2005 covered 2,410 persons (lower than the population reported at the 2001 Census) and 667 households. At the Census of 2001, the village had 834 households and a population of 3,100 persons. Our definition of a household is the same as the one used by the Census, that is, a group of persons generally belonging to the same family, living together and eating from a com-

Table 1 *Number of households and average household size, Ananthavaram village, December 2005 and March 2001*

Source	Number of households	Average household size
PARI survey	667	3.62
Census of India 2001	834	3.72

Note: PARI = Project on Agrarian Relations in India.
Source: Survey data and Census of India 2001.

Table 2 *Distribution of population by caste, Ananthavaram village, December 2005*

Caste	Male	Female	Total	% of total population
Mala (SC)	284	292	576	23.9
Madiga (SC)	250	234	484	20.1
Other Scheduled Castes	4	7	11	0.5
All Scheduled Castes	**538**	**533**	**1071**	**44.5**
Yanadi (ST)	34	31	65	2.7
Yerukala (ST)	46	47	93	3.9
All Scheduled Tribes	**80**	**78**	**158**	**6.6**
Kamma	222	256	478	19.8
Other Castes	89	100	189	7.8
BC	220	231	451	18.7
Muslim	32	29	61	2.5
Unspecified	1	1	2	0.1
Total	**1182**	**1228**	**2410**	**100.0**

Note: (i) "Other Castes" include Brahmin, Kapu, Naidu, Nayar, Reddy, Telaga, Vaishya.
(ii) SC = Scheduled Caste.
(iii) BC = Backward Class.
(iv) "Backward Class" includes Chakali/Rajaka, Dudekula, Yadava, Gouda, Mangali, Nai Brahmin, Kamsali, Mudiraj, Surya Vansha (Rajulu), Padmasali.

Source: Survey data.

mon kitchen. The difference suggests some emigration from the village between 2001 and 2005.

Ananthavaram is a multi-caste village with a significant Dalit population (Table 2). Members of Dalit households constituted 44.5 per cent of the population, while members of Adivasi households formed 6.6 per cent of the population and members of households of the Kamma caste (the dominant landholding caste) constituted 19.8 per cent of the population.

Land use, irrigation and cropping pattern
According to official statistics on land use reported in the Census of India, 2001, 87 per cent of the village land area was available for cultivation. There was no culturable waste land, forest land or unirrigated land in the village.

A detailed account of cropping patterns and irrigation has been provided in chapter 6. Survey data from the census-type survey of December 2005 indicate that the index of multiple cropping in the village in the preceding agricultural year was 1.7. Such an intensity of cropping was achieved because 79 per cent of the gross cropped area in the village covered by the sample survey was irrigated.

Ananthavaram is irrigated by the waters of the Krishna river. The entire net sown area of the village is, by official records, cultivated in the kharif season. The surface irrigation system is fed by the Varalapuram canal, which comes from the Prakasam barrage on the Krishna river in Vijayawada. Water is not released for irrigation from December through June, and the Irrigation Department ensures that Krishna water is not used for irrigation during these months. In response to petitions from the people and from legislators, water is sometimes released during these months to serve drinking-water ponds. There are no village-level institutions for water-sharing between villages or between cultivators in the village.

Although official data suggest that almost the entire extent of cultivated land in the village was classified as being under canal irrigation, data from our census-type survey of December 2005 show that supplementary irrigation from ground-water was almost the norm on area officially classified as solely under the canal irrigation system. Only 12 per cent of gross cropped area was solely under surface irrigation, 24 per cent was solely dependent on groundwater irrigation and 55 per cent was under irrigation from both sources.

Ananthavaram was selected as being characteristic of a village from the paddy-dominated tracts of south coastal Andhra. In the kharif season, paddy cultivation dominated the sown area of the village. The two most important crops in the rabi season were maize and black gram. Sugarcane was cultivated through the year. Although a total of twenty-five crops were listed in our 2005 survey as having been cultivated in the village, four crops — paddy, maize, black gram and sugarcane — accounted for 95 per cent of the gross cropped area. Ananthavaram differed from the district-level cropping pattern in having almost no cultivation of oilseeds, cotton or tobacco.

The average yield of paddy (Table 3) in Ananthavaram at our sample survey

Table 3 *Average yields of selected crops, India, Andhra Pradesh and Ananthavaram, 2005–06* (tonnes per hectare)

Crop	India	Andhra Pradesh	Ananthavaram
Paddy	3.5	4.9	4.7
Maize	1.9	4.1	6.2

Source: Survey data and Government of India (2008).

was around 4.7 tonnes per hectare, which is similar to the average production of the state in 2005–06, which was 4.9 tonnes per hectare.[2] The average yield of rabi maize in the village at our survey, 6.2 tonnes per hectare, was substantially higher than the state average of 4.1 tonnes per hectare.[3]

Bukkacherla

Map 3 *Bukkacherla village, Raptadu mandal, Anantapur district*

[2] Government of India (2008).
[3] *Ibid.*

Location

Bukkacherla village is located in Raptadu mandal, Anantapur district. The mandal headquarters, Raptadu, is 9 km away, and Anantapur, the nearest town and rail-head, is 15 km away. The approach road to the village is a katcha road and difficult to travel on during the monsoon. There is no bus to the village, though autorickshaws and motor-vans from Gandlaparthy village pass through, depending on passenger demand.

There is a post office in the village, a ration shop and one pay-telephone booth. There are no regular stores but there is a weekly market. There is a cooperative bank in the village of Gandlaparthy, 6 km away. The nearest commercial bank is in Anantapur. The nearest Primary Health Centre is at Raptadu. For any other medical services, private and public, people have to go to Anantapur.

The area of the village, according to the Census of India 2001, is 1944.9 hectares.

Population

At the Census of 2001, the population of Bukkacherla was 1,383 persons (712 males and 671 females). Bukkacherla had the lowest population density among the three survey villages, 71 persons per sq km. In 2001, the sex ratio for the village population was 942 for all persons and 1000 for Scheduled Caste persons.

Our census survey of 2005 covered 292 households and 1,228 persons (Table 4). At the Census of 2001, the village reported a population of 296 households and 1,383 people.

Members of households of the dominant landholding Kapu caste constituted 39.3 per cent and members of Dalit households constituted 19.5 per cent of the population in Bukkacherla. People from the three caste groups — Kapu, Dalit and Kuruba — constituted some 71 per cent of the population.

According to data from the Census of India 2001, 88 per cent of the village land area was cultivated land and the rest was not available for cultivation. The village had 79 hectares of culturable waste land but no forest land. The important feature of land use was, of course, that unirrigated land accounted for 89 per cent of the land under cultivation. Bukkacherla was and remains a dry village, dependent on rainfall for irrigation.

The main source of irrigation in the district of Anantapur has always been groundwater. Official data on the village indicate that the major source of irrigation is water from wells fitted with electric pump-sets. Residual irrigation is pro-

Table 4 *Number of households and average household size, Bukkacherla village, December 2005 and March 2001*

Source	Number of households	Average household size
PARI survey	292	4.18
Census of India 2001	296	4.67

Note: PARI = Project on Agrarian Relations in India.
Source: Survey data and Census of India 2001.

Table 5 *Distribution of population by caste, Bukkacherla village, December 2005*

Caste	Male	Female	Total	% of total population
Kapu	252	231	483	39.3
Other Castes	47	40	87	7.1
Mala (SC)	33	30	63	5.1
Madiga (SC)	80	97	177	14.4
All Scheduled Castes	**113**	**127**	**240**	**19.5**
Boya (BC)	37	46	83	6.8
Yadava/Golla (BC)	35	31	66	5.4
Kuruba/Kuruma (BC)	76	76	152	12.4
Other BC	43	42	85	6.9
Muslim	17	15	32	2.6
Total	**620**	**608**	**1228**	**100.0**

Note: (i) "Other Castes" include Kamma, Karawal, Komati, Reddy, Vaishya.
(ii) SC = Scheduled Caste.
(iii) BC = Backward Class.
(iv) "Other Backward Class" includes Ediga, Balija, Chakali/Rajaka, Ekila, Gouda, Mangali, Kummara, Vaddelu.
Source: Survey data.

vided by tanks. Between 1991 and 2001, according to Census of India data, there was a steep decline in total irrigated area, from 292 hectares to 178 hectares.

Only 9 per cent of gross cropped area in Bukkacherla was irrigated in 2005–06.[4] Typically, therefore, there was a single agricultural season in the village, with cultivation occurring mainly in kharif.

A major shift in cropping pattern occurred in the district in the 1980s towards

[4] Survey data 2006.

Table 6 *Average yields of selected crops, India, Andhra Pradesh and Bukkacherla, 2005–06* (tonnes per hectare)

Crop	India	Andhra Pradesh	Bukkacherla
Paddy	3.5	4.9	4.7
Groundnut	1.2	7	7

Source: Survey data and Government of India (2008).

the cultivation of oil seeds (in this case, mainly groundnut). In 1980–81, according to official statistics, 40 per cent of the cropped area in Anantapur was sown to oilseeds. By 1990–91, the share of oilseeds was 77 per cent and it remained 78 per cent in 2000–01. The expansion of area under oilseeds was counterbalanced by a decline in the area under cotton, pulses and cereals such as sorghum (jowar).

As the data in chapter 6 show, 74 per cent of gross cropped area in the village was planted to groundnut intercropped with red gram, with another 5 per cent covered by the sole cultivation of groundnut. In addition to land in the command area of a tank (the major source of the little surface irrigation present in the village), there was a small, dynamic sector of drip irrigation, where chilli, water-melon, tomato, brinjal, orange, sweet lime and musk melon were grown.

Groundnut yields in Bukkacherla were in the vicinity of the state average (official data for groundnut yields are, of course, for stand-alone crops, while our survey data are mainly for intercropped groundnut), as were paddy yields (see Table 6).

Kothapalle P. N.

Location

Kothapalle village is located in Thimmapur (Lower Maner Dam Colony) mandal, Karimnagar district. The village is 5 km away from the mandal headquarters at Thimmapur. The road to Thimmapur is a pucca road, constructed recently under the Pradhan Mantri Gram Sadak Yojana scheme. The nearest town is Karimnagar, which is 16 km away. The village is situated on the main Hyderabad to Karimnagar highway, a fact that has major consequences for the village economy. There is a bus stop in the village, and a bus passes through every 10 minutes. It is also easy to find an autorickshaw or motor-van passing through the village en route to the

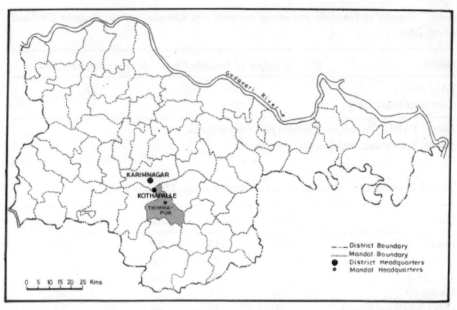

Map 4 *Kothapalle village, Thimmapur mandal, Karimnagar district*

district headquarters. The village is well-connected in terms of road transport, but the nearest railhead is at Kazipet, about 84 km away.

The village has a post office, a ration shop and two pay-telephone services. There is a weekly market. The nearest commercial bank branch is at Thimmapur. Thimmapur has a Primary Health Centre and Nustlapur (6 km away) has a subdivisional hospital. Karimnagar has a district hospital, and several private hospitals and nursing homes. There are two medical stores in the village.

The area of the village, according to the Census of India, is 715.5 hectares.

Population

At the Census of 2001, as Table 7 shows, the population of Kothapalle was 390 households and 1,534 persons (751 males and 783 females). The population density was 214 persons per sq km. In 2001, the sex ratio for the village population was 1,043 females per 1000 males. Our village census survey covered 1,436 persons and 372 households.

This is a multi-caste village. The village has an almost equal number of persons from the two major landholding castes, Reddys and Goudas. Members of Dalit households comprised 30 per cent of the population (Table 8).

Table 7 *Number of households and average household size, Kothapalle village, December 2005 and March 2001*

Source	Number of households	Average household size
PARI survey	372	3.8
Census of India 2001	390	3.9

Note: PARI = Project on Agrarian Relations in India.
Source: Survey data and Census of India 2001.

Table 8 *Distribution of population by caste, Kothapalle village, December 2005*

Caste	Male	Female	Total	% of total population
Reddy	147	142	289	20.1
Other Castes	27	29	56	3.9
Mala (SC)	79	90	169	11.8
Madiga (SC)	101	114	215	15.0
Other Scheduled Castes	20	25	45	3.1
All Scheduled Castes	**200**	**229**	**429**	**29.9**
Gouda (BC)	165	163	328	22.8
Yadava/Golla (BC)	54	93	147	10.2
Other BC	64	59	123	8.6
Kuncha yerukala (ST)	7	10	17	1.2
Yerukala (ST)	9	11	20	1.4
Other Scheduled Tribes	1	2	3	0.2
All Scheduled Tribes	**17**	**23**	**40**	**2.8**
Muslim	13	10	23	1.6
Unspecified	1	0	1	0.1
Total	**688**	**748**	**1436**	**100.0**

Note: (i) "Other Scheduled Castes" include Nethakani.
(ii) SC = Scheduled Caste.
(iii) BC = Backward Class.
(iv) "Other Backward Class" includes Padmasali, Chakali/Rajaka, Goldsmith, Kamsali, Kummari, Mangali, Vadrangi, Viswabrahmin.
(v) "Other Castes" include Kamma, Kapu (Munnuru Kapu), Vaisya, Brahmin.
Source: Survey data.

Land use, irrigation and cropping pattern

According to official statistics on land use (cited in the Census of India 2001), there has been a more than four-fold increase in area under irrigation, and a corresponding fall in unirrigated area, between 1991 and 2001. This change is explained by the construction of the Lower Maner Dam (LMD). The extent of cultivable waste land and land not available for cultivation also increased, the latter having also to do with the submergence of large tracts of village land in the LMD reservoir. Open wells and borewells are the main sources of groundwater.

Construction of the dam raised the water table in the village, and according to the Census, irrigated area of the village increased by 232 acres between 1991 and 2001 on account of increased groundwater irrigation.

Although there has been an expansion of irrigation in the village, our survey shows that the quality of groundwater irrigation was unreliable. Kharif thus continues to dominate seasonal cropping in the village.

The two most important crops were maize and paddy. Maize was sown separately and was also intercropped with pulses. Groundnut, cowpea and cotton were also sown in the village. Orchards of mango and other fruit trees (lime, mango, coconut and pomegranate) accounted for almost 5 per cent of gross cropped area. Tapping toddy from palmyra trees was an important village occupation.

Paddy yields in Kothapalle (4.3 tonnes per hectare in kharif) were lower than in Ananthavaram and Bukkacherla (Tables 3, 6 and 9). Maize yields were also lower than the state average.

Table 9 *Average yields of selected crops, India, Andhra Pradesh and Kothapalle, 2005–06* (tonnes per hectare)

Crop	India	Andhra Pradesh	Kothapalle
Maize	1.9	4.1	1.9
Paddy	3.5	4.9	4.3 (kharif)
Paddy	3.5	4.9	3.2 (rabi)

Source: Survey data and Government of India (2008).

Annexure

Sampling Procedures

In each village, households were divided into different strata using data on landhold-ings from the census-type study of December 2005. The criteria used for identifi-cation of different strata are listed in Tables A, B and C. In each village, sampling proportions for each stratum were chosen to ensure that households in the stratum were adequately represented in the sample. Within each stratum, households were sorted by caste and the actual size of ownership holding. Then a circular systematic sample with a random start was drawn.

Table A *Description of sample, Ananthavaram village, 2006*

Stratum No.	Stratum description	No. of households	No. of sample households
1	Landless (no ownership, no operational holding)	317	40
2	Landless tenants	124	31
3	Landowner cum tenants	66	17
4	Small landowners (ownership holding less than 5 acres)	127	32
5	Medium and large landowners (ownership holding of 5 acres or more)	32	32
6	Largest landowner	1	1
	All strata		153

Source: Survey data.

Table B *Description of sample, Bukkacherla village, 2006*

Stratum No.	Stratum description	No. of households	No. of sample households
1	All households except the largest landowner	291	98
2	Largest landowner	1	1
	All strata		99

Source: Survey data.

Table C *Description of sample, Kothapalle village, 2006*

Stratum No.	Stratum description	No. of households	No. of sample households
1	Households with less than 5 acres of ownership holding	345	87
2	Medium and large landowners (ownership holding of 5 acres or more)	26	14
3	Largest landowner	1	1
	All strata		102

Source: Survey data.

Since non-uniform sampling proportions were used in all villages, a multiplier (weight) was used for each observation when estimates were made either for the village as a whole or for any group that cut across more than one stratum. For any household, the value of the multiplier was the ratio of total number of households to the number of sample households in the stratum to which the household belonged.

2

A Note on Socio-Economic Classes in the Survey Villages

This chapter describes the criteria that were used to classify households in the three villages into socio-economic classes.

LANDLORDS

Landlord households own the most land and generally the best land in all three villages, and the members of landlord households do not participate in the major agricultural operations on the land. Their land is cultivated either by tenants, to whom land is leased out on fixed rent or share, or by means of the labour power of hired workers.[1] Landlord families are, in general, historical participants in the system of land monopoly in the village. Landlords dominate not just economic, but also traditional social and modern political hierarchies in the village. It is absolutely essential to remember that — to quote E.M.S. Namboodiripad — "landlordism is not only an economic category but also social and political."

Big Capitalist Farmers

Capitalist farmers also do not participate in the major manual operations on the land. The main difference between these capitalist farmers and landlords is that the former did not traditionally belong to the class of landlords. Some of them came from rich peasant or upper-middle peasant families that had a tradition of family labour, whose members, in fact, actually worked at major manual tasks even in the present or previous generation. Such families invested the surplus they

---

[1] Those landlords whose surpluses come mainly from the labour of hired manual workers are called capitalist landlords.

gained from agriculture or other activities — including moneylending, salaried employment, trade and business — in land. Agriculture was or became the focal point of their activity, and the basis of their economic power.

Capitalist farmers of this type may be of the traditionally dominant caste. They may also be from castes designated officially as Backward Classes. In any case, although their position in the ritual hierarchy may not be equivalent to the traditional dominant or ritually 'superior' castes, big capitalist farmers are also entrenched in positions of social and political dominance.

We have termed the biggest landholders in this category "big capitalist farmers". Their landholdings are in the same size bracket as that of the landlords, as are their incomes and overall ownership of the means of production and other assets.

This class — that is the class of landlords and "big capitalist farmers" — is the main pillar of the class power of the ruling classes and the state in the villages. It follows, then, that it is the mainstay of the power of political parties of the ruling classes in the villages.

We have generally included capitalist farmers other than big capitalist farmers (a few in number) in the class of rich peasants (for rich peasants, see discussion below).

MANUAL WORKERS

At the other end of the spectrum of classes involved in agricultural production is the class of manual workers, whose major income comes from working as hired workers on the land of others and at tasks outside crop production. Many manual worker households are landless (the proportion of landless households within this class was 90 per cent in Ananthavaram, 15 per cent in Bukkacherla and 58 per cent in Kothapalle). About 5 per cent of manual worker households were tenant cultivators in Ananthavaram and 2 per cent in Kothapalle. In Bukkacherla there were no tenant cultivators belonging to this class. Agricultural workers work at non-agricultural tasks as well, and it is not possible to distinguish a class of non-agricultural workers from agricultural workers in any of the villages. In general, manual workers work on a wide range of tasks, and the set of skills necessary for most tasks is to be found among most manual workers. One crop that employs a more specialised group of workers is betel leaf, cultivated in the *lanka* (river island) land near Ananthavaram.

Some Case Studies

The wealth and assets of a landlord in Ananthavaram cannot be judged by looking at his house in the village — large and imposing (in absolute terms and relative to the houses of the poor) though it may be. It is likely that such a landlord has a house in Tenali, Guntur, Hyderabad or elsewhere; that his wealth goes beyond that which is to be found in the village itself; and that the sources of his overall income go well beyond agriculture and allied activity in Ananthavaram (the diverse sources of landlord/big capitalist farmer income have been discussed in chapter 5). At the same time, landed wealth remains an important part of his asset wealth, an important source of income (and household provision) and a foundational feature of his social status. Land and landed income are likely to have served as the means for further expansion, and the basis for diversification.

In south coastal Andhra Pradesh, landlords and the rural rich (and sections of rural society other than the very poor and socially oppressed) seem to have realised, about a generation earlier than others, the value of investment in modern technical and high-income-return higher education, particularly medicine and computer engineering. About 15 persons born in the village were working in the United States, and more in Europe, Singapore and other places. It would be interesting to see the share of persons who come from rural landed families among those who migrate to the United States from Andhra Pradesh, and the corresponding share among migrants from other states of India. Investment in high-expenditure and high-income-yielding higher education appears to be more a part of the strategic planning of an upper stratum of the privileged in rural Andhra Pradesh than in the rural areas of other states.

In Anantapur village, the main landlord family owned 280 acres of land in the village. The siblings who constitute the present generation of the family had control over the village panchayat. Professionally, one was in politics and held a cabinet-rank position in Hyderabad; another was a representative in the mandal-level administration; and the family also had representation in the bureaucracy in the state capital and in the legal profession in the district headquarters. The overall income of this family came from land, contracts from small-scale civil construction, moneylending (while simultaneously being in debt), and salaried and professional incomes. The head of the household said that incomes from leasing urban property existed in the past, but had ceased by the time of the survey.

For this landlord family, land is not so much a source of income as of socio-political influence and power. Large tracts of land in the village are left fallow. Large tracts of land in other villages are not taken into account at all. Socio-political involvement is now such that very little attention is paid to cultivation. There are no attempts at large-scale land improvement or changes in land use. Almost all productive land is left to tenants. Production itself is thus conducted on a very small scale. Attempts to increase incomes through horticulture, particularly papaya and mango by means of drip irrigation, have been made by rich peasants and smaller landlords, not by the big landlord.

The family migrated to the village "one or two centuries ago". It now owns land in at least four mandals, although it is only the land in the village that is under their effective control. Every village in this vicinity, the head of the household says, has a landlord who owns more than 100 acres, although no family in the region has holdings as large as those of his family.

The family in this generation pays careful attention to the quality of school education for the next generation. Their children are enrolled in schools in Hyderabad, and in residential schools of perceived high quality elsewhere in the state.

The two houses in the village, though not luxurious, are the most prominent. The landlord collects his rent there, meets people who come to pay 'respect' and to petition him for a variety of favours, and to facilitate a variety of tasks. The primary foundation of the landlord's political base and that of his family — they are close to the top echelons of the Congress leadership — is the power that he wields in the village, and the primary source of that power is land.

This village is also the site of a rural factional conflict of the type for which the Rayalaseema area in general is well known. The main landlord family is the head of one faction. The source of the factional division is not clear, but the respondent said that it had begun generations ago, and that it perhaps originated from conflict over the use of water in the fields.

Our experience in Kothapalle showed another aspect of landlordism. The largest landlord had this in common with the landlords in the other villages: he owns and operates the largest landholding in the village, a holding that covers the best land in the village. The family maintains an establishment in Hyderabad where his grandchildren are educated in expensive English medium schools.

The family has real estate interests (this source of income is managed by the son of the head of the household), and they receive incomes for contracts for civil construction and sand contracts.

A feature of this family is that it takes advantage of all the facilities available to agriculture and sideline activities in the village. They grow regular field crops, and make use of special government schemes for the cultivation of vegetables, oranges and mango, and sheep, goat and dairy farming.

There appears to be a certain loosening of the traditional social grip of the landlords over the day-to-day social life of the village. The combined effect of the political activity of the Telengana separatists and the naxalites, particularly the latter, appears to have encouraged the landlords to seek new avenues of investment outside the village, particularly in real estate.

Manual workers also have other small sources of income. These include animal husbandry, small businesses, toddy-tapping and miscellaneous low remuneration jobs in the private sector.

Most manual workers are casual workers who work at daily-rated tasks or for piece-rates. Some, however, are annual workers: farm servants who do agricultural, non-agricultural and some domestic tasks for a single employer for a monthly wage (and generally on an annual contract). There were 16 such households in Ananthavaram, 3 households in Bukkacherla and 12 households in Kothapalle.

The Peasantry

Peasant households, whose members work on all or some of the major manual operations on the land, constitute the sector of petty producers that lies between landlords and big capitalist farmers on the one hand, and manual workers on the other.

The peasantry is heterogeneous, and the criteria we have used to identify strata among the peasantry in the survey are discussed below. All classes of the peasantry together (including capitalist farmers not included in the landlord/big capitalist farmer class) constituted 39 per cent of all households in Ananthavaram, 54 per cent of all households in Bukkacherla, and 28 per cent of all households in Kothapalle.

We classified each peasant household into a class category on the basis of the broad criteria that follow.

1. Ownership of the means of production and other assets.
2. The labour ratio, defined as the ratio between the sum of number of days of family labour, and the number of days of labouring out of members of the household in agricultural and non-agricultural work (in the numerator) and the number of days of labour hired in by the household (in the denominator).
3. Rent exploitation, that is, rent received or paid by the household.
4. Net income of the household, making separate note of the gross value of output from agriculture and the investment in agriculture per hectare.
5. The sources of income of the household.

We emphasise here the problems of classifying the peasantry on the basis of a single year's data, when socio-economic circumstances typically fluctuate from year to year. We use, in other words, static data to study dynamic circumstances. This problem affects income particularly, since peasant incomes typically fluctuate from year to year.

With regard to the labour ratio, the extent of participation of working members of peasant households in the labour process in agriculture depends on economic and social status, and on the nature of land use and cropping pattern in the village. For example, in Ananthavaram, paddy is cultivated through intensive employment of large groups of workers. Betel-leaf cultivation requires intensive supervision and a specialised labour force, thus limiting the number of days of actual family labour deployed by the peasant household. In Kothapalle, the nature of lift irrigation is such that it absorbs a high absolute level and a substantial share of the family labour that peasants deploy. Labour absorption in Bukkacherla across all crops and seasons was only 70 days per hectare against 275 days per hectare in Ananthavaram and 173 days per hectare in Kothapalle. Among many Other Castes in the villages, in peasant households characterised by the hard labour of male workers, women worked at domestic tasks and animal husbandry, but for reasons of traditional social status, did not work outside the household, thus bringing down the total number of days of family labour. (This was the case, for instance, among women from Kamma households in Ananthavaram.)

We then classified households into rich, upper-middle, lower-middle and poor, on the basis of their ownership of the means of production, labour ratios and incomes.

Rich peasant households had the highest levels of ownership of means of production, particularly land and other productive assets, while at the other end of the spectrum, poor peasants hardly had any productive assets at all other than small plots of land. In Ananthavaram, most poor and lower-middle peasants were tenants, so they did not even have any land. With respect to the labour ratio, the coefficient was above 0 but very low for rich peasants, generally in the vicinity of 1 among middle peasants (less than 1 for upper-middle and greater than 1 for lower-middle peasants), and greater than 1 among poor peasants.

Incomes ranged from high surpluses based on relatively heavy investments among the rich, to subsistence and even negative incomes among the poor. The income criterion was particularly important in resolving borderline problems in the classification of the middle peasantry into upper and lower sections.

A very important feature of the situation in Ananthavaram was that even middle peasants — particularly from Dalit, but also Backward Class — households laboured out heavily. In Ananthavaram, poor peasants and all tenants were substantially and characteristically semi-proletarians with respect to days of labouring out, but with respect to hiring in, they were relatively heavy employers of labour. In fact in two villages, of all the days of labour worked by hired labour for wages, a very large share came from the peasantry, particularly poor and lower-middle peasants: 42 per cent in Ananthavaram and 26 per cent in Bukkacherla.

In all the villages, it was difficult to draw an exact line differentiating between the poor peasantry and manual workers. There were many households now classified as poor peasants, who, if classified by either an income criterion or the labour ratios, would have been classified as manual workers. They were classified eventually as poor peasants because of the absolute number of labour days they hired in and because the extent of their operational holdings was non-negligible (sometimes, particularly in Ananthavaram, because of leased-in land).

Rich peasants were a class set distinctly apart from the rest of the peasantry, particularly in Ananthavaram. Their households were characterized by substantial accumulation of capital, low labour ratios and high incomes. A striking feature of the distribution of operational holdings of land in Ananthavaram was that the largest operational holding in the village was cultivated by a rich peasant, not a landlord. The household operated about 47.5 acres, of which 42 acres were leased in. It also owned 8 acres, of which 2.5 acres were leased out. It cultivated traditional crops — paddy, sesamum, pulses and oilseeds — but the main work of the head of the household was as an award-winning sugarcane farmer. The household was among the top in the village with respect to assets and incomes, but was also a rare case of a top rich peasant participating in every single manual operation on the land and in animal husbandry.

In Ananthavaram, households of the upper-middle sections are also distinctly demarcated from other peasants by their average incomes and average levels of ownership of productive assets. All other classes in the three villages lived in precarious economic conditions. In Bukkacherla, cross-over occupations were more common than elsewhere — particularly among poor peasants, manual workers and other income-poor — as survival strategies among the poor. In Kothapalle, animal husbandry and (for one caste) toddy-tapping were important alternative sources of income.

Other Households

Other classes have been classified on the basis of the main sources of their incomes, although, as can readily be understood, it can be very difficult to assign to a household a single category of occupation in circumstances where the incomes of households derive from diverse occupations.[2]

The categorisation of other households is presented here with an important qualification. These are broad occupational groups classified on the basis of the main sources of household incomes. In the categories titled "Business activity/ Self-employed", "Rents/Moneylending", "Salaried person/s", and "Remittances/ Pensions" in the fact cover households with different levels of income — and consequently, different class interests — and need further to be classified on the basis of their internal stratification. That is, however, a task that we leave for future writing on the subject.

1. *Artisan work and work at traditional caste calling.* This class includes carpenters, blacksmiths, potters, service castes and temple priests.
2. *Business activity/ self-employed.*

---

[2] The statistical tables on different sources of income in each class are in chapter 5.

3. *Rents/moneylending*. This class typically includes small rent receivers, and small and medium moneylenders.

4. *Salaried persons*. Salaried persons in a village are invariably from households that have multiple sources of income and generally have links to the land. They have been able to gain access to salaried employment because they have had access to education. Many would have remained trapped in village employment but for progressive policies of affirmative action and reservation. Other Caste people who have received education in more exclusive institutions of higher education and who go to high-end jobs generally migrate out of the village.

5. *Remittances/pensions*. Pensions covered a wide spectrum, from Rs 1,300-a-year government old-age pensions, generally received by poverty-stricken, low-literacy households, to more than Rs 9,000 a month — the latter reflecting access to more well-paid organised-sector employment and high levels of household education. There was a marked prevalence of female-headed households, particularly of older women, in this class.

The distribution of households into classes is provided in Tables 1, 2 and 3. Each chapter that follows discusses different aspects of the socio-economic condition of these classes.

Table 1 *Distribution of households, by class, Ananthavaram village, 2005–06*

Socio-economic class	Households	
	No.	%
Landlord/Big capitalist farmer	11	2
Capitalist farmer/Rich peasant	12	2
Peasant: upper-middle	24	3
Peasant: lower-middle	93	14
Peasant: poor	131	20
Hired manual worker	164	25
Artisan work and work at traditional caste calling	28	4
Business activity/Self-employed	39	6
Rents/Moneylending	35	5
Salaried person/s	61	9
Remittances/Pensions	58	9
Unclassified households	8	1
All households	664	100

Source: Survey data.

Table 2 *Distribution of households, by class, Bukkacherla village, 2005–06*

Socio-economic class	Households	
	No.	%
Landlord/Big capitalist farmer	10	3
Capitalist farmer/Rich peasant	33	11
Peasant: upper-middle	45	16
Peasant: lower-middle	39	14
Peasant: poor	39	14
Hired manual worker	59	20
Artisan work and work at traditional caste calling	3	1
Business activity/Self-employed	12	4
Rents/Moneylending	12	4
Salaried person/s	18	6
Remittances/Pensions	21	7
All households	289	100

Source: Survey data.

Table 3 *Distribution of households, by class, Kothapalle village, 2005–06*

Socio-economic class	Households	
	No.	%
Landlord/Big capitalist farmer	5	1
Capitalist farmer/Rich peasant	33	9
Peasant: upper middle	24	6
Peasant: lower middle	28	8
Peasant: poor	20	5
Hired manual worker	163	44
Artisan work and work at traditional caste calling	4	1
Business activity/Self-employed	30	8
Rents/Moneylending	4	1
Salaried person/s	42	11
Remittances/Pensions	20	5
All households	370	100

Source: Survey data.

3

Land, Assets
and Property Inequality

The basis of class power in the countryside is the control of land and other means of production and forms of wealth. By this criterion, the data show unequivocally that class power in the three villages is firmly in the grip of the landlords and big capitalist farmers.

At one end of the distribution, landlords and big capitalist farmers controlled the lion's share of land and other immovable property, and a disproportionately high share of other production assets. At the other end of the distribution, poor peasants and manual worker households, and Dalit, Adivasi and Muslim households, were characterized by the very small share of production assets that they held.

DATABASE

As the list of categories of assets below show, the PARI database covers a very wide range of household assets. For each type of asset, respondents are asked the number of assets owned by the household and the price they are likely to get if the asset is sold in its present condition in the market. Assets are valued by the investigators in consultation with members of the respondent household. While posing questions on assets to members of the household, investigators make a clear distinction between the present value of the existing asset, the price at which the asset was purchased, and the price the household may have to pay to buy a new asset at the time of the survey. The survey team also does, as far as possible without offending the respondents, an overall visual inspection to ensure that all major assets are covered.

Two items of information do not appear in our database. We did not collect data on the financial assets of households, on bank deposits, small savings, stocks and shares, and so on, or on gold and jewellery. We also excluded the value of some small assets, such as small hand implements and light-bulbs, as these were difficult to value and had trivial value or no value at all. The exclusion of gold, jewellery and financial assets is likely most to affect our estimates of the asset holdings of the rich; to that extent the data that follow underestimate their wealth and understate inequality.

Data on asset holdings were collected for all households in December 2005. In this chapter, all data except when presented across classes are based on information collected through that census of households.

Determining the class status of households required information that was collected through the sample survey conducted in May 2006. As a result, the class status of households could be determined only for those households that were covered in the sample survey (see chapter 2). In view of this, the class-wise analysis of asset holdings is based on the information for households covered by the sample survey of May 2006. In such cases, appropriate multipliers have been used to arrive at estimates of asset holdings for different classes in the village as a whole.

For the purpose of analysis, assets have been grouped into the following categories:

- Land (including homestead), trees and water-bodies
- Houses and other buildings
- Animals other than draught animals
- Other means of production (including draught animals and assets related to non-agricultural activities)
- Means of transport
- Other domestic durables
- Other assets

In this and all subsequent chapters, the category "Other Caste" refers to Hindus that are not Scheduled Caste (Dalit), Scheduled Tribe (Adivasi) or Backward Class.

LAND OWNERSHIP

Land constitutes the primary instrument and means of production in agriculture, and the distribution of land lays the basis for the pattern of distribution of other productive assets and forms of wealth in the countryside.

Ownership of land was concentrated in the hands of landlords and big capitalist farmers, and of Other Castes. Detailed data on the distribution of land between classes and social groups are given in the Appendix.

About 65 per cent of households in Ananthavaram and 47 per cent of households in Kothapalle did not own any land (Table 1). Landlessness is not as prominent a feature of land distribution in Bukkacherla as in the other villages. Bukkacherla is, of course, predominantly unirrigated, and the loss of land by poor and middle peasants is, as a rule, more pronounced in villages where a high proportion of the cropped area is irrigated.

The Gini coefficient for distribution of landholdings shows very high levels of inequality: a staggering 0.86 for Ananthavaram and 0.76 for Kothapalle. Although landlessness is less in Bukkacherla than in Ananthavaram, the Gini coefficient for the distribution of land, 0.55, is still indicative of a very unequal distribution. The distribution of land in Bukkacherla is influenced greatly by the fact

Table 1 *Proportion of households that do not own any land, study villages, 2005*

Village	Proportion of households that do not own any land
Ananthavaram	65
Bukkacherla	15
Kothapalle	47

Source: Survey data.

Table 2 *Gini coefficients of ownership holding, study villages, 2005*

Village	Ownership holding
Ananthavaram	0.86
Bukkacherla	0.55
Kothapalle	0.76

Source: Survey data.

Table 3 *Share of different classes in ownership and operational holding of land, study villages, May 2006 (%)*

Socio-economic class	Ananthavaram			Bukkacherla			Kothapalle		
	Proportion of households	Share in ownership holdings	Share in operational holdings	Proportion of households	Share in ownership holdings	Share in operational holdings	Proportion of households	Share in ownership holdings	Share in operational holdings
Landlord/Big capitalist farmer	2	25	9	3	22	16	1	19	12
Capitalist farmer/ Rich peasant	2	16	18	11	18	20	9	31	32
Peasant: upper middle	4	20	14	15	16	23	6	8	10
Peasant: lower middle	14	8	18	13	8	13	7	4	8
Peasant: poor	20	4	17	13	7	14	5	2	10
Hired manual worker	25	1	1	20	9	8	44	15	13
Non-agricultural classes	33	26	22	23	19	6	27	21	14
Unclassified households	1	0	1	0	0	0	0	0	0
All households	100	100	100	100	100	100	100	100	100

Source: Survey data.

that the largest landowning family owns 280 acres of agricultural land, an extent that far outstrips the land held by any other household.

Landlords and big capitalist farmers, who accounted for only 2 per cent of households in Ananthavaram, owned 25 per cent of land (Table 3). In Bukkacherla, landlords accounted for 3 per cent of households and owned 22 per cent of land. In Kothapalle, landlord households accounted for 1 per cent of households and owned 19 per cent of land.

Landlords were net lessors of land, while all peasant classes operated more land than they owned. A very high proportion of land operated by lower-middle peasants and poor peasants was leased in. In the capitalist farmer/rich peasant and upper-middle peasant classes, there were some households that leased in land in order to cultivate high-income crops. While tenants among poor and lower-

Table 4 *Extent of land leased out as a proportion of total land owned and the share of different classes in total land leased out, study villages, May 2006* (%)

Socio-economic class	Share in total extent of land leased out			Area leased out as a proportion of total land owned		
	Ananthavaram	Bukkacherla	Kothapalle	Ananthavaram	Bukkacherla	Kothapalle
Landlord/Big capitalist farmer	21	37	37	36	44	32
Capitalist farmer/ Rich peasant	20	3	19	54	5	10
Peasant: upper middle	2	0	0	4	0	0
Peasant: lower middle	0.5	0	0	2	0	0
Peasant: poor	2	0	0	19	0	0
Hired manual worker	0.5	7	0	18	22	1
Non-agricultural classes	54	53	44	88	74	34

Note: Various non-agricultural classes together account for 33 per cent of households in Ananthavaram, 23 per cent of households in Bukkacherla and 27 per cent of households in Kothapalle.

Source: Survey data.

Table 5 *Incidence of tenancy, study villages, 2005* (%)

	Ananthavaram	Bukkacherla	Kothapalle
Land leased in as a proportion of total operated area	52	11	16
Tenants as a proportion of households operating land	65	15	15
Tenants as a proportion of all households	29	15	8

Source: Survey data.

middle peasants were small cultivators, some tenants in the capitalist farmer/rich peasant class leased in very large amounts of land. Landlords, various non-agricultural classes and, in Ananthavaram and Kothapalle, the capitalist farmer/rich peasant class, constituted the major lessors of land (Table 4).

The incidence of tenancy was very high in Ananthavaram (Table 5). Land leased in constituted about 52 per cent of total land operated by households in Ananthavaram; the corresponding ratios were 11 per cent for Bukkacherla and 16 per cent for Kothapalle.

In Ananthavaram, the pattern of land ownership was also associated with stark social disparities. About 80 per cent of Dalit households, 98 per cent of Adivasi households and 89 per cent of Muslim households in Ananthavaram did not own any agricultural land.

Asset Holdings

Some Features of Property Inequality

Ownership of assets was also deeply unequal (see Appendix Tables). Inequality in household wealth was particularly pronounced in Ananthavaram, where the richest 10 per cent of households owned 75 per cent of all household wealth. By contrast, the poorest 80 per cent of households together owned only about 12 per cent of household wealth. The top decile accounted for 54 per cent of all household wealth in Bukkacherla and 58 per cent of all household wealth in Kothapalle. In Bukkacherla, the poorest 80 per cent of households together owned about 32 per cent of wealth. In Kothapalle, the poorest 80 per cent of house-

Table 6 *Gini coefficients of household and per capita asset holdings, study villages, 2005*

Village	Household assets	Per capita assets
Ananthavaram	0.83	0.84
Bukkacherla	0.65	0.61
Kothapalle	0.69	0.67
All villages	0.77	0.77

Source: Survey data.

holds together owned about 27 per cent of wealth. The Gini coefficient of distribution of household wealth was 0.83 in Ananthavaram, 0.65 in Bukkacherla and 0.69 in Kothapalle (Table 6).

Land constituted the single most important asset of households. It accounted for 74 per cent of total household wealth in Ananthavaram, 63 per cent of total household wealth in Bukkacherla and 66 per cent of total household wealth in Kothapalle (Table 7). More detailed data show that agricultural land accounted for 70 per cent of total household wealth in Ananthavaram, 54 per cent of total household wealth in Bukkacherla and 47 per cent of total household wealth in Kothapalle.

Homestead land was valued the highest in Kothapalle, where high land prices were associated with its location on a state highway. The median reported price of 0.01 acre of homestead land was Rs 4,000 in Kothapalle, Rs 3,000 in Ananthavaram and Rs 2,000 in Bukkacherla.

Table 7 *Share of different types of assets in total household wealth, study villages, 2005* (%)

Categories of assets	Ananthavaram	Bukkacherla	Kothapalle
Land and water bodies (including trees)	74	63	66
Houses and other buildings	19	21	25
Animals (excluding draught animals)	1	2	2
Other means of production	1	7	3
Means of transport	1	2	1
Other domestic durable goods	3	2	2
Other assets	0.3	1	0.4
All assets	100	100	100

Source: Survey data.

Table 8 *Gini coefficients of distribution of different types of assets, study villages, 2005*

Categories of assets	Ananthavaram	Bukkacherla	Kothapalle
Land and water bodies (including trees)	0.89	0.72	0.79
Houses and other buildings	0.77	0.67	0.61
Animals (excluding draught animals)	0.81	0.88	0.84
Other means of production	0.96	0.75	0.87
Means of transport	0.94	0.84	0.93
Other domestic durable goods	0.63	0.51	0.55
Other assets	0.88	0.81	0.81
All assets	0.83	0.65	0.69

Source: Survey data.

Table 9 *Median and average values of assets of different types, study villages, 2005*

Categories of assets	Median value of assets			Average value of assets for households owning the assets		
	Ananthavaram	Bukkacherla	Kothapalle	Ananthavaram	Bukkacherla	Kothapalle
Land and water bodies (including trees)	12,000	74,000	40,000	385,033	196,984	214,649
of which, Agricultural land	0	60,000	8,000	906,116	190,161	264,721
Houses and other buildings	15,000	30,000	40,000	98,859	72,621	89,290
Animals (excluding draught animals)	0	0	0	14,157	20,219	13,672
Other means of production	0	0	0	44,537	42,875	20,975
Means of transport	200	0	400	9,256	15,526	6,745
Other domestic durable goods	4,950	4,320	3,800	11,482	6,734	6,485
Other assets	90	580	240	1,804	4,110	1,425
All assets	34,604	23,375	82,040	447,675	296,369	299,592

Source: Survey data.

The next most important constituent of asset holdings, houses and buildings, constituted 19 per cent of total household wealth in Ananthavaram, 21 per cent of total household wealth in Bukkacherla and 25 per cent of total household wealth in Kothapalle (Table 7).

It is noteworthy that the shares of animal holdings (that is, animals other than draught animals) and other means of production in total household asset holding were very small. Animals (other than draught animals) accounted for only about 2 per cent of household wealth in Bukkacherla and Kothapalle, and 1 per cent of household wealth in Ananthavaram (Table 7). All other means of production accounted for about 1 per cent of household wealth in Ananthavaram, 7 per cent of household wealth in Bukkacherla and 3 per cent of household wealth in Kothapalle.

In all three villages, the ownership of non-land means of production (that is, animals and other means of production) and means of transport was even more concentrated in the hands of the rich than the distribution of land (Table 8). With regard to buildings and domestic durable goods, however, although the Gini coefficients were very high in an absolute sense, they were lower than the Gini coefficients for land. This is primarily because of the prevalence of some home ownership, however poorly appointed the home, among the poor.

More than half of all households in Ananthavaram owned no land, and more than half of all households in all three villages owned no animals or other means of production (Table 9).

ASSET HOLDINGS BY CLASS AND SOCIAL GROUP

There were sharp disparities in levels of asset holdings across classes and social groups (see Appendix Tables). Among agricultural classes, the average levels of asset holdings fell sharply as one moved from landlords to hired manual workers (Table 10). The asset holdings of a single household in the class of manual workers was 1 per cent of the value of assets of a landlord household in Ananthavaram, 2 per cent in Bukkacherla and 3 per cent in Kothapalle (Table 10).

The pattern of inequality in Ananthavaram was interesting. The average asset holdings of lower-middle and poor peasants, manual workers and artisans were consistently less than 5 per cent of the average asset holdings of landlord households. The data also show that, although the average rich peasant and upper-middle peasant household owned a fraction of the wealth of a landlord house-

Table 10 *Average household asset holdings, by class, study villages, May 2006*

Socio-economic class	Ananthavaram	Bukkacherla	Kothapalle
Landlord/Big capitalist farmer	5,161,579 (100)	3,097,431 (100)	4,659,341 (100)
Capitalist farmer/Rich peasant	2,643,843 (51)	654,776 (21)	1,021,948 (22)
Peasant: upper middle	1,952,972 (38)	290,865 (9)	328,301 (7)
Peasant: lower middle	236,800 (5)	161,482 (5)	126,523 (3)
Peasant: poor	120,493 (2)	78,644 (3)	101,708 (2)
Hired manual worker	39,872 (1)	71,229 (2)	120,446 (3)
Artisan work and work at traditional caste calling	32,130 (1)	402,150 (13)	140,740 (3)
Business activity/Self-employed	641,530 (12)	117,798 (4)	179,845 (4)
Rents/Moneylending	907,679 (18)	1,090,895 (35)	179,150 (4)
Salaried person/s	311,805 (6)	139,747 (5)	457,948 (10)
Remittances/Pensions	232,539 (5)	94,835 (3)	316,076 (7)

Note: (i) Population estimates based on data for sample households.
(ii) Figures in parentheses give the average level of asset holding of each class as a percentage of the average level of asset holdings of the "landlord/big capitalist farmer" class.
Source: Survey data.

Table 11 *Average household asset holdings, by social group, study villages, 2005*

Social group	Ananthavaram	Bukkacherla	Kothapalle
Dalit households	64,670(5)	65,380(13)	107,468(13)
Adivasi households	19,444(1)		27,102(3)
Muslim households	47,264(4)	126,721(24)	163,558(20)
BC households	228,565(18)	154,293(30)	187,069(23)
Other Caste households	1,300,830(100)	519,306(100)	798,550(100)

Note: Figures in parentheses give the average level of asset holding of each social group as a percentage of the average level of asset holdings of the Other Caste households.
Source: Survey data.

hold, some accumulation of wealth and property has indeed occurred among the upper sections of the peasantry, especially rich peasants. In Bukkacherla and Kothapalle, the gap between the asset holdings of the rich peasantry and land-lords was much wider than in Ananthavaram. In Bukkacherla, the highest average household asset holding after landlords was among moneylender households, an interesting phenomenon in a drought-prone region where access to modern technology is unequal and indebtedness levels are very high.

Data on average levels of asset holdings across different social groups show that Dalit, Adivasi, Muslim and Backward Class households had substantially lower levels of asset holdings than Other Caste households (Table 11). The average level of asset holdings of Dalit households was only 5 per cent of the average level of asset holdings of Other Caste households in Ananthavaram, and 13 per cent of the average level of asset holding of Other Caste households in Bukkacherla and Kothapalle. The average asset holdings of Adivasi households was 1 per cent of the average asset holdings of Other Caste households in Ananthavaram and 3 per cent of the average asset holdings of Other Caste households in Kothapalle.

Animal Resources

The number of milch cattle per 100 households was 58 in Ananthavaram, 49 in Bukkacherla and 62 in Kothapalle (Table 12). With high levels of mechanisation in agriculture, very few households in Ananthavaram maintained draught animals. There were only eight head of draught animals per 100 households in Ananthavaram.[1] The stock of both cattle and sheep and goats, in terms of the number of animals owned per 100 households, was much bigger in Bukkacherla than in the other two villages.

The pattern across classes shows that, in Ananthavaram, the number of milch cattle per 100 households declines as one moves from capitalist farmers and rich peasants to the class of hired manual workers (Table 13).

Cattle holdings in Kothapalle were bigger than in the other villages, mainly because there was grazing land along the banks of the lake of the Lower Maner Dam. Poor peasants and hired manual workers in Kothapalle were able to main-tain much larger cattle holdings than corresponding classes in Ananthavaram and Bukkacherla (Table 13).

---

[1] Eight pairs of draught animals are bred for competition. We watched hefty Ongole bulls being exercised by dragging a heavy stone slab along the road every day.

Table 12 *Number of animals of different types per 100 households, study villages, 2005*

	Ananthavaram	Bukkacherla	Kothapalle
Milch cattle	58	49	62
Adult male cattle	8	68	35
Calves	35	24	34
Goats and sheep	5	218	111
Pigs	3	0	9
Poultry	62	54	78

Source: Survey data.

Table 13 *Number of cattle of different types per 100 households, by class, study villages, 2006*

Socio-economic class	Ananthavaram		Bukkacherla		Kothapalle	
	Adult female	Adult male	Adult female	Adult male	Adult female	Adult male
Landlord/ Big capitalist farmer	127	0	60	80	145	85
Capitalist farmer/ Rich peasant	211	106	73	45	157	77
Peasant: upper middle	375	4	127	113	167	83
Peasant: lower middle	128	8	23	115	71	86
Peasant: poor	67	18	62	92	240	60
Hired manual worker	22	5	0	10	32	12
Non-agricultural classes	15	7	17	0	21	8

Source: Survey data.

In all the villages, Dalit, Adivasi and Muslim households had much smaller holdings of milch cattle than Other Caste households. Data also show that pigs were owned in Ananthavaram and Kothapalle only by Adivasi households (Table 14). In Ananthavaram and Kothapalle, household-based poultry were raised mainly by Dalit and Adivasi households. In Bukkacherla, poultry was maintained by households belonging to all social groups and, among all social groups, the number of

Table 14 *Number of animals of different types per 100 households, by social group, study villages, 2005*

Village	Social group	No. of animals					
		Milch cattle	Adult male	Calf	Goats and sheep	Pigs	Poultry
Ananthavaram	Dalit households	47	7	35	1	0	87
	Adivasi households	7	0	0	0	48	123
	Muslim households	22	22	11	0	0	0
	BC households	56	4	23	24	0	72
	Other Caste households	91	13	56	0	0	11
Bukkacherla	Dalit households	2	26	5	9	0	19
	Muslim households	0	25	0	0	0	63
	BC households	38	80	12	251	0	19
	Other Caste households	83	81	42	302	0	97
Kothapalle	Dalit households	64	26	35	5	0	135
	Adivasi households	9	9	0	0	291	100
	BC households	35	26	21	171	0	75
	Other Caste households	117	69	63	172	0	11

Source: Survey data.

Figure 1 *Average number of cattle vs. operational holdings in acres*

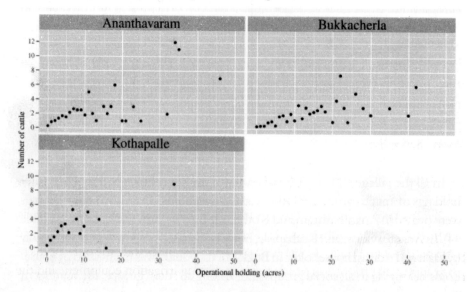

birds per hundred households was highest for Other Caste households (Table 14).

Figure 1 shows the average number of head of cattle owned by households operating different sizes of landholdings. The figure shows that there was a clear positive relationship between the average number of cattle owned by a household and the size of operational holding of land in all the villages. The figure shows that, with the shrinking availability of grazing areas, access to fodder from land operated by households has become critical for maintaining cattle. As a result, households with larger operational holdings were able to maintain larger stocks of cattle.

Other Means of Production

The proportion of households that owned different types of agricultural machinery was very small (Table 15).

In Ananthavaram, only 12 per cent of households owned any agricultural machinery at all. About 8 per cent of households owned borewells, 5 per cent of households owned sprayers, 3 per cent of households owned ploughs and levellers, and less than 1 per cent of households owned tractors and related accessories. Low levels of ownership of agricultural machinery in Ananthavaram were related to the unequal distribution of land, and the fact that a large proportion of land was cultivated by poor tenants who did not have the means to buy agricultural machinery. It was also related to the fact that the main source of irrigation was canal water from the Krishna river, as a consequence of which ownership of irrigation equipment was not critical. Agriculture was highly mechanized in Ananthavaram, and most cultivators used rented tractors for agricultural tasks.

The proportion of households owning different types of machinery was somewhat greater in Bukkacherla and Kothapalle. Since there was no surface irrigation in these villages, 28 per cent of households in Bukkacherla and 23 per cent of households in Kothapalle owned borewells. The proportion of households that owned ploughs, levellers and other equipment used with draught animals was also higher in Bukkacherla and Kothapalle than in Ananthavaram.

Table 16 shows the distribution of irrigation equipment — including borewells, pumps and pipes — across classes. The table shows that in both Bukkacherla and Kothapalle, two villages where privately owned sources were the only means of irrigation, the proportion of households owning irrigation equipment and the

Table 15 *Proportion of households that owned specified means of production and share of different categories of equipment in total value, study villages, 2005 (%)*

Category of means of production	Proportion of households that owned different types of assets			Share of different types of assets in total value		
	Anantavaram	Bukkacherla	Kothapalle	Anantavaram	Bukkacherla	Kothapalle
Agricultural machines						
Tractors, power tillers and accessories	1	9	2	22	8	19
Borewells, pumps and other irrigation equipment	8	28	23	16	28	19
Machines for harvesting and post-harvest operations	0.1	5	4	0.2	1	0.2
Sprayers	5	10	7	2	1	1
Ploughs, levellers and other equipment for use with draught animals	3	39	20	0.2	3	1
Other equipment	0.3	0.0	0.0	1	0.0	0.0
All agricultural machines and equipment	12	47	32	40	41	40
Draught animals	3	34	18	12	18	18
Implements related to toddy-tapping	0.1	0.3	3	0.0	0.0	0.1
Assets related to non-agricultural activities	1	1	4	8	0	1
Total	100	100	100	100	100	100
Number of households/average value (Rs.)	667	292	372	10,487	36,026	13,704

Source: Survey data.

Table 16 *Proportion of households that own irrigation equipment and average value of irrigation equipment, by class, study villages, 2006*

Socio-economic class	Ananthavaram		Bukkacherla		Kothapalle	
	Proportion of households	Average value*	Proportion of households	Average value*	Proportion of households	Average value*
Landlord/Big capitalist farmer	45	42,400	100	42,997	100	20,758
Capitalist farmer/ Rich peasant	49	31,500	82	29,778	64	12,880
Peasant: upper middle	60	22,042	73	26,355	50	5,000
Peasant: lower middle	0		23	24,333	43	4,111
Peasant: poor	6	25,000	8	25,000	0	
Hired manual worker	0		10	7,500	7	6,500
Non-agricultural classes	10	14,114	9	47,250	10	11,627

Note: * Average value calculated over households that owned borewells, pumps and other irrigation equipment.
Source: Survey data.

average value of irrigation equipment declined sharply as one moved from the landlord class towards the class of hired manual workers.

The low general level of assets in this category reflects the age or obsolescence of existing holdings of agricultural machinery, and the fact that many of the tractors that are brought to work on fields in villages often come from nearby towns. It also reflects, most importantly, the general absence of modern manufacture of productive non-agricultural enterprise in the villages.

CONCLUSIONS

Data on asset holdings show an extremely high level of inequality in the ownership of assets. In particular, a large proportion of households belonging mainly to poor peasant, hired manual worker and artisan households owned very few productive assets. The most important productive assets were concentrated in the hands of landlords in all three villages. That said, there were interesting differences in patterns of differentiation with respect to assets between the three villages. Ananthavaram, in particular, showed substantial accumulation of productive assets and wealth in the hands of rich peasants and capitalist farmers. Levels of ownership of assets among upper-middle peasants were also markedly higher than among lower-middle and poor peasants, and manual workers.

Across social groups, there was a sharp disparity in the ownership of assets between Other Caste households on the one hand, and Dalit, Adivasi and Muslim households on the other.

Of all the villages, inequality with respect to ownership of assets was highest in the coastal Andhra village of Ananthavaram. The Gini coefficients of total asset holdings of households were 0.83 in Ananthavaram, 0.65 in Bukkacherla and 0.69 in Kothapalle (Table 6). Land and buildings dominated the asset portfolios of households. Land and buildings accounted for about 93 per cent of total assets in Ananthavaram, 84 per cent of total assets in Bukkacherla, and 91 per cent of total assets in Kothapalle.

Inequality in the distribution of ownership of assets was very high in respect of land, animal wealth and other means of production.

The extent of landlessness was very high in Ananthavaram and Kothapalle. About 65 per cent of households in Ananthavaram and about 47 per cent of households in Kothapalle did not own any land (Table 1). In Ananthavaram, about 52 per cent of total operated area was cultivated by tenants (Table 5).

Holdings of draught animals were the smallest in Ananthavaram and the biggest in Bukkacherla, a phenomenon clearly related to higher levels of mechanization in agriculture in Ananthavaram and a relatively high use of draught animals in agriculture in Bukkacherla. Average holdings of milch cattle, in terms of the number of cattle per 100 households, were the highest in Kothapalle, followed by Ananthavaram and then Bukkacherla (Table 12). In Kothapalle, access to grazing land along the lake of the Lower Maner Dam stimulated larger holdings of milch cattle among poor peasant households than elsewhere. There were very sharp disparities in the ownership of cattle across classes in Ananthavaram: cattle wealth tended to decline as one moved from capitalist farmer/rich peasant households towards hired manual worker households. Across social groups, Adivasi and Muslim households in Ananthavaram owned very little cattle. Dalit households, particularly Madiga households, who cultivated land on lease, were able to maintain larger stocks of cattle than Adivasi and Muslim households.

The proportion of households owning different types of agricultural machinery was lowest in Ananthavaram (Table 15). This was likely to be related to a greater degree of landlessness and high incidence of tenancy in Ananthavaram. Since privately owned sources of groundwater were the only source of irrigation in Bukkacherla and Kothapalle, a substantial proportion of households (28 per cent in Bukkacherla and 23 per cent in Kothapalle) owned some irrigation equipment. Ownership of these assets, however, was concentrated in the hands of the landlord and capitalist farmer/rich peasant classes.

Other reasons for low holdings of modern means of production in the villages are the low general development of rural industry and non-agricultural enterprise, the very low replacement of old machinery including tractors, and the shift of rental services for farm machinery (including tractors and harvesters) from villages to semi-urban and urban areas.

4

Tenancy Relations in Ananthavaram 1974 to 2005–06

In the articles that he wrote on his landmark 1974 survey of Ananthavaram, P. Sundarayya provided a detailed account of tenancy in Ananthavaram, and described the exploitative nature of tenancy relations in the village at some length (Sundarayya 1977). This chapter examines aspects of tenancy based on our surveys and compares them with Sundarayya's observations.

CHANGES IN LAND DISTRIBUTION

Sundarayya (1977) noted that in 1974, there was a "tremendous concentration of land in Ananthavaram". Table 1 shows that there was an increase in the degree of landlessness and the extent of inequality in the distribution of land between 1974 and 2005–06. The proportion of households that did not own any land increased from 50 per cent in 1974 to 60 per cent in 2006 (Table 2). There was also an increase in the proportion of landless households among Adivasi households, Backward Class households and Other Caste households. The Gini coefficient of distribution of ownership holdings increased from 0.835 in 1974 to 0.856 in 2006.

Table 2 shows a relative decline in the share of landless households among Dalits and an increase in landlessness among Other Castes in the period between the Sundarayya and PARI surveys. The difference may be because of various factors. First, the 1974 survey covered 818 single families against 667 households (or 931 "single families" by Sundarayya's definition) covered by the 2005 survey. The decline in landlessness among Dalit households in the village may be as a result of the emigration of landless Dalit households from Ananthavaram (which did occur), just as the rise in landlessness among Other

Table 1 *Distribution of land across size classes of holdings, 1974 and May 2006*

Size-classes of ownership holding	1974			2006		
	Proportion of households (%)	Proportion of area (%)	Average land holding (acres)	Proportion of households (%)	Proportion of area (%)	Average land holding (acres)
0	50.4	0.0	0.0	60.5	0.0	0.0
0.5 aces and below	11.5	1.9	0.3	12.6	3.5	0.3
0.5–1.0 acres	10.9	4.9	0.9	8.9	7.4	0.9
1.0–1.5 acres	4.0	2.8	1.4	1.8	2.5	1.5
1.5–2.0 acres	5.4	5.2	2.0	4.8	8.8	2.0
2.0–2.5 acres	1.7	2.0	2.4	1.2	2.8	2.5
2.5–3.0 acres	2.9	4.4	3.0	1.8	4.9	3.0
3.0–4.0 acres	1.5	2.7	3.7	1.5	5.2	3.7
4.0–5.0 acres	1.6	3.9	5.0	0.2	0.7	5.0
5.0–6.0 acres	1.2	3.6	5.9	1.9	10.6	6.0
6.0–7.0 acres	1.7	5.8	6.9	0.9	5.5	6.7
7.0–8.0 acres	1.3	5.0	7.5	1.2	8.7	7.9
8.0–9.0 acres	0.2	1.0	8.7	0.5	3.7	8.8
9.0–10.0 acres	0.7	3.6	10.0	1.1	10.0	10.0
10.0–12.5 acres	0.5	2.9	12.0	0.2	1.5	10.8
12.5–15.0 acres	1.3	10.0	15.0	0.3	4.0	14.5
15.0–20.0 acres	1.1	9.8	18.0	0.3	4.7	17.0
More than 20 acres	2.0	30.4	31.4	0.6	15.4	27.7
All households	100.0	100.0	2.0	100.0	100.0	1.1
Gini coefficients		0.835			0.856	

Source: Sundarayya (1977), and estimates based on sample survey, May 2006.

Table 2 *Proportion of households that did not own any land, by social group, Ananthavaram village, 1974 and May 2006* (%)

Social group	1974	2006
Dalit households	80.6	72.6
Adivasi households	81.4	89.8
Muslim households	–	100
BC households	49.7	56.5
Other Caste households	17.7	33.6
All households	50.3	60.4

Source: Sundarayya (1977), and estimates based on sample survey, May 2006.

Caste households may be because of the emigration of landed households from the village (which also occurred, particularly among Kamma households).

Secondly, the main ownership holdings of Dalit households are of *lanka* lands on the Krishna river and adjacent to the boundaries of the revenue village of Ananthavaram. The PARI survey covered these holdings, since they were owned by households resident in the village and within or in the vicinity of the village. It is not clear whether the 1974 survey covered these holdings. If it did not — which seems likely, since Sundarayya's surveys were generally restricted to the village boundaries — the "decline" in landlessness would be explained, in substantial measure, by the difference in coverage of the surveys.

Thirdly, Sundarayya used the "single family" as the unit of accounting, while we used the "household" (that is, persons generally of the same family living together and eating from a common kitchen) as the unit of accounting. In other words, if there were four adult males in a single family (a man and his three sons, for example), Sundarayya considered them to be four separate families. When we recomputed the data by Sundarayya's "single family" criterion, it made no difference to the change in the proportion of landless households among Dalit and Muslim families, but it did increase the proportion of landless among Adivasi familes, and brought down the proportion of landless among Other Caste families by 5 percentage points.

The differences in the proportion of the landless among households of different social groups in 1974 and 2005 may thus be the result of differences in statistical method, and of migration. There may also be other processes of economic differentiation at work that need to be examined further.

INCIDENCE OF TENANCY

As is typical of the paddy-dominated tracts of south coastal Andhra Pradesh, tenancy was widely prevalent in Ananthavaram in 2006. A comparison with data from 1974 shows that there was an expansion in the area cultivated by tenants between 1974 and 2006, and that the proportion of households participating in tenancy, both as lessors and as tenants, increased greatly (Table 3).

In 1974, 19 per cent of landowning households leased out all their land. This proportion had increased to 30 per cent in 2005–06. Land leased out by these households accounted for 13.8 per cent of total owned land in 1974 and 29.8 per cent of total owned land in 2005–06. In 1974, about 3 per cent of landowning

Table 3 *Incidence of tenancy in Ananthavaram village, 1974 and May 2006*

Land leased out	1974	2006
A. Households that leased out all their land		
Number of households as a proportion of landowning households (%)	19	30
Number of households as a proportion of all households (%)	9	12
Land leased out as a proportion of total land owned (%)	13.8	29.8
B. Households that leased out part of their land		
As a proportion of cultivating households (%)	3	5
As a proportion of all households (%)	1	2
Land leased out as a proportion of total land owned (%)	3.5	5.7
Land leased in (%)		
Tenants as a proportion of cultivating households		71
Tenants as a proportion of all households	18	37
Land leased in as a proportion of total land operated	22	67

Source: Sundarayya (1977), and estimates based on sample survey, May 2006.

households leased out a part of their ownership holdings. The proportion of such households was 5 per cent in 2005–06. The land leased out by such households increased from 3.5 per cent of total land owned to 5.7 per cent of total land owned.

Data on land leased in also show a huge expansion in tenancy. In 1974, tenants comprised 18 per cent of all households. In 2005–06, they comprised 37 per cent of all households. In 1974, about 22 per cent of land cultivated in the village by households resident in Ananthavaram was leased in. In 2005–06, 67 per cent of the total area of operational holdings cultivated by households resident in Ananthavaram was leased in.

Tenants in Ananthavaram, then and now, paid fixed rents to lessors. In other words, sharecropping was not a feature of tenancy in this village. What did happen between 1974 and 2005–06 was the emergence and expansion of cash-paid tenancy. The practice of paying rent in kind for paddy-producing land remained widespread; at the same time, many households paid rents in cash. In general, relatively affluent sections of the peasantry paid cash rents while lower-middle and poor peasants paid rents in kind. Cash rents were paid on land on which paddy and other seasonal crops were grown, and also land on which high-value crops like sugarcane and betel leaves were grown.

To What Classes and Social Groups Do Tenants and Lessors Belong?

In 2006, lessors and tenants came from different socio-economic classes and social groups, and the character of tenancy varied according to the classes to which the lessor and lessee belonged, and their relative economic power.

Among tenants, those who leased in land for the cultivation of paddy and maize for rents in kind came primarily from the poor and lower-middle peasantry, and belonged mainly to the Madiga and Mala Dalit castes. About 54 per cent of tenants who paid rent in kind came from the ranks of poor peasants; another 30 per cent belonged to the class of lower-middle peasants (Table 4). In general, these were economically the poorest among peasants in Ananthavaram. As we shall see in the next section, these households got meagre incomes from leased-in land. These peasants typically leased in land from landlords and capitalist farmers/rich peasants.

Table 4 *Distribution of tenant households, area leased in, lessor households and area leased out, by class, Ananthavaram, 2005–06*

Class	Land leased in on rent-in-kind tenancy		Land leased in on rent-in-cash tenancy		Land leased out	
	Proportion of households	Proportion of area	Proportion of households	Proportion of area	Proportion of households	Proportion of area
Landlord/Big capitalist farmer	1	2	0	0	7.5	26
Capitalist farmer/ Rich peasant	1	1	8	33	2.5	24
Peasant: upper middle	3	3	5	6	0	2
Peasant: lower middle	30	37	28	11	0	0.5
Peasant: poor	54	45	35	7	0	0
Hired manual labour and other wage-work	6	2	0	0	10	0.5
Non-agricultural classes	6	11	16	41	80	47
Unclassified households	0	0	8	2	0	0
All households	100	100	100	100	100	100

Source: Estimates based on sample survey, May 2006.

Table 5 *Distribution of tenant households, area leased in, lessor households and area leased out, by social group, Ananthavaram, 2005–06*

Social group	Land leased in on rent-in-kind tenancy		Land leased in on rent-in-cash tenancy		Land leased out	
	Proportion of households	Propor-tion of area	Proportion of households	Propor-tion of area	Proportion of households	Propor-tion of area
Madiga households	33	42	16	4	0	0
Mala households	22	22	16	5	30	3
Other Dalit households	0	0	0	0	0	0
Adivasi households	8	4	0	0	5	0
Muslim households	3	2	0	0	0	0
BC households	26	16	19	7	17	9
Other Caste households	8	14	49	84	48	88
All households	100	100	100	100	100	100

Source: Estimates based on sample survey, May 2006.

Land was leased in for cash rents by households belonging to different peasant classes and various social groups (Tables 4 and 5). Among them were those who leased in land for the cultivation of paddy, maize and black gram. These were, primarily, households from among the ranks of poor peasant and lower-middle peasant classes who had access to some cash either from occasional windfall incomes or credit, and were able to pay advance cash rent for small plots of land. The next section shows that the incomes of these tenants were also small.

Among those who leased in land for cash rents were also households that belonged to the capitalist farmer/rich peasant class and Other Castes (and, in particular, the Kamma caste) (Tables 4 and 5). These households, however, primarily leased in land for the cultivation of high-value crops such as betel leaves and sugarcane. These were often cases of reverse tenancy, in which land owned by small landowners — in particular, those belonging to the Mala caste — was leased in by households belonging to capitalist farmer/rich peasant and upper-middle peasant classes and Other Castes. The data presented in the next section show that these households got substantial returns from leased in land.

There were also some cases where Kamma households belonging to the rich peasant and upper-middle sections of the peasantry leased in land on cash rents, and cultivated paddy, maize and black gram. These households typically leased land on relatively low cash rents from either very poor Dalit households who were unable to cultivate their lands because of lack of capital, or from households belonging to their own caste who were unable to cultivate land for various reasons (for example, because they lived elsewhere, or because they were engaged in other occupations, or because the lessor household had no member of working age). Such rich tenant households often leased in a large amount of land from several landowners.

In Ananthavaram, Scheduled Caste families belonging to the Mala caste had gained title to small plots of *lanka* lands in the 1940s. These lands, on islands in the Krishna river, are suitable for the cultivation of betel leaves, turmeric and other high-value crops. However, most Dalit landowners did not have the resources to invest in the cultivation of these crops. A specific feature of tenancy relations in Ananthavaram was that these households, belonging to the class of hired manual workers and the Mala caste, leased out small plots of land, typically to Kamma upper-middle and rich peasants, for cash rents.

CHANGES IN TENANCY CONTRACTS

In 1974, land in Ananthavaram was leased in by tenants who paid a fixed annual rent in kind at the end of the kharif season. The tenants paid a fixed rent of 16 bags (12 quintals) of paddy per acre as rent. All costs of cultivation were met by the tenant. In 1974, the normal yield of paddy, cultivated in the kharif season, was 14 quintals per acre. Tenants also cultivated black gram in the rabi season, for which no additional rent was paid. The normal yield of black gram was about 2 quintals per acre. In 1974, the total value of produce was Rs 1,660 per acre (Rs 1,260 from paddy and Rs 400 from black gram). The rent, valued at Rs 1,080, constituted about 65 per cent of total output (Sundarayya 1977).

In 1974, the tenant got 2 quintals of paddy (value equivalent to Rs 180) and 2 quintals of black gram (value equivalent to Rs 400) from every acre of land cultivated on lease. The remaining paid-out expenses, assuming that the household of the tenant provided all the labour for the crop, amounted to Rs 250 (Rs 200 for paddy and Rs 50 for black gram). In other words, a tenant who cultivated the land only with family labour received about 20 per cent of gross value of output as profit. On the other hand, if all labour was hired, the net profit was about 11 per cent of the gross value of output (Sundarayya 1977).

There were a number of important changes between 1974 and 2006 in the nature of tenancy contracts for land on which kharif paddy was grown.

First, in 2005–06, rent was paid either in paddy or in cash. In fact, in 2005–06, a larger proportion of gross cropped area was cultivated under contracts in which rent was paid in cash (36 per cent) than contracts in which rent was paid in terms of grain (28 per cent) (Table 6).

Secondly, between 1974 and 2005–06, rent increased substantially. The average rent in kind was 21 bags (16.2 quintals) of paddy per acre of land. This was about 4.2 quintals per acre, or 35 per cent, more than the rent paid in 1974. In the case of cash rents, the average rent was Rs 9,371 per acre (Table 8). At current prices of paddy (in 2005–06), this was marginally lower than 21 bags of paddy.

Thirdly, with fierce competition among landless and small landowning house-holds for obtaining land on lease, rents became negotiable. Of the total area under rent-in-kind tenancy reported in the sample, 40 per cent was leased for 22 bags of paddy (17 quintals) per acre, 10 per cent for 23 bags of paddy (17.7 quintals) per acre, and another 9 per cent for 24 bags of paddy (18.5 quintals) per acre (Table 7). Of the total land leased in on cash rent, 28 per cent was leased in on rents less than or equal to Rs 8,000 per acre, 11 per cent for rents of Rs 9,000 per acre, 51 per cent for rents of about Rs 10,000 per acre and the rest for more than Rs 10,000 per acre (Table 8).

Table 6 *Proportion of leased in and owned land in area cultivated with different crops, Ananthavaram village, 2005–06* (%)

| Crop | Leased in | | Owned land | Total |
	Rent in cash	Rent in kind		
Paddy	36	28	36	100 (1128)
Maize	28	41	31	100 (663)
Black gram	59	1	40	100 (286)
Betel leaves	100	0	0	100 (32)
Sugarcane	55	3	42	100 (95)
Turmeric	33	0	67	100 (9)
Fruits and vegetables	71	0	29	100 (7)
Other crops	27	12	61	100 (155)
All crops	38	26	37	100 (2375)

Notes: Figures in parentheses give area under different crops in acres.
Source: Estimates based on sample survey, May 2006.

Table 7 *Distribution of area under rent-in-kind lease across different rates of rent, Ananthavaram, 2005–06*

Rate of rent	Proportion of area (%)
Less than 20 bags per acre	9
20 bags per acre	24
21 bags per acre	8
22 bags per acre	40
23 bags per acre	10
24 bags per acre	9
Total	100

Source: Estimates based on sample survey, May 2006.

Table 8 *Distribution of paddy land leased in on cash rents, Ananthavaram village, May 2006*

Size-class of cash rent	Proportion of area (%)	Average value of rent (Rupees)
Less than or equal to Rs 8,000 per acre	28	7,476
Rs 9,000 per acre	11	9,000
Rs 9,000 to 10,000 per acre	51	9,963
Greater than Rs 10,000 per acre	10	11,864
Total	100	9,371

Source: Sample estimates based on survey data, May 2006.

An account of the average income of tenants who paid rent in kind and cultivated paddy and maize is provided in Table 9.

The average level of yield of paddy on leased-in land was 18.9 quintals (24 bags) per acre. This was about 4.9 quintals per acre more than the average yield in 1974. The average rate of rent was 16.2 quintals (21 bags) per acre. At the end of the kharif season, the tenant was left with only 2.6 quintals of paddy per acre. It may be noted that while the yield level increased by 4.9 quintals per acre between 1974 and 2005–06, the quantity retained by the tenants increased only by 0.6 quintals per acre. Almost the entire increase in yields was taken away by the land-owners in the form of rent. At the end of the kharif season, the value of grain and straw retained by the tenant was way short of the investment of Rs 4,346 in procuring inputs and Rs 2,564 for hiring labour. The average loss at this stage was about Rs 4,384 per acre.

Table 9 *Accounts of average income from paddy and maize cultivated by tenants who paid rent in kind, 2005–06*

Item	Rupees
Average account for paddy	
Value and production of paddy	11,055 (18.9 quintals)
Value of paddy straw	840
Total value of output	11,895
Cost of inputs	4,346
of which	
Seeds	369
Manure	339
Fertilizer	1,742
Plant protection chemicals	673
Irrigation expenses	85
Rent for machines	1,138
Cost of hired labour	2,564
Value and quantity of rent	9,368 (16.2 quintals)
Value and quantity of grain retained by tenant after paying rent	1,687 (2.6 quintals)
Net income from paddy crop	–4,384
Average account for maize	
Value of output	11,261 (19.5 quintals)
Cost of inputs	4,120
of which	
Seeds	754
Manure	6
Fertilizer	2,001
Plant protection chemicals	319
Irrigation expenses	903
Rent for machines	138
Cost of hired labour	1,773
Net income from maize crop	5,368
Total net income over paid-out cost	984

Note: (i) This account is based on a simple average of all tenant households in the sample who paid rents in kind and cultivated paddy and maize on the leased-in land.

(ii) The cost items considered here include only those items on which the cultivator actually incurred expenditure. No costs of interest, depreciation, cost of family labour or rental income of own land have been included in these costs.

Source: Survey data.

This was the stage when tenants faced a severe financial crunch. In our sample, four tenants, accounting for 9.5 per cent of total land leased under such contracts in the sample, were unable to cultivate land in the rabi season because of lack of further funds to invest in the rabi crop.

For cultivating maize in the rabi season, tenants had to make a further investment of Rs 4,120 per acre on purchase of inputs and Rs 1,773 for hiring labour. The average net income of tenants from maize was Rs 5,368 per acre.

Table 9 shows that the net income of tenants from both paddy and maize put together was Rs 984 per acre. In other words, a tenant who leased in land and paid rent in kind just managed to break even after the maize harvest.

Table 10 provides accounts of households who cultivated paddy followed by black gram and households who cultivated paddy followed by maize on rent-in-cash tenancy contracts. In the case of land sown with paddy in the kharif season and black gram in the rabi season, average net income was Rs 1,123 per acre. In the case of land sown with paddy in the kharif season and maize in the rabi season, the income was slightly higher, Rs 1,680 per acre.

How did these levels of income compare with incomes in 1974?

In terms of paddy equivalents, a cash income of Rs 250 per acre in 1974 was equivalent to 278 kilograms of paddy. In 2005–06, the average income from tenancy contracts where rent was paid in kind (Rs 984 per acre) in 2005–06 was equivalent to only 168 kilograms of paddy. The average income from the paddy-black gram cycle on a rent-in-cash tenancy contract was equivalent to 192 kilograms of paddy. The average income from a paddy–maize cycle on a rent-in-cash tenancy contract was equivalent to 287 kilograms of paddy.

Between 1974 and 2005–06, the gross value of output on leased paddy land went up substantially. In 1974, the total gross value of output from paddy and black gram was, given the prevailing paddy prices, equivalent to 1,844 kilograms of paddy. In 2005–06, the gross value of output in terms of paddy equivalents was about 4,000 kilograms of paddy for the cases described in Tables 9 and 10. The increase in gross value of output occurred on account of both increases in yields of paddy and the cultivation of maize instead of black gram in the rabi season. While the gross value of output in paddy equivalents more than doubled between 1974 and 2005–06, the income of the tenant in paddy equivalents fell for most tenants. The increased gross value of output was taken away in part by the increased rent and spent in part on much greater expenditure on inputs. On the whole, the income of an average tenant who cultivated leased-in land and

Table 10 *Accounts of average per acre income from rent-in-cash tenants who cultivated paddy in the kharif season followed by black gram and maize in the rabi season, Ananthavaram village, 2005–06*

	Paddy and Black gram cycle	Paddy and Maize cycle
	Kharif (paddy)	*Kharif (paddy)*
Value and production of paddy	14,678	10,104
Value of paddy straw	1,619	977
Total value of output	16,297	11,081
Cost of inputs	4,817	3,975
of which		
Seeds	216	247
Manure	154	235
Fertilizer	1,336	1,435
Plant protection chemicals	1,480	863
Irrigation expenses	92	31
Rent for machines	1,538	1,163
Cost of hired labour	1,866	2,784
	Rabi (Black gram)	*Rabi (maize)*
Value of output	5,896	12,753
Cost of inputs	2,596	4,006
of which		
Seeds	596	792
Manure	0	0
Fertilizer	70	2,027
Plant protection chemicals	1,851	379
Irrigation expenses	46	627
Rent for machines	33	182
Cost of hired labour	1,217	1,977
Annual rent	10,573	9,412
Net income over paid-out expenses	1,123	1,680

Note: (i) These accounts are based on a simple average of all tenant households in the sample who paid rents in cash and cultivated these crop combinations on leased-in land.

(ii) The cost items considered here include only those items on which the cultivator actually incurred expenditure. No costs of interest, depreciation, cost of family labour or rental income of own land have been included in these costs.

Source: Survey data.

paid a rent in kind, fell from about 11 per cent of gross value of output in 1974 to about 4 per cent in 2005–06.

It may be noted that these accounts of the costs of cultivation include only those items on which the cultivator incurred an actual expense. No costs have been imputed for interest on working capital, for the depreciation of owned capital, for the rental cost of owned capital, or for family labour. The inclusion of some or all of these costs, as is done for estimation of costs by CACP, would give substantially lower net incomes (see chapter 6).

In 2005–06, a number of households in Ananthavaram also leased in land for the cultivation of crops like sugarcane, betel leaf and turmeric. These crops were cultivated only on cash-paid tenancy contracts. Land was leased for the cultivation of these crops by households that were, in general, more affluent than tenants who leased land on rent in kind.

In particular, note should be made of land leased for the cultivation of betel leaf. In Ananthavaram, betel leaf was cultivated on *lanka* (islands in the Krishna river) lands. A number of households belonging to the Mala caste in Ananthavaram owned these lands. These lands, provided by the government in the 1940s, were held under a land title that did not allow households to sell them. At the same time, since these households did not have resources to invest in betel-leaf cultivation, they leased out their land for cash rents to other households. In addition to land leased from households belonging to the Mala caste, some of the betel-leaf cultivators also leased land suitable for betel-leaf cultivation from Other Caste households in neighbouring villages.

Table 11 gives data on the average value of output, cost of cultivation and income from land leased for betel-leaf cultivation. The table shows that the average rent on land leased for betel-leaf cultivation was very low in relation to the gross value of output. It constituted, on average, only 1 per cent of the gross value of output.

While land leased on tenancy contracts, when cultivated with paddy in the kharif season and maize or black gram in the rabi season, gave meagre incomes to tenants, they gave very substantial incomes in rent to landowners. In particular, large landowners belonging to landlord or rich peasant classes, who leased out a substantial extent of land, received very large quantities of paddy or a large amount in cash as rent. Given the average rates of rent, a landowner who leased out 20 acres of land received between 300 and 370 quintals of paddy valued at over Rs 2 lakhs. In order to gain such handsome incomes, these landowners in Ananthavaram

Table 11 *Value of output, cost of cultivation and net income from betel leaf cultivation on leased-in land, Ananthavaram village, 2005–06*

	Rupees	Per cent
Value of output	27,98,000	100
Cost of inputs	1,58,225	6
Cost of hired labour	1,16,329	4
Rent	17,630	1
Net income	25,05,816	89

Note: (i) These accounts are based on a simple average of all tenant households in the sample who paid rents in cash and cultivated these crop combinations on leased-in land.

(ii) The cost items considered here include only those items on which the cultivator actually incurred expenditure. No costs of interest, depreciation, cost of family labour or rental income of own land have been included in these costs.

Source: Survey data.

were neither required to make any investment in fixed capital, nor contribute to working capital, nor supervise crop operations on the land.

It is clear from the foregoing discussion that in Ananthavaram, land leased on tenancy contracts, except when leased to cultivate specific high-value crops, gave meagre incomes to tenants.

Let us now look at the aggregate levels of incomes of tenant and lessor households in Ananthavaram.

Table 12 shows that landless tenant households that paid rent in kind incurred an average loss (over Cost A2) of Rs 2,286 from crop production.[1] In contrast, tenants who cultivated high-value crops like betel leaf received on average an income of Rs 3.6 lakhs.

Table 12 also shows that tenant households have substantial incomes from animal resources. A landless household that took land on lease was able to earn an average of about Rs 13,049 from animal resources. In comparison, a landless household that did not cultivate any land earned only about Rs 795 from animal resources. The average income of non-cultivating lessor households from animal resources was also only Rs 1,222.

An important aspect of tenancy contracts in Ananthavaram was that even for

[1] See the definition of Cost A2 in the Annexure to chapter 6.

Table 12 *Average annual income by source for households belonging to selected tenurial categories, Ananthavaram village, 2005–06* (rupees)

Source of income	Non-cultivating landless households	Owner culti-vators	Tenant cultivators of high-value crops	Other tenants		Lessors	
				Land-less	Land-owning	Non-cultivating	Cultivator-cum-lessor
Crop production	0	19,331	3,65,923	–2,286	16,568	0	25,172
Animal resources	795	23,573	2,971	13,049	72,490	1,222	7,723
Rental income from agricultural land	0	0	11,787	56	3,347	21,759	15,440
Agricultural labour earnings	7,964	2,955	413	9,038	4,935	227	1,165
Non-agricultural casual labour earnings	1,472	0	0	4,165	2,815	105	0
Income from other sources*	13,339	27,482	2,652	2,595	28,377	32,589	43,258
Total income	23,570	73,341	383,746	26,618	128,533	55,902	92,757

Note: *These include all other sources of income like salaried jobs, artisanal activities, remittances and pensions, and non-farm businesses.

Source: Estimates based on sample survey, May 2006.

Table 13 *Number of cattle per hundred households, landless tenant households, households that neither own nor cultivate land, and non-cultivating lessor households, Ananthavaram village, May 2006*

Type of animals	Households that neither own nor operate land	Landless tenants	Non-cultivating lessors
Milch cattle (adult)	11	71	13
Draught animals (adult)	3	10	0
Female calf	12	32	7
Male calf	0	8	6

Source: Estimates based on sample survey, May 2006.

Table 14 *Average annual income by source for tenants belonging to different classes, Ananthavaram village, 2005–06* (rupees)

Source of income	Tenants belonging to lower-middle peasant, poor peasant, hired manual labour and artisan classes	Tenants belonging to other classes
Crop production	−3,464	74,683
Animal resources	34,321	33,237
Rental income from agricultural land	57	4,693
Agricultural labour earnings	6,979	6,895
Non-agricultural casual labour earnings	3,898	2,714
Income from other sources*	5,800	19,862
All sources	47,591	1,42,084

Note: *These include all other sources of income like salaried jobs, non-farm businesses, artisan activities, remittances and pensions.

Source: Estimates based on sample survey, May 2006.

rent-in-kind tenancy contracts, the tenant was allowed to keep all the straw from the paddy crop. This enabled tenants to maintain a much larger stock of animals than other households (Tables 13 and 14). While their incomes from crop production were low, by-products of crop production in the form of straw enabled them to keep milch cattle. Incomes from these animals, most importantly in the form of milk production, were a substantial component of the total annual income of tenant households.

CONCLUSIONS

This chapter analysed changes in tenancy relations in Ananthavaram village from 1974 to 2006.

There was a clear increase in the degree of landlessness and in inequality in the distribution of ownership of land in Ananthavaram between 1974 and 2006. The proportion of households that did not own any land increased from 50 per cent in 1974 to 60 per cent in 2005–06 (Table 2).

Sundarayya (1977) showed that the cultivation of land under tenancy was widespread in Ananthavaram. Our data indicate that the incidence of tenancy increased sharply over the last three decades. The proportion of households that cultivated land on lease increased from 18 per cent in 1974 to 37 per cent in 2006. The proportion of land cultivated under tenancy contracts increased from 22 per cent to 67 per cent during the same period (Table 3).

Several changes in tenancy relations took place in Ananthavaram between 1974 and 2005–06.

One important change was the emergence of fixed rent-in-cash tenancy contracts for leasing paddy land as well as land used for the production of other high-value crops. Relatively better-off sections of the peasantry leased in land on rent-in-cash contracts. Capitalist farmers/rich peasants leased in substantial amounts of land for the cultivation of high-value crops like betel leaf and sugarcane. The returns from cultivation of these crops were high and these cultivators earned a substantial income from their operational holdings.

On the other hand, a majority of tenants, in particular tenants from poor peasant and lower-middle peasant classes, leased land on which they cultivated paddy in the kharif season, and maize or black gram in the rabi season. Most of these tenants leased land on rent-in-kind contracts. An important change that took place between 1974 and 2005–06 was that tenants cultivated maize rather than black gram in the rabi season.

P. Sundarayya has described the extremely oppressive nature of tenancy contracts in Ananthavaram. In 1974, a tenant produced 14 quintals of paddy and 2 quintals of black gram from an acre of land, and paid 12 quintals of paddy as rent. The income of a tenant, after deducting costs, and given prevailing paddy prices, was equivalent to 278 kilograms of paddy per acre.

The average yield of paddy increased between 1974 and 2005–06 by about 5 quintals per acre. The gross value of output per acre increased further on account of a shift from black gram to maize. However, a comparison of the average cost of cultivation and incomes of tenants in 1974 and 2005–06 shows that these gains were almost entirely lost because of a steep rise in rents and the increased costs of inputs. In fact, the incomes of tenants in terms of paddy equivalents and in terms of shares of gross value of output fell sharply. The net income of a tenant from an acre of land in 1974 was equivalent to 278 kilograms of paddy. In 2005–06, a tenant who paid rent in terms of paddy earned an income that was the equivalent of only 168 kilograms of paddy from an acre of land.

In Ananthavaram, landowners made no contribution to the costs of cultivation. In 2005–06, a tenant who leased land on a rent-in-kind tenancy contract produced about 18.9 quintals from an acre of land. Of this, 16.2 quintals were given away as rent (Table 9). Having made a large investment in the production of paddy, tenants incurred a huge loss in the kharif season. The loss was so high that some tenants were unable to make a further investment in the cultivation of the rabi crop. Those of them who did manage to cultivate the second crop still had very low incomes.

While incomes from crop production under these tenancy contracts were meagre, the incomes were augmented to some extent by incomes from the animal resources that these tenants were able to maintain because of access to land, and therefore to straw (which was retained entirely by the tenant), through these tenancy contracts. Production from animal resources made a small but important contribution to the total income of tenant households (Tables 13 and 14).

A comparison of the terms of tenancy between 1974 and 2005–06 shows that, over this period, tenancy contracts in Ananthavaram became even more exploitative than they were when Sundarayya and others surveyed the village.

In 1977, P. Sundarayya wrote:

There is great competition for leasing land and hence rents are exorbitant . . . So long as 40 to 50 per cent of the rural families remain completely landless or own nominal small plots of land, they have to run to the landlords for leasing land or to get work, paying exorbitant rents and surrendering to low wages. This situation cannot be changed unless and until land is distributed to them or their unemployment problem is solved by providing them with work in other occupations. (Sundarayya 1976: 28)

That analysis remains relevant today.

5

Household Incomes

From the study of incomes in the three villages emerges a picture of widespread income-poverty amidst very high levels of inequality. An overwhelming majority of cultivators get only meagre returns from crop production, while a few get very large incomes through profits and rent. Dalits, Adivasis and Muslims have substantially lower incomes than Other Castes. Hired manual worker and poor peasant classes have substantially lower incomes than rich sections of the peasantry and, of course, landlords and big capitalist farmers.

The village economies of Ananthavaram in Guntur district and Bukkacherla in Anantapur district are primarily agrarian. By comparison, greater diversification to non-agricultural activities has taken place in Kothapalle, a village situated on a major highway.

METHODOLOGY OF ESTIMATION OF INCOMES

There are no official sources of serial data on household incomes in rural India.[1] The National Sample Survey Organisation (NSSO) provides regular data on monthly per capita household expenditure, and the Comprehensive Scheme for the Study of Cost of Cultivation of Principal Crops in India (CCPC) provides regular data on farm business incomes for selected crops. Estimates of income in the PARI database, by contrast, include household incomes from all sources of tangible household income, under the following heads:

- Income from crop production
- Income from animal resources

[1] For a discussion, see Bakshi (2008b).

- Income from agricultural and non-agricultural wage labour
- Income from salaries
- Income from business and trade, rent, interest earnings, pensions, remittances, scholarships and all other sources

The estimates of income in the PARI database account for all receipts in cash and kind other than from borrowing and from the sale of assets. All incomes are net of costs incurred by the households in the process of production or income generation.

A large number of rural households are self-employed, particularly in crop production, but also in a variety of non-agricultural occupations. Most such households do not maintain any accounts. Accounting for incomes from different economic activities of these households is a complex task, not least because a substantial part of the produce is not marketed and many inputs used in the process of production are not purchased from the market. For some of these products and inputs, either no markets or only very thin markets exist. Given the complexities of valuation and the absence of recorded accounts, detailed data have to be collected on production processes, input use, costs of production, levels of production and prices in order to arrive at estimates of net income.

With respect to data on incomes from crop production and on the cost of cultivation, the PARI database includes household-wise data on the following variables:

- Cost of hired labour
- Cost of hired and owned bullock labour
- Cost of hired and owned machinery
- Value of home-produced and purchased seed
- Value of insecticides and pesticides
- Value of home-produced and purchased manure
- Value of fertilisers
- Cost of irrigation
- Land revenue
- Miscellaneous expenses
- Rent paid for leased in land
- Interest on working capital
- Depreciation of owned implements and machinery

The income from crop production for a household is calculated for individual crops over paid-out cost. The cost of cultivation estimated for this purpose closely resembles Cost A2 as defined by the CCPC of the Commission of Agricultural Costs and Prices (CACP).[2] Cost A2 includes, broadly speaking, the costs of all material inputs used (purchased as well as home-produced), hired labour, rental payments, the imputed value of interest on working capital, and the depreciation of owned fixed capital other than land. No cost is imputed for family labour and no rent is imputed for owned land. Conceptual and methodological problems in imputing the costs of family labour and owned land have been discussed at length in the writings on CCPC data (see Sen and Bhatia 2004 for a summary), and shall not detain us here. We shall, however, note the consequences of the exclusion of these items of costs from our calculations. As a result of the exclusion of the cost of family labour, a household using a greater share than others of family labour incurs a lower cost of cultivation than a household that uses relatively more hired labour. Similarly, the cost of cultivation is higher for a tenant than for a landowner because rental payments of a tenant are included in the costs while no rental cost is imputed for owned land.

It is not uncommon for costs and revenues from different sources of income to be connected. For example, by-products of crop husbandry are used as fodder to maintain animal resources and by-products of animal husbandry are used as manure on the fields. As a result, in the accounting of household incomes in this example, part of the income from crop production is entered as a cost of animal husbandry and vice versa.

The PARI database does not include information on incomes from financial assets, that is, on stocks and shares, small savings, fixed deposits, and so on. We do not collect these data on a statistical basis because of problems of concealment and misreporting. Data on large-scale moneylending are also likely to be inaccurate. Thus, to the extent to which the data exclude such sources of income, our income estimates are likely to be underestimates. This is a problem that is likely to affect our estimates of the incomes of rich households. Similarly, since our surveys are based on recall and not, say, on diaries maintained throughout the year, wages and incomes from odd jobs and certain types of casual labour may go unrecorded. This is a less frequent problem than that of unreported incomes

[2] Comprehensive Scheme for the Study of Cost of Cultivation of Principal Crops in India.

among the rich, but where it occurs, it results in underestimates of incomes among the relatively poor.

Data pertaining to incomes of households were collected in the second round of surveys in the study villages. In this round, conducted in May 2006, a sample of households, selected through stratified random sampling, was covered. Population stimates presented in this chapter are prepared on the basis of data for this sample of households and multipliers derived from the stratification scheme used for sampling.

LEVELS OF HOUSEHOLD AND PER CAPITA INCOMES

Estimates of incomes for the study villages show that the average levels of household and per capita incomes are very low, and that the large mass of people in the villages live at a very low level of per capita income. Table 1 shows that the median annual per capita income was only Rs 5,895 in Kothapalle, Rs 6,308 in Bukkacherla and Rs 8,537 in Ananthavaram. The Planning Commission recently announced a new set of poverty lines.[3] Although these are, as before, consumption-poverty lines, it is instructive to compare the data on per capita incomes from the study villages with these poverty lines. Table 2 shows that about 32.3 per cent of the population in Ananthavaram, 44 per cent of the population in Bukkacherla, and 44.1 per cent in Kothapalle had per capita incomes below the official poverty line.

A significant proportion of households in all three villages had negative incomes in the reference year (Table 2). Households that made a net income-loss over the reference year had incurred losses mainly in crop production.[4] A household with negative incomes made a loss over paid-out costs. Such households used past savings, sold assets accumulated in the past or borrowed to meet their consumption requirements.

Households that make losses in one year may not do so in the next. Incomes from agriculture are subject to large fluctuations, both on account of fluctuations in physical yields (due, for example, to weather shocks or pests or other factors) and fluctuations in input and output prices. A village that faces adverse weather conditions one year may not face the same the next year. Nevertheless, the fact

[3] Planning Commission (2009).

[4] The source-wise composition of income is discussed in greater detail in Section 7.

Table 1 *Median household and per capita incomes, study villages, 2005–06* (in rupees)

Villages	Household income	Per capita income
Ananthavaram	25,629	8,537
Bukkacherla	19,517	6,308
Kothapalle	22,309	5,895

Source: Survey data.

Table 2 *Proportion of persons with annual per capita income of less than 0, less than Rs 5,400 and less than Rs 12,000 per annum, study villages, 2005–06*

Villages	Less than 0	Between 0 and Rs 5,400 per annum*	Between Rs 5,400 and Rs 12,000 per annum
Ananthavaram	2.5	29.8	30.9
Bukkacherla	2.8	41.2	32.7
Kothapalle	2.5	41.6	42.0

Note: * This is based on the assumption of Rs 433 per capita per month at 2004–05 prices, as recommended by the Tendulkar Committee (Planning Commission 2009). This poverty line is adjusted to 2005–06 prices using the Consumer Price Index for Agricultural Labourers (CPIAL) and then for a standard household by assuming an average family size of 4.1 persons.

Source: Survey data.

that negative income occurs across all the villages, that is, three villages with very different irrigation and agricultural cropping patterns, suggests that there is a serious problem with respect to the profitability of agriculture in Andhra Pradesh (see chapter 6). Our data suggest that a certain proportion of rural households are likely to suffer losses from cultivation in any given year.[5]

INCOME DISTRIBUTION

The distribution of household and per capita incomes in the survey villages was extremely unequal.

---

[5] The occurrence in an income distribution of a significant number of households with negative incomes also raises a series of methodological questions in statistics.

In the international literature on inequality, India is often — and incorrectly, we believe — considered to be a country with relatively low levels of economic inequality (Palma 2006). This is, in part, on account of the fact that the measurement of inequality in India is based on consumer *expenditure*, which is expected to be less unequally distributed than income (Swaminathan and Rawal 2009). In such a context, the estimates of income inequality from the survey villages are striking indeed.

Table 3 shows the distribution of households across deciles of household income. The table shows that the top 10 per cent of households accounted for about 52 per cent of the total income of households in Ananthavaram, and about 43 per cent of the total income of households in the other two villages. By contrast, the lowest 40 per cent of households accounted for only 7.8 per cent of household income in Ananthavaram, 7.4 per cent of household income in Bukkacherla and 9.3 per cent of household in come in Kothapalle (Table 3). The distribution of per capita income across deciles was similarly unequal (Table 4).

A noteworthy feature of the distribution of income across deciles is that there is very high concentration at the very top end of the distribution. In all the villages, there is a very large gap in the income share of the top and ninth decile. Such concentration at the very top end of the distribution of income is characteristic

Table 3 *Distribution of total household income across deciles of households, study villages, 2005–06* (%)

Decile	Ananthavaram	Bukkacherla	Kothapalle
1	0.2	-0.7	-0.1
2	2.1	1.4	2.4
3	2.2	3.0	3.0
4	3.3	3.7	3.9
5	3.3	5.1	6.7
6	5.7	8.0	9.0
7	7.3	9.4	8.1
8	10.7	10.7	12.2
9	13.4	16.5	11.0
10	51.8	42.9	43.8
All	100.0	100.0	100.0
Decile10/Decile9	3.9	2.6	4.0

Source: Survey data.

THE PUBLIC DISTRIBUTION SYSTEM: EXCLUSION PERSISTS

In 1997, following the advice given in an influential document of the World Bank, the Government of India introduced the Targeted Public Distribution System (TPDS). The most distinctive feature of the TPDS is the division of the entire population into below-poverty-line (BPL) and above-poverty-line (APL) categories, based on the poverty line defined by the Planning Commission.

This BPL–APL division has now become all-pervading, and a wide range of government schemes (housing benefits, loan schemes, student scholarships and others), not related to the PDS in any way, use this distinction to identify potential "beneficiaries".

Exclusion and targeting errors

The procedures by which the poor are identified for poverty line analyses in India are unjust, arbitrary and invidious. It is now also well established that narrow targeting has led to the large-scale exclusion of genuinely needy households from the PDS. All India and state-wise data from the National Sample Survey conducted in 2004–05 show that a large proportion of agricultural labour and other manual labour households, Dalit and Adivasi households, households with little or no land, and households in the lowest expenditure classes, are excluded from the PDS (Swaminathan 2008).

Andhra Pradesh has done better in terms of targeting errors than many other states, primarily because the state government categorised more households as "poor" than notified by the Planning Commission. Targets were thus not as narrowly defined in Andhra Pradesh as in many other states.

We use our survey data to examine problems of exclusion of households in the three study villages from the PDS.

Households that do not possess any ration card at all or possess APL ration cards can be said to be excluded form the PDS, and households with Antyodaya or BPL cards can be said to be included in the PDS.

Table B1 shows that, in aggregate, Andhra Pradesh performs better than the rest of India in respect of inclusion in the PDS. According to official data, 71 per cent of households in rural India are excluded from the PDS. The corresponding official figure for rural Andhra is 43 per cent, which is far better than the abysmal record of the country as a whole, but still represents a substantial degree of exclusion. Exclusion as shown in our survey data was, as Table B1 indicates, actually less than the official figures for rural Andhra Pradesh.

Table B1 *Distribution of households by type of ration card possessed, rural India, Andhra Pradesh and study villages, 2006*

Region/village	Antyodaya	BPL	Antyodaya plus BPL	APL/ Other	No ration card	All
All India (rural)	3	26	29	52	19	100
Andhra Pradesh (rural)	3	54	57	16	27	100
Ananthavaram	6	54	60	18	21	100
Bukkacherla	3	67	70	12	18	100
Kothapalle	3	57	60	19	21	100

Note: APL = Above Poverty Line; BPL = Below Poverty Line.
Sources: The figures for the state and India are taken from GOI (1997), and for the study villages from survey data.

Table B2 shows the extent of exclusion of households below the official poverty line from the PDS in the study villages.

Table B2 *Proportion of households below the official poverty line that possess either an APL card or no ration card at all, study villages, May 2006* (%)

Villages	BPL households excluded from PDS
Ananthavaram	29
Bukkacherla	29
Kothapalle	32

Note: APL = Above Poverty Line.
Source: Survey data.

Table B3 shows the extent to which manual labour households were excluded from the PDS.

Table B3 *Proportion of manual labour households that possess either an APL card or no ration card at all, study villages, May 2006* (%)

Villages	Manual labour households excluded from PDS
Ananthavaram	26
Bukkacherla	20
Kothapalle	30

Note: APL = Above Poverty Line.
Source: Survey data.

To summarize, although in aggregate the coverage of the village population by PDS is better in the study villages than in rural Andhra Pradesh as a whole (which, in turn, performs far better than the rest of rural India), a very substantial section of the income-poor (as measured by the government's own poverty line) in the study villages is excluded from the PDS.

Table 4 *Distribution of per capita income across deciles of population, study villages, 2005–06* (%)

Decile	Ananthavaram	Bukkacherla	Kothapalle
1	0.4	-0.4	-0.1
2	1.6	2.0	2.2
3	2.6	3.0	3.1
4	3.4	4.2	4.4
5	4.4	5.9	5.7
6	5.9	6.9	6.9
7	7.7	9.2	8.7
8	9.9	11.9	10.2
9	14.3	17.6	12.3
10	49.7	39.8	46.6
All	100.0	100.0	100.0
Decile 10/Decile 9	3.5	2.3	3.8

Source: Survey data.

Table 5 *Gini coefficients for household and per capita income distributions, study villages, 2005–06*

Villages	Gini coefficient of household incomes	Gini coefficient of per capita incomes
Ananthavaram	0.656	0.602
Bukkacherla	0.608	0.540
Kothapalle	0.578	0.565
All villages	0.641	0.596

Note: In view of presence of negative incomes, we have estimated adjusted Gini coefficients as proposed by Chen, Tsaur, and Rhai (1982).
Source: Survey data.

of income distribution in the most unequal societies in the world (Palma 2006).

Estimates of Gini coefficients also suggest very high levels of inequality. Gini coefficients of income distribution in most countries of the world tend to vary between 0.3 and 0.6.[6] In such a context, the Gini coefficients for the distribution of household incomes in the study villages — about 0.66 for Ananthavaram, 0.61 for Bukkacherla and 0.58 for Kothapalle — indicate extremely high levels of income inequality.

INCOME DISPARITIES

Data from the study villages show very clear and sharp caste and class divisions with respect to incomes. Tables 6 and 7 show the disparities in income levels across different classes in the three villages. The major conclusions from the tables are as follows. Firstly, landlords/big capitalist farmers and capitalist farmers/rich peasants had the highest levels of per capita income in all three villages. In Ananthavaram, these classes accounted for about 5 per cent of the population and about 25 per cent of total income. In Bukkacherla, landlord households accounted for about 5 per cent of the population and about 20 per cent of income. In Kothapalle, landlord households accounted for 1.4 per cent of the population and over 21.8 per cent of income.

Secondly, per capita income declined as one went from capitalist farmer/rich peasants to poor peasants and hired manual workers.

Thirdly, in general, of all classes, poor peasants and hired manual workers had the lowest levels of income. In Ananthavaram, hired manual workers and poor peasants accounted for about 45 per cent of the population and only about 14 per cent of income. In Bukkacherla, they accounted for about 34 per cent of the population and about 20 per cent of income. In Kothapalle, hired manual workers and poor peasants accounted for 49 per cent of the population and about 36 per cent of income.

Fourthly, in Ananthavaram, the median per capita income among households engaged in artisan work and traditional caste occupations was very low.

Fifthly, in Ananthavaram and Kothapalle, the median per capita income of poor peasants was slightly higher than the median per capita income of hired manual workers. Bukkacherla, a village with uncertain rain-fed agriculture, reported higher wage rates than the other villages: the median per capita income of hired manual workers was higher than the median per capita income among poor peasants. In all three villages, a considerable proportion of poor peasants, exposed to the vagaries of nature and of the market, had incomes lower than high earners among the class of hired manual workers.

In all the villages, the incomes of Dalit and Adivasi households were substan-

Table 6 *Median per capita income, by class, study villages, 2005–06* (in rupees)

Socio-economic class	Ananthavaram	Bukkacherla	Kothapalle
Landlord/Big capitalist farmer	45,189	47,607	12,357
Capitalist farmer/Rich peasant	1,59,544	13,561	7,011
Peasant: upper middle	23,456	6,354	4,959
Peasant: lower middle	13,729	4,180	3,258
Peasant: poor	4,958	3,709	6,411
Hired manual workers	4,175	4,762	5,108
Artisan work and work at traditional caste calling	3,517	14,796	10,176
Business activity/Self-employed	25,448	9,600	7,443
Rents/Moneylending	9,491	4,700	12,240
Salaried person/s	11,600	10,185	7,157
Remittances/pensions	14,970	3,792	2,127

Source: Survey data.

Table 7 *Share of different classes in population and in total income, study villages, 2005–06* (%)

Socio-economic class	Ananthavaram		Bukkacherla		Kothapalle	
	Share in population	Share in income	Share in population	Share in income	Share in population	Share in income
Landlord/Big capitalist farmer	2	5	5	20	1	22
Capitalist farmer/ Rich peasant	3	20	11	16	9	8
Peasant: upper middle	4	7	17	16	7	4
Peasant: lower middle	15	14	15	9	8	4
Peasant: poor	20	6	15	7	6	7
Hired manual workers	25	8	19	13	43	29
Artisan work and work at traditional caste calling	4	1	2	3	1	1
Business activity/ Self-employed	6	15	4	3	8	6
Rents/Moneylending	4	6	4	5	0	0.4
Salaried person/s	12	11	6	6	14	17
Remittances/pensions	5	6	3	3	3	2
Unclassified households	1	1				
All	100	100	100	100	100	100

Source: Survey data.

tially lower than the incomes of Other Caste households. The disparities across castes were particularly high in Ananthavaram, where the average per capita income of Adivasis (Rs 4,831) was only 14 per cent of the average per capita income of Other Castes (Rs 35, 224), and the average per capita income of Dalits (Rs 8,840) was only 25 per cent of the average per capita income of Other Castes. Average levels of income of persons from Backward Class households were also lower than average levels of incomes of Other Caste households. In Ananthavaram, Muslims had the lowest average levels of per capita income among all social groups (Table 8).

An important aspect of income disparities across social groups was that not only were the median levels of income among Muslims, Dalits and Adivasis low, there were also no Muslims, Dalits and Adivasis anywhere near the top end of the

Table 8 *Average and median per capita income, by social group, study villages, 2005–06* (in rupees)

Villages	Average per capita income			Median per capita income		
	Ananthavaram	Bukkacherla	Kothapalle	Ananthavaram	Bukkacherla	Kothapalle
Dalit households	8,840	5,521	7,192	6,838	4,268	4,939
Adivasi households	4,831			3,913		
Muslim households	4,407			2,802		
BC households	10,179	7,873	7,065	8,255	6,114	5,895
Other Caste households	35,224	12,271	18,233	18,000	8,322	7,249

Note: BC = Backward Class.
Source: Survey data.

Table 9 *Average annual per capita household income of the top five sample households, by social group, study villages, 2005–06* (in rupees)

Villages	Ananthavaram	Bukkacherla	Kothapalle
Dalit households	22,430	11,013	17,080
Adivasi households	5,108		
Muslim households	4,717		
BC households	33,173	26,064	19,934
Other Caste households	1,30,663	39,448	83,823

Note: (i) BC = Backward Class.
         (ii) "Top five households" here means the five households for which average annual per capita household income is the highest.
Source: Survey data.

distribution of income. In Ananthavaram, the average per capita income of the richest five Adivasi households was 4 per cent of the average per capita income among the richest five Other Caste households. The average annual per capita household income of the five richest Dalit households as a proportion of the average per capita income of the five richest Other Caste households was 17 per cent in Ananthavaram, 28 per cent in Bukkacherla and 20 per cent in Kothapalle (Table 9). The average annual per capita household income of the five richest Muslim households in Ananthavaram was only 3.6 per cent of the average income of the five richest Other Caste households.

COMPOSITION OF INCOMES

Tables 10 and 11 present data on the participation of households in different income-bearing activities and the share of these activities in total household income in the three villages. In these tables, economic activities are grouped into primary sector-based, secondary sector-based and tertiary sector-based activities, and other activities. Primary sector-based activities include crop production, rents from agricultural land, agricultural wage labour and toddy-tapping. Secondary sector-based and tertiary sector-based activities include non-agricultural casual labour, non-agricultural salaried jobs, rental incomes from machinery, and various kinds of businesses and trade. The main components of "other incomes" are financial transfers such as remittances, scholarships, pensions, and rents from houses and other buildings.

These tables show that a very large proportion of households derive incomes from the primary sector and, in particular, from agriculture. The proportion of households that participated in some primary sector-based activity was as high as 88 per cent in Ananthavaram, 94 per cent in Bukkacherla and 89 per cent in Kothapalle. About 53 per cent of households in Ananthavaram, 74 per cent of households in Bukkacherla and 43 per cent of households in Kothapalle were engaged in crop production. About 61 per cent of households in Ananthavaram, about 48 per cent of households in Bukkacherla, and about 54 per cent of households in Kothapalle derived income from agricultural labour (casual or long-term). About 55 per cent of households in Ananthavaram, 49 per cent of households in Bukkacherla and 59 per cent of households in Kothapalle maintained animals, and nearly 14 per cent of households in Kothapalle worked at toddy-tapping (Table 10).

A substantial proportion of households — 52 per cent in Ananthavaram, 38 per cent in Bukkacherla and 54 per cent in Kothapalle — also participated in economic activities that could be classified as part of the secondary and tertiary sectors (Table 10).

In terms of shares of income, primary sector-based incomes accounted for 68 per cent of household incomes in Ananthavaram, 59 per cent of household incomes in Bukkacherla and 44 per cent of household incomes in Kothapalle. Thus, Ananthavaram and Bukkacherla can still be characterized as agricultural economies, with more than 50 per cent of the household incomes being generated from agriculture and allied activities (Table 11).

Table 10 *Proportion of households engaged in different economic activities, study villages, 2005 –06* (%)

	Sources of income	Ananthavaram	Bukkacherla	Kothapalle
1	Crop production	53	74	43
2	Rental income from agricultural land	15	18	6
3	Animal resources	55	49	59
4	Agricultural labour (casual) earnings	59	47	51
5	Earnings from long term labour in agriculture and allied activities	2	1	3
6	Toddy-tapping	0	1	14
7	Primary sector (1–6)	88	94	89
8	Non agricultural casual labour earnings	21	18	21
9	Government salaried jobs	5	9	9
10	Private salaried jobs	11	3	23
11	Business and trade earnings	18	10	17
12	Rental income from machinery	1	4	1
13	Secondary and tertiary sectors (8 –12)	52	38	54
14	Pensions scholarships and insurance claims	12	10	10
15	Remittances	12	6	8
16	Rental income from other assets	1	0.3	4
17	Any other source	10	4	4
18	Other incomes (14–17)	32	19	22
19	All sources	100	100	100
20	Total number of households	664	286	370
	Average number of sources of income per household	3.07	2.73	2.97

Source: Survey data.

Diversification into non-agricultural activities was greatest in Kothapalle, situated on a major highway and close to Karimnagar town. Access to non-agricultural employment in commercial establishments (including shops and restaurants) along the road and in Karimnagar resulted in much greater diversification into secondary-sector-based and tertiary-sector-based employment in Kothapalle than in the other two villages. The share of secondary-sector-based and tertiary-sector-based income in total household income was 54 per cent in

Table 11 *Share of different economic activities in total household income, study villages, 2005–06* (%)

	Sources of income	Ananthavaram	Bukkacherla	Kothapalle
1	Crop production	25	21	9
2	Rental income from agricultural land	6	8	2
3	Animal resources	28	17	18
4	Agricultural labour (casual) earnings	9	10	7
5	Earnings from long term labour in agriculture and allied activities	1	0.2	1
6	Toddy tapping	0	2	7
7	Primary sector (1–6)	68	59	44
8	Non agricultural casual labour earnings	3	4	6
9	Government salaried jobs	5	17	13
10	Private salaried jobs	4	1	11
11	Business and trade earnings	6	9	22
12	Rental income from machinery	1	1	2
13	Secondary and tertiary sectors (8–12)	20	32	54
14	Pensions scholarships and insurance claims	4	1	1
15	Remittances	5	3	1
16	Rental income from other assets	0	3	0.3
17	Any other source	4	2	1
18	Other incomes (14–17)	12	9	3
19	Total income (7+13+18)	100	100	100
20	Average household income (Rupees)	59,173	36,572	33,987

Source: Survey data.

Kothapalle, compared to 32 per cent in Bukkacherla and 20 per cent in Ananthavaram (Table 11).

Incomes from manual labour (agricultural and non-agricultural) contributed 13 to 14 per cent of household incomes in all three villages. Incomes from salaried employment were higher in Bukkacherla and Kothapalle than in Ananthavaram (Table 11). Incomes from business and trading activities were significant in Kothapalle, providing, on average, an annual income of Rs 7,610 (22 per cent) per household.

The estimates of average incomes and shares by source confirm that Kothapalle is more diversified in respect of the income-generating activities of its residents than Ananthavaram and Bukkacherla. In Ananthavaram, a region of canal irriga-

tion and high-yielding paddy cultivation, crop production and rearing milch cattle
remained the two major sources of livelihood. In Bukkacherla, agriculture is risky
and relatively low-yielding, but there has been very limited diversification of
activity within the village. Interestingly, when households were ranked by the share
of non-farm or non-primary sector income in their aggregate incomes, the
median value for Bukkacherla was 0, that is, the median household had no non-
farm incomes at all. The corresponding values for the share of non-farm income
of the median household were 26 per cent in Ananthavaram and 34 per cent in
Kothapalle. One way of interpreting this finding is that some people emigrate

Table 12 *Share of primary, secondary and tertiary sectors in total income of households in different
agricultural classes, study villages, 2005–06* (%)

Village/Socio-economic class	Primary sector	Secondary and tertiary sectors	Other incomes
Ananthavaram			
Landlord/Big capitalist farmer	78	9	13
Capitalist farmer/Rich peasant	97	0.1	3
Peasant: upper middle	97	2	2
Peasant: lower middle	87	11	3
Peasant: poor	72	26	2
Hired manual labour and other wage-work	74	25	2
Bukkacherla			
Landlord/Big capitalist farmer	24	63	14
Capitalist farmer/Rich peasant	85	15	0
Peasant: upper middle	99	0.3	0.5
Peasant: lower middle	70	23	7
Peasant: poor	72	28	0
Hired manual labour and other wage-work	63	32	5
Kothapalle			
Landlord/Big capitalist farmer	22	78	0
Capitalist farmer/Rich peasant	88	11	1
Peasant: upper middle	69	31	0
Peasant: lower middle	92	6	2
Peasant: poor	79	21	0
Hired manual labour and other wage-work	58	39	3

Source: Survey data.

from the drought-prone village of Bukkacherla, but those who remain in the village remain trapped in agriculture and agriculture alone.

Table 12 shows the shares of primary-sector-based, secondary-sector-based, tertiary-sector-based, and other incomes, for agricultural classes in each village. The table shows that there are some important differences between villages in the pattern of variation in composition of the incomes of these classes.

Landlord households in Bukkacherla and Kothapalle derived substantial incomes from secondary-sector-based and tertiary-sector-based sources. In contrast, incomes of landlords/big capitalist farmers in Ananthavaram were mainly from agriculture (Table 12).

In Ananthavaram, the share of secondary-sector-based and tertiary-sector-based incomes in total income increased as one moved from the capitalist farmer/rich peasant class to the poor peasant and hired manual worker classes. In Kothapalle, substantial dependence on secondary-sector-based and tertiary-sector-based incomes was a general feature of all classes other than lower-middle peasants (Table 12).

CROP INCOMES AND AGRICULTURAL RENTS

Although the reference period of this study was officially a normal year in all three survey villages, incomes from crop production were very low for a very large proportion of cultivating households. A substantial proportion of cultivating households in all three villages incurred losses in agriculture.

The proportion of cultivating households that incurred losses in agriculture was 29 per cent in Ananthavaram, 36 per cent in Bukkacherla and 30 per cent in Kothapalle (Table 13). Some of these households were able to cover these losses through earnings from other economic activities. Others had to fall back on past savings, borrow or sell some assets to cover the losses.

There were two major factors behind losses in crop production. In Ananthavaram, losses in crop production were incurred mainly by households that leased in paddy land on rent in kind. This is discussed in detail in chapter 6. In Bukkacherla and Kothapalle, losses were mainly on account of lack of irrigation and crop failures.

Table 13 also shows that, for more than 80 per cent of cultivating households in all three villages, per capita income from crop production was less than the official consumption-poverty line (Rs 5,400 per capita per annum).

Some Rich Farmers of Ananthavaram

NVN, Capitalist Farmer/Rich Peasant

NVN, a capitalist farmer belonging to the Kamma caste, owned 10 acres of paddy land, which he leased to his son-in-law for cultivation. His son-in-law, RL, who owned 10 acres of unirrigated land in Cuddapah district, migrated to Ananthavaram and cultivated land leased in from NVN. RL paid a cash rent of Rs 50,000 per year to NVN for 10 acres of land. The rent charged by NVN was relatively low in comparison with prevailing rates of cash rent for paddy land in the village, which were Rs 8,000 to 10,000 per acre.

In 2004 NVN leased in, from two other Kamma households, a total of 5 acres of land that was suitable for the cultivation of betel leaf. NVN leased this land in Epur village for an annual rent of Rs 95,000. In 2005–06, betel leaves plucked from the land were sold for about Rs 24.7 lakhs. The total cost of production was about Rs 10.8 lakhs.

NVN's total income, Rs 13.9 lakhs from crop production and Rs 50,000 in rent, was the highest in the village.

RPVD, Landlord

RPVD, aged 75 years, owned 24.75 acres of land. At the time of the survey in May 2006, the land was valued at Rs 3 lakhs per acre. RPVD and his wife were the only members of their household. His son, RS, lived separately with his family.

Until 2004–05, RPVD cultivated 12 acres of land himself and leased out the rest to his nephew, RMN. Since 2004–05, in view of his age, he has leased out all his land. In 2005–06, he had six tenants, of whom two belonged to the Kamma caste, one to the Yadava caste, one to the Mala caste and two to the Madiga caste. RMN cultivated 7 acres of his land and paid him 22 bags of paddy per acre in rent. RPVD advanced him interest-free credit for cultivation. All other tenants paid 24 bags of paddy per acre in rent, though they received no similar advance. Like most other lessors of land in Ananthavaram, RPVD did not contribute anything towards the cost of cultivation.

In 2005–06, RPVD got 435 quintals of paddy, valued at Rs 2.26 lakhs, as rent for his land.

RPVD's son, RS, owned a poultry farm in Vellabdu (Vemuru mandal, Guntur). In 2006, RS was establishing another poultry farm in Ananthavaram.

RSD, Capitalist Farmer/Rich Peasant

The largest operational holding in Ananthavaram was cultivated by RSD, a capitalist farmer/rich peasant. RSD owned only 8 acres of land, of which he leased out 2.5 acres because of its inconvenient location. He leased in 42 acres of land from 13 landowners on cash rent. Of the land leased in, 19.85 acres were leased in for Rs 8,000 per acre, 5.5 acres for Rs 8,500 per acre, 13.05 acres for Rs 9,000 per acre, 1 acre for Rs 9,500 per acre and 2.6 acres for Rs 10,000 per acre. The persons from whom he leased in land included two large landowners belonging to the Kamma caste, two salaried persons who had migrated from the village, medium landowners belonging to Chakali caste, a small land-owner belonging to the Kamma caste, a person who worked as an agricultural labourer, and a person who was a small tenant peasant.

On his total operational holding, he cultivated sugarcane (27 acres, annual), paddy (22 acres, kharif), maize (10 acres, rabi), black gram (4 acres, rabi) and sesamum (10 acres, rabi).

In 2005–06, RSD had two long-term workers. They were paid an annual wage of Rs 21,600 each. He spent about Rs 3.8 lakhs on wages paid to daily-rated and piece-rated workers.

In August 2008, RSD took a loan of Rs 42,000 from the Andhra Bank to meet the expenses of kharif cultivation. In November 2008, he took a loan of Rs 1 lakh from the bank to meet rabi expenses.

RSD himself was a major moneylender in the village. In May 2006, he reported having lent Rs 2.37 lakhs to peasants and agricultural workers. His interest earnings from moneylending for 2005–06 were estimated to be Rs. 42,660. His household had five buffalo and his income included Rs 1.18 lakhs from crop production, Rs 99,445 from animal resources and Rs 22,000 from rent on land leased out.

Table 13 *Proportion of households that incurred losses in crop production and number of households than earned less than Rs 5, 400 per annum from crop production, study villages, 2005–06* (%)

	Households with negative crop production income		Households with <Rs 5400 per capita per annum crop production income	
	As a proportion of cultivating households	As a proportion of all households	As a proportion of cultivating households	As a proportion of all households
Ananthavaram	29	15	81	43
Bukkacherla	36	27	82	61
Kothapalle	30	13	92	40

Source: Survey data.

Table 14 shows the distribution of incomes from agriculture obtained in the form of profits and rent. The table shows that while agricultural incomes were low for a very large proportion of households, some households in each of the three villages gained substantial incomes from agriculture in the form of profits and rent. The proportion of households with an income of more than Rs 48,000 per annum was 12 per cent in Ananthavaram, 9 per cent in Bukkacherla and 3 per cent in Kothapalle. In Ananthavaram, these households, on average, got Rs 1.74 lakhs in profit and Rs 27,390 as rent from agriculture. In Bukkacherla, households in the highest size class, on average, earned Rs 68,295 as profit and Rs 28,507 as rent. In Kothapalle, these households earned Rs 73,665 as profit and Rs 12,610 as rent.

Of all sample households in the three villages, the highest income from crop production, a staggering Rs 13.9 lakhs, was gained by a household belonging to the capitalist farmer/rich peasant class in Ananthavaram. Among all sample households in the three villages, the highest receipt of rent for agricultural land, Rs. 2.26 lakhs, was reported by a landlord household in Ananthavaram.

Table 15 shows the average income from crop production per acre of operational holding for different agricultural classes in the three study villages. It shows that in Ananthavaram and Bukkacherla, average per acre income from crop production of the capitalist farmer/rich peasant class was higher than the corresponding average for landlords. Capitalist farmer/rich peasant households operated substantial amounts of land, had access to irrigation and were able to culti-

Table 14 *Distribution of households cultivating land or receiving rent from agricultural land, by size category of income from crop production and rents from agricultural land, study villages, 2005–06 (in rupees)*

Size-classes of income from crop production and agricultural land	Ananthavaram			Bukkacherla			Kothapalle		
	Proportion of households (%)	Average income from crop production	Average rental income from agricultural land	Proportion of households (%)	Average income from crop production	Average rental income from agricultural land	Proportion of households (%)	Average income from crop production	Average rental income from agricultural land
Less than 0	24	(–)10,892	196	30	(–)8,963	626	24	(–)6,366	0
0–12000	45	2,653	1,229	38	4,101	1,621	50	4,787	735
12000–24000	10	12,283	4,319	14	13,330	2,080	18	14,652	0
24000–36000	5	22,661	6,235	7	26,995	0	6	20,734	9,230
36000–48000	3	25,659	14,674	1	40,670	0	0	NA	NA
>48000	12	1,73,657	27,390	9	68,295	28,507	3	73,665	12,610
All households	100 (416)	23,171	5,214	100 (247)	9,250	3,619	100 (166)	5,405	2,144

Note: Figures in parentheses give number of households cultivating land or receiving rent from agricultural land.
Source: Survey data.

Table 15 *Average income from crop production per acre of operational holding, by agricultural class, study villages, 2005–06* (in rupees)

Socio-economic class	Ananthavaram	Bukkacherla	Kothapalle
Landlord/Big capitalist farmer	4,731	403	4,120
Capitalist farmer/Rich peasant	28,468	2,328	2,615
Peasant: upper middle	8,020	1,488	1,327
Peasant: lower middle	2,438	872	–217
Peasant: poor	–1,304	358	4,060
Hired manual worker	1,338	1,258	655

Source: Survey data.

vate crops that gave high returns; some even leased in substantial amounts of land in order to grow profitable crops. It is clear that, in Ananthavaram and Bukkacherla, capitalist farmers/rich peasant households, rather than landlords, represented, as a class, the most modern sector of the agrarian economy.

In Kothapalle, by contrast, the biggest landlord had an extremely profitable farm on which he had, in addition to field crops, large mango and orange orchards. In contrast with landlords in Ananthavaram and Bukkacherla, this landlord in Kothapalle took advantage of his dominant social and economic position in the village, and opportunities available outside the village, to modernize farming on his land and start new enterprises.

Table 15 also shows that, in Ananthavaram, on average, rich peasant/capitalist farmers earned the highest income per acre of land operated. The average per acre income from crop production declined sharply as one went from rich peasants to upper-middle peasants and lower-middle peasants, and is negative for poor peasants. Many poor peasants paid rents in kind on leased land and therefore incurred losses (see chapters 4 and 6). Among hired manual labour households, some households cultivated small plots of owned land and earned small positive incomes from such cultivations.

Bukkacherla showed a somewhat similar pattern. The average income went down as one moved from the rich peasant class towards the class of poor peasants (Table 15). In Kothapalle, however, on account of an extremely diversified cropping pattern and limited access to irrigation, incomes from crop production varied a great deal within each class (see Annexure), and, as a result, no clear pattern of variation across different peasant classes (as we have classified them) emerged.

CONCLUSIONS

We summarize below the major findings of our analysis of household incomes in the study villages.

Firstly, the data show that average levels of household and per capita incomes were very low, and that a large proportion of people in the villages lived at a very low level of per capita income. The per capita incomes of 32.3 per cent of the population in Ananthavaram, 44 per cent of the population in Bukkacherla and 44 per cent of the population in Kothapalle were below the official consumption-poverty line (Table 2).

Secondly, there were clear regional variations. The highest average incomes were in the south coastal village of Ananthavaram. Next in rank was Kothapalle in Karimnagar district (Table 8), where proximity both to a state highway served to diversify and raise average incomes.

Thirdly, the distribution of household and per capita incomes in the survey villages was, by all international standards, extremely unequal. The Gini coefficients of household incomes were 0.66 in Ananthavaram, 0.61 in Bukkacherla and 0.58 in Kothapalle (Table 5). Thus Ananthavaram, where average incomes were the highest, was also characterized by the highest degree of income inequality. The distribution of incomes was particularly concentrated at the top end: the top 10 per cent households accounted for 51.8 per cent of total income in Ananthavaram, 42.9 per cent of total income in Bukkacherla and 43.8 per cent of total income in Kothapalle (Table 3).

Fourthly, data from the study villages show that there were sharp income disparities across various social groups. As was the case with average incomes, Ananthavaram had the highest average incomes and the highest levels of income inequality among social groups.

Average annual income per capita among Dalits in Ananthavaram (Rs 8,840) was only 25 per cent of the average annual income per capita among Other Castes in the village (Rs 35,224). The corresponding figures for Kothapalle and Bukkacherla were 39 per cent and 45 per cent. The average income per capita among Adivasis in Ananthavaram (Rs 4,831) was 14 per cent of the corresponding average for Other Castes (Table 8).

Inequality is particularly sharp if we consider the richest in each distribution. The average income of the top five Dalit households in respect of per capita household incomes was only 17 per cent of the income of the top five house-

holds among Other Castes in Ananthavaram, 20 per cent of the top five households among Other Castes in Kothapalle and 28 per cent of the top five households among Other Castes in Bukkacherla (Table 9).

Per capita incomes among the "richest" Adivasi households were only 4 per cent
of per capita incomes among the richest Other Castes. The worst off in our sample
was the small community of Muslims (16 households out of 667) in Ananthavaram.
The average income among the "richest" Muslim households was about 3.6 per
cent of the average income of the five richest Other Caste households.

Fifthly, across classes, landlords/big capitalist farmers and capitalist farmers/
rich peasants had the highest levels of per capita income in all three villages. Per
capita income tends to decline as one goes from the capitalist farmer/rich peasant class to poor peasants and hired manual workers. The median per capita
income of capitalist farmers/rich peasants in Ananthavaram was about 1.59 lakhs.
The median per capita income of poor peasants and hired manual workers was
only about 3 per cent of the median per capita income of capitalist farmers/rich
peasants (Table 6).

Sixthly, our analysis of the composition of incomes showed that about 90 per
cent of households in all the villages participated in some way in primary sector-
based activities. In Ananthavaram and Bukkacherla, the primary sector accounted
for more than 50 per cent of total income. In terms of its share in total income,
the primary sector was relatively less important in Kothapalle (Tables 11 and 12).,
which is situated close to a major highway. Access to employment in shops and
commercial establishments along the road and in non-agricultural activities in
Karimnagar town resulted in a substantially lower share of primary sector-based
activities in aggregate household incomes in Kothapalle.

Finally, incomes from crop production were very low for an overwhelming
majority of cultivating households. About 29 per cent of cultivating households
in Ananthavaram, 36 per cent of households in Bukkacherla and 30 per cent of
cultivating households in Kothapalle actually incurred losses in crop production
(Table 13). Moreover, in each village, the per capita income from agriculture of
over 80 per cent of cultivating households was lower than the official consumption-poverty line (Table 13). At the other end of the distribution, a few households belonging to the landlord and capitalist farmer/rich peasant classes, particularly in Ananthavaram, obtained large profits from crop production, and received substantial rental incomes from agricultural land (Table 14). In Ananthavaram,
poor peasants on average made a loss of Rs 1,304 per acre of land operated,

while capitalist farmers/rich peasants made an average profit of Rs 28,468 per acre of land operated (Table 15). Among all sample households, the highest income from crop production, Rs 13.9 lakhs, was of a capitalist farmer/rich peasant in Ananthavaram and the highest income from rent, Rs 2.26 lakhs, was of a landlord in Ananthavaram.

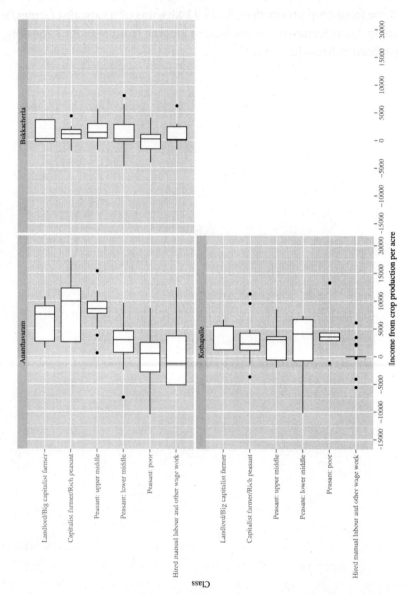

Annexure

Income from crop production per acre of operational holding, by agricultural classes, Ananthavaram, Bukkacherla and Kothapalle, 2005–06

6

Is Agriculture Profitable?

The focus of this chapter, as the title suggests, is crop incomes. The chapter examines the gross value of outputs, costs of inputs and net incomes from the cultivation of selected crops by different socio-economic classes in Ananthavaram, Bukkacherla and Kothapalle. As we shall see, differences in crop incomes mirrored the pattern of socio-economic differences in the village.

A NOTE ON METHODOLOGY

For each crop, we have computed the gross value of output (sometimes abbreviated as GVO). This is simply the value of total production, that is, of the main product and all by-products.

The cost of cultivation considered here are the costs paid out by the cultivators. More specifically, we have used the category of "Cost A2" as defined by the Commission on Agricultural Cost and Prices (CACP). The full definition of A2 is in Annexure 1. In brief, Cost A2 covers all paid-out costs, such as the costs of seed, manure, fertiliser, plant protection, irrigation and labour. Cost A2 includes some imputed costs, such as the cost of depreciation and interest on working capital. Rental payments are also included in Cost A2 though no cost is imputed for family labour or the rental value of owned land.

All references in this chapter to "costs" are to Cost A2 as defined in the preceding paragraph and in Annexure 1. All references to "net income" or "crop incomes" are to the gross value of output minus such costs.

Different kinds of rental arrangements prevail in the villages. These include sharecropping with the share paid in kind (in Bukkacherla), and fixed rent with rent paid in cash or kind (in all three villages). Rent may be paid in full after the first crop or may be paid in instalments. In the computations that follow, annual rent payments have been divided across all crops cultivated on the rented land during the year in the ratio of the gross values of output of the crops. In other words, even though tenants cultivating paddy in Ananthavaram pay the rent in bags of paddy at the end of the kharif harvest, and are in deficit till they reap the rabi harvest, we have divided the rent paid across all crops grown in both seasons.

We have calculated crop incomes from the cultivation of the major crops in the three villages, namely, paddy, maize, groundnut, black gram, sugarcane and cotton. All costs and incomes are reported in rupees per hectare and refer to the agricultural year 2005–06.

CROPPING PATTERN

In Ananthavaram (Annexure 2, Table A), 462.8 hectares (ha) were sown with paddy in the kharif season. In the rabi season, 268.3 hectares were sown with maize and 121.8 hectares were sown with black gram. These three crops accounted for 87 per cent of total cropped area during the year (paddy covered 98 per cent of kharif area, and maize and black gram together covered 91 per cent of rabi area).

In total, 79 per cent of the gross cropped area was irrigated. Paddy, maize, sugarcane, millet and betel leaf were all irrigated crops. Black gram, sesame and other crops sown in the rabi season were generally not irrigated.

In Bukkacherla, groundnut was the major crop and was sown on 506.7 hectares in the kharif season (Annexure 2, Table B). Most of the groundnut cultivated in kharif was unirrigated. Some irrigation was available in kharif and such land was sown with paddy. Groundnut was sown as a sole crop on some plots in kharif, but it was more commonly intercropped with red gram, cowpea, green gram, sesame, bajra, jowar and beans.

As there was very little irrigation in this village, the area under rabi crops was small. The irrigated rabi crops were paddy, groundnut, and a variety of fruit and vegetable. There was a very small sector of drip-irrigated agriculture in the village.

In Kothapalle, the gross cropped area was only 221.6 hectares. As noted in chapter 5, non-agricultural activity dominated income-generation in Kothapalle. Maize, paddy, cotton and fodder crops were the major kharif crops, and maize and paddy were the major rabi crops (Annexure 2, Table C). A range of other crops, including oilseeds, fruit and vegetables, were also cultivated on a small scale on irrigated land in kharif.

PADDY

Gross and Net Incomes

The average gross value of output of paddy for all cultivators in each village in the kharif season was of the order of Rs 30,000 per hectare (Table 1). The gross value of output was Rs 29,939 per hectare in Kothapalle, Rs 31,734 per hectare in Ananthavaram and Rs 33,917 per hectare in Bukkacherla for paddy sown in kharif. The gross value of output was lower for paddy sown in rabi (Rs 27,333 in Bukkacherla and Rs 28,777 in Kothapalle), mainly on account of lower output prices.

The costs of cultivation were also very high (Table 1). According to our surveys, Cost A2 per hectare ranged from around Rs 21,000 in Kothapalle to Rs 29,000 in Ananthavaram.

As a result, crop incomes (gross value of output minus Cost A2) in our surveys were extremely low. On average, the net income from paddy cultivation was Rs 8,555 per hectare in Kothapalle and Rs 6,332 per hectare in Bukkacherla. In Ananthavaram, the average net income was extremely low: Rs 2,441 per hectare.

While costs in the rabi season were lower than costs in the kharif season, gross incomes were also lower. Paddy cultivation in rabi was profitable in Kothapalle,

Table 1 *Gross value of output (GVO), Cost A2 and net income from paddy cultivation, study villages, 2005–06* (Rs/ha)

Crop season	Location	GVO	Cost A2	Net income
Kharif	Andhra Pradesh	32,108	16,320	15,788
	Ananthavaram	31,734	29,293	2,441
	Bukkacherla	33,917	27,585	6,332
	Kothapalle	29,939	21,385	8,555
Rabi	Bukkacherla	27,333	25,563	1,770
	Kothapalle	28,777	18,691	10,086

Source: Survey data; estimates for Andhra Pradesh are from the CACP Report (GOI 2009).

providing a net income of Rs 10,086 per hectare, but it was a low-return crop in Bukkacherla.

The only national sources of information on crop-wise costs and returns are the reports of the CACP, which are based on data collected through cost of cultivation surveys. The estimate of costs and incomes given in these reports are important, as they form the basis for determination of minimum support prices.

According to the CACP, the gross value of output from paddy cultivation in Andhra Pradesh in 2005–06 was Rs 32,108 per hectare. At an aggregate level, then, the estimates of gross value of output obtained in our village surveys were similar to the CACP estimate for the same year.

However, Cost A2 per hectare, according to the CACP, was only Rs 16,320. Thus, according to the CACP, the average cultivator of paddy in Andhra Pradesh made a net income of Rs 15,788 per hectare. It is clear that, while the survey estimates and CACP estimates concur with respect to the gross value of output, they vary hugely with respect to costs. The costs per hectare in Ananthavaram, for instance, were almost Rs 16,000 higher in our database than in the CACP estimates. We believe that the CACP data represent a huge underestimation of costs, an issue that we discuss below.

A Class-Wise Analysis

Ananthavaram

Table 2 reports the gross value of output, Cost A2 and net incomes from paddy cultivation for cultivators from different socio-economic classes. The most striking finding from these data is of very big losses from paddy cultivation incurred by poor peasant households, and substantial incomes earned by big capitalist farmers and landlords. Rich peasants, upper-middle peasants and poor peasants earned a positive income from paddy cultivation, though much less than the incomes gained by landlords and big capitalist farmers. Village-level averages thus conceal huge differences in the incomes gained by different classes.

The gross value of output per hectare (GVO) from paddy was broadly similar across socio-economic classes. In other words, paddy yields and the prices of output received by cultivators were broadly similar across classes, with some variation. Lower and upper-middle peasant households received around Rs 30,000 per hectare from the paddy crop before costs were deducted. Landlords and big capitalist farmers gained a gross income of Rs 30,374 per hectare. Poor peasants

Table 2 *Gross value of output (GVO), Cost A2 and net income for kharif paddy, by class, Ananthavaram village, 2005–06* (Rs/ha)

Socio-economic class	GVO	A2	Net income
Peasant: poor	29,142	33,578	(–)4,436
Peasant: lower-middle	30,230	27,625	2,606
Peasant: upper-middle	30,466	21,875	8,591
Capitalist farmer/Rich peasant/Peasant: upper*	35,521	31,772	3,748
Landlord/Big capitalist farmer	30,374	19,065	11,308
All classes (average)	31,734	29,293	2,441

Note: * A significant proportion (40 per cent) of land cultivated by households in this class was leased in.

Source: Survey data.

obtained the lowest gross value of output, Rs 29,000 per hectare. The highest gross value of output from paddy, Rs 35,521 per hectare, was gained by rich peasants.

Aggregate costs, however, varied significantly by class. Poor peasants incurred costs of more than Rs 33,000 per hectare, while landlords and big capitalist farmers incurred costs of about Rs 19,000 per hectare. In other words, per hectare-costs for landlords and big capitalist farmers were almost one-half of per hectare-costs incurred by poor peasants.

As a consequence, net incomes were negative, (–)Rs 4,436 per hectare, for poor peasants; and net incomes were positive and substantial, Rs 11,308, for landlords and big capitalist farmers. Nevertheless, even the net income per hectare gained by landlords was lower than the CACP estimate for Andhra Pradesh. Net incomes were positive but low for lower-middle peasants and rich peasants. The relatively low income from paddy among rich peasants, as explained later, is on account of the high share of leased-in land in the operational holdings of this class.[1]

Bukkacherla

Net incomes from paddy cultivation follow a similar pattern of variation across socio-economic classes in Bukkacherla, though absolute levels are different

---

[1] As shown in Table 8, when the calculation is done exclusively for owner-cultivators among rich peasants, net incomes rise to Rs 12,831 per hectare.

Table 3 *Gross value of output (GVO), Cost A2 and net income for kharif paddy, by class, Bukkacherla village, 2005-06* (Rs/ha)

Socio-economic class	GVO	Cost A2	Net income
Peasant: poor	37,103	33,618	3,485
Peasant: lower-middle	30,178	27,973	2,205
Peasant: upper-middle	33,666	23,621	10,044
All classes (average)	33,917	27,585	6,332

Note: There were only two observations for rich peasants and so they have been excluded.
Source: Survey data.

(Table 3). In Bukkacherla, gross value of output was the highest among poor peasants (Rs 37,103 per hectare). However, costs were also the highest among poor peasants.

According to computations from our survey data, lower-middle peasants obtained Rs 2,205 per hectare, poor peasants obtained Rs 3,485 per hectare, and upper-middle peasants obtained Rs 10,044 per hectare from paddy cultivation in 2005–06. Thus, in the same village, for the same crop and same season, upper-middle peasants received an income per hectare that was three times higher than that of poor peasants.

Kothapalle

In Kothapalle, too, there were sharp variations in costs and incomes across socio-economic classes (Table 4). The lowest net income, around Rs 8,000 per hectare,

Table 4 *Gross value of output (GVO), Cost A2 and net income for kharif paddy, by class, Kothapalle village, 2005–06* (Rs/ha)

Socio-economic class	GVO	Cost A2	Net income
Peasant: poor	29,638	21,409	8,229
Peasant: lower-middle	34,679	25,216	9,463
Peasant: upper-middle	23,472	15,348	8,124
Capitalist farmer/Rich peasant/Peasant: upper	34,473	20,255	14,218
All classes	29,939	21,385	8,555

Note: There were only two observations for landlord/big capitalist farmers and so they have been excluded.
Source: Survey data.

was obtained by poor and upper-middle peasants and the highest income was obtained by capitalist farmers and rich peasants (Rs 14,218 per hectare).

Costs of Production: Levels and Shares of Different Components

Our estimates of paddy accounts showed that there were huge class differences in net incomes from paddy cultivation in all three villages. The underlying explanation is to be found in tenancy and the payment of rent. We examine item-wise costs of cultivation for different classes and show how costs of cultivation — rent payments in particular — wipe out the profits of poor and middle peasants.

The main point to emerge from an item-wise comparison of costs of paddy cultivation as reported by the CACP and our survey data is the large expenditure on rent or rental payments in the study villages.

For the paddy crop, in Ananthavaram, on average, rental payments amounted to Rs 9,447 per hectare; the corresponding figures were Rs 4,770 for Bukkacherla and Rs 875 for Kothapalle (Table 5). By contrast, in the CACP data, rental payments are estimated to be very low: merely Rs 369 per hectare. In Bukkacherla, rental payments per hectare were thirteen times the amount reported in the CACP; and in Ananthavaram, rental payments per hectare were twenty-six times the amount reported in the CACP.

The CACP data thus seriously underestimate rent. This is because the CACP data essentially exclude tenant cultivation (indeed, the CACP methodology excludes unregistered tenant cultivators from the CACP sample).

Table 5 *Costs of cultivation by type of cost for kharif paddy, survey village, 2005–06* (Rs/ha)

Item of cost	CACP data for Andhra Pradesh	Ananthavaram	Survey data for Bukkacherla	Kothapalle
Seed	891	762	1,164	923
Manure	383	907	5,536	2,525
Fertiliser	2,579	3,755	2,452	3,993
Pesticide	900	2,335	922	312
Irrigation	665	261	50	8
Labour	9,130	10,138	8,407	9,511
Rent	369	9,447	4,770	875
Other costs	1,402	1,688	4,284	3,238
Cost A2	16,319	29,293	27,585	21,385

Source: Survey data; figures for Andhra Pradesh are from the CACP report (GOI 2009).

Table 6 *Share of specific components of cost in total Cost A2 for kharif paddy, survey villages, 2005–06* (%)

Item of cost	CACP data for Andhra Pradesh	Survey data for		
		Ananthavaram	Bukkacherla	Kothapalle
Seed	5	3	4	4
Manure	2	3	20	12
Fertiliser	16	13	9	19
Pesticides	6	8	3	1
Irrigation	4	1	0	0
Labour	56	35	30	44
Rent	2	32	17	4
Other cost	9	6	16	15
Cost A2	100	100	100	100

Source: Survey data; figures for Andhra Pradesh are from the CACP report (GOI 2009).

Our survey data also showed higher expenditures on manure and fertilizers than the CACP data.

Expenditure on hired labour was the biggest component of costs incurred in the cultivation of paddy. However, rent was a major component of the costs in Ananthavaram (32 per cent of total costs) and Bukkacherla (17 per cent). According to the CACP, rent was only 2 per cent of the total cost of cultivation of paddy. The share of manure costs in total expenditure was much higher in Bukkacherla and Kothapalle than in the CACP estimate (Table 6).[2]

Tenants and Owner-Cultivators in Ananthavaram

Ananthavaram provides an instructive study of the differences in costs of cultivation for tenants and owner-cultivators, and of the punishing rents paid by tenants in parts of south coastal Andhra Pradesh.

In Ananthavaram, land was leased in by all classes of cultivators; the ratio of area leased in to total cultivated area fell as we moved from the poor peasantry to the rich peasantry and landlord/big capitalist farmer class. The proportion of land operated under tenancy to total land operated was the highest among poor

---

[2] It is not surprising that the number of head of cattle per household was higher in Bukkacherla and Kothapalle than in Ananthavaram.

peasants (81 per cent), followed by lower-middle peasants (74 per cent), and the least among landlords and big capitalists (6 per cent).

It is worth repeating that gross incomes from paddy cultivation did not vary significantly across sections of the peasantry, although landlords and big capitalist farmers received the highest gross incomes per hectare.

However, the data confirm a large difference in the cost of cultivation as between tenant-cultivators and owner-cultivators. Cost A2 averaged Rs 35,773 per hectare for poor peasants operating land under tenancy (Table 7). For land-lords cultivating their own land, the cost incurred was Rs 18,516 per hectare (Table 8). The difference in costs for these two categories of cultivators was over Rs 17,000 per hectare. Poor peasants cultivating paddy on leased-in land made a loss of Rs 6,733 per hectare even though they obtained the same output per hectare as landlords and big capitalist farmers. The latter made a positive gain of Rs 11,372 per hectare. Punishing rent payments ensured that paddy cultivation was loss-making for tenants from the poor and lower-middle sections of the peasantry.

Table 7 *Gross value of output (GVO), Cost A2 and net income from kharif paddy for tenant-cultivators, by class, Ananthavaram village, 2005–06* (Rs/ha)

Tenant cultivators among	GVO	Cost A2	Net income
Poor peasants	29,040	35,773	(–)6,733
Lower-middle peasants	30,371	29,782	589

Source: Survey data.

Table 8 *Gross value of output (GVO), Cost A1 and net incomes from kharif paddy for owner-cultivators, by class, Ananthavaram village, 2005–06* (Rs/ha)

Owner cultivators among	GVO	Cost A1	Net income
Peasants: poor	29,739	20,654	9,085
Peasants: lower-middle	29,705	19,572	10,132
Peasants: upper-middle	30,829	20,971	9,858
Capitalist farmers/Rich peasants/Peasants: upper	34,262	21,431	12,831
Landlords/Big capitalist farmers	29,888	18,516	11,372

Note: Cost A1 is Cost A2 minus rental payments. Rental payments are zero for cultivation on own land.

Source: Survey data.

OTHER CROPS

Gross and Net Incomes from Other Crops

In general, net incomes from maize (grown in Ananthavaram and Kothapalle), groundnut (grown in Bukkacherla and Kothapalle), sugarcane (grown in Ananthavaram) and black gram (grown in Ananthavaram) were low. The only exception was sugarcane cultivation in Ananthavaram, where average net income was Rs 13,527 per hectare (Table 9).[3]

In Ananthavaram, maize gave a net income of Rs 6,355 per hectare. Cultivators of black gram suffered a loss of Rs 404 per hectare. Most tenant-cultivators sowed paddy during the kharif and maize during the rabi season, whereas owner-cultivators tended to sow black gram after paddy.

In the survey year, the yield of black gram in Ananthavaram was lower than the state average. There are several reasons for this outcome. Some cultivators, especially poor and lower-middle peasants, reported unseasonal rain and pest attacks as reasons for low yields. This also explains the high expenses on plant protection chemicals reported in our survey. Some upper-middle and rich peasant cultivators grew black gram in order to improve soil fertility (through nitrogen fixation), and neither incurred heavy costs on the crop nor expected a high income from it.

Table 9 *Gross value of output (GVO), Cost A2 and net income for maize, black gram and sugarcane, Ananthavaram village, 2005–06* (Rs/ha)

Crop	Crop season	Location	GVO	Cost A2	Net income
Maize	Kharif	Andhra Pradesh	20,940	10,636	10,304
	Rabi	Ananthavaram	30,985	24,629	6,355
Black gram	Kharif	Andhra Pradesh	26,457	5,305	21,152
	Rabi	Ananthavaram	12,064	12,467	(–)404
Sugarcane	Annual	Andhra Pradesh	82,615	35,261	47,354
		Ananthavaram	1,11,562	98,035	13,527

Source: Survey data; estimates for Andhra Pradesh are from the CACP report (GOI 2009).

---

[3] Incomes from the small but dynamic, investment-intensive and high-income drip irrigation sector in Bukkacherla are not discussed here.

Table 10 *Gross value of output (GVO), Cost A2 and net income for kharif groundnut, Bukkacherla village, 2005–06* (Rs/ha)

Crop	Location	GVO	Cost A2	Net income
Groundnut	Andhra Pradesh	15,349	11,707	3,643
	Bukkacherla	15,110	10,572	4,538
Groundnut intercropped	Bukkacherla	12,683	9,579	3,104

Source: Survey data; estimates for Andhra Pradesh are from the CACP report (GOI 2009).

Table 11 *Gross value of output (GVO), Cost A2 and net income for kharif maize and groundnut, Kothapalle village, 2005–06* (Rs/ha)

Crop	Location	GVO	Cost A2	Net income
Maize	Andhra Pradesh	20,940	10,636	10,304
	Kothapalle	15,958	11,637	4,321
Groundnut	Andhra Pradesh	15,349	11,707	3,643
	Kothapalle	20,256	15,377	4,879

Source: Survey data; estimates for Andhra Pradesh are from the CACP report (GOI 2009).

Groundnut occupied the largest single share of gross cropped area in Bukkacherla. When sown separately, an average income of Rs 4,538 per hectare was obtained from groundnut cultivation. However, groundnut was usually intercropped, and on such plots the average income (for all crops cultivated) was a little lower, Rs 3,104 per hectare (Table 10).

In Kothapalle, maize was an important crop. Average incomes from maize cultivation were only Rs 4,321 per hectare. The average income from groundnut cultivation was Rs 4,879 per hectare (Table 11).

With two exceptions — groundnut in Bukkacherla and Kothapalle — the estimates of incomes from crop cultivation reported by the CACP are consistently higher than our estimates. The main reason for this is that our estimates of costs are higher than those of the CACP (Tables 9, 10 and 11).

Costs of Cultivation: An Illustration from Maize Cultivation

Differences in costs vary across socio-economic classes for other crops, too. In this section, we examine the differences between tenant-cultivators and owner-cultivators of maize in Ananthavaram, where there were a substantial number of households growing maize on leased-in land (Table 12).

For both tenant-cultivators and owner-cultivators in Ananthavaram, the gross value of output of maize was higher than the state average, but the costs were higher too. On average, on leased-in land, the paid-out costs incurred were Rs 27,446 per hectare, whereas on land owned by the cultivator, the costs incurred were Rs 18,452 per hectare. It is noteworthy that all paid-out costs other than rent were lower for tenant-cultivators than for owner-cultivators. Despite

Table 12 *Gross value of output (GVO), Cost A2, Cost A1 and net income for maize, by ownership of land, Ananthavaram village, 2005–06* (Rs/ha)

	Crop season	Ownership status	GVO	Cost A2	Cost A1	Net income (GVO – A2)
Andhra Pradesh	Kharif	All	20,940	10,636	10,636	10,304
Ananthavaram	Rabi	Leased in	29,993	27,446	16,033	2,547
		Owned	33,159	–	18,452	14,707

Source: Survey data; figures for Andhra Pradesh are from the CACP report GOI (2009).

Table 13 *Costs of cultivation by type of cost and type of land ownership, maize, Ananthavaram village, 2005–06*

Item of cost	CACP data for Andhra Pradesh Kharif	Survey data for Ananthavaram Rabi	
		Leased in	Owned
Seed	675	1,965	1,990
Manure	419	9	112
Fertiliser	2,353	5,028	5,342
Pesticide	204	916	794
Irrigation	167	2,013	2,265
Labour	4,746	4,546	6,821
Rent	0	11,413	0
Other costs	2,071	1,556	1,128
Cost A2/Cost A1	10,635	27,446	18,452

Note: Cost A1 is Cost A2 minus rental payments. Rental payments are zero for cultivation on own land.

Source: Survey data; figures for Andhra Pradesh are from the CACP report GOI (2009).

this, the net income was much lower for tenant-cultivators (Rs 2,547 per hectare) than for owner-cultivators (Rs 14,707 per hectare).

The differences in net incomes derive from the heavy burden of rent (Table 13). When maize was cultivated on leased-in land, a tenant, on average, paid a rent of Rs 11,413 per hectare.

The pattern of input use suggests that the higher yields of maize in Ananthavaram, relative to the state average, may be on account of better quality seeds, and higher manure and fertiliser application, as well as use of irrigation water.

To sum up, despite obtaining high yields from the cultivation of maize, returns to tenant-cultivators were low, and were only 17 per cent of the income obtained by owner-cultivators.

CONCLUDING REMARKS

In this chapter, we estimated incomes from agriculture for all households engaged in crop cultivation in our study villages. The analysis was undertaken for the major crops grown in each village, namely, paddy, maize, black gram and sugarcane in Ananthavaram; groundnut and paddy in Bukkacherla; and paddy, maize and groundnut in Kothapalle.

As paddy was a major crop in two villages, we began our analysis with estimates of incomes and costs of paddy cultivation. In Ananthavaram, a major paddy-growing village, the gross incomes from paddy averaged Rs 31,734 per hectare (Table 1). The high average costs of cultivation, amounting to Rs 29,293 per hectare, meant that net incomes from a hectare of paddy were very low indeed, merely Rs 2,441 (Table 5). Net incomes, on average, were higher in Kothapalle, at Rs 8,555 per hectare, but even this estimate was lower than the average for the state reported by the Commission for Agricultural Costs and Prices (CACP), Rs 15,788 per hectare (Table 1).

Next, we examined incomes and costs of cultivation for cultivators belonging to different socio-economic classes. The results of this analysis were striking: there were systematic differences in costs, and hence in net incomes, across classes. Specifically, poor and lower-middle peasants, predominantly tenant-cultivators, incurred significantly higher costs than landlords and big capitalist farmers. Paid-out costs amounted to Rs 33,578 per hectare for poor peasants and Rs 19,065 for landlords in Ananthavaram (Table 2).

An item-wise analysis of costs of cultivation was then undertaken (Table 6), and we found that rent payments accounted for a significant proportion of total costs (32 per cent of total costs in Ananthavaram and 17 per cent in Bukkacherla). It follows that the problem of low incomes for a large number of cultivators was not on account of low production but on account of the distribution of output, that is, of rack-rents imposed on the poor.

On account of exorbitant rent payments, the class of poor peasants, most of whom were tenant-cultivators, incurred huge losses from paddy production. A poor peasant leasing in land for paddy cultivation in Ananthavaram ended up, on average, with a loss of Rs 6,733 per hectare. Owner-cultivators, on the other hand, could keep the surplus and thus get a reasonable return. Lower and upper-middle peasants cultivating owned land received a net income of around Rs 10,000 per hectare from paddy, while rich peasants and landlords received Rs 11,000 to 12,000 (Tables 7 and 8).

A similar analysis was undertaken for maize in Ananthavaram. While the losses were not as severe as in the case of paddy, the net incomes of tenant-cultivators were much lower than those of owner-cultivators (Table 12).

To sum up, our data showed, first, that gross incomes and costs, and, consequently, net incomes, varied by village, crop, season and, most dramatically, by socio-economic class. Secondly, estimates of costs in our surveys were consistently higher than those reported in the CACP. As a result, our estimates of net incomes were consistently lower than those reported in the CACP.

An important policy implication of these findings is that official data reporting a single "average" for gross value of outputs, costs and net incomes are highly misleading. Official data do not take into account variations in the costs of a crop, for example rice, across seasons. Official data disregard class differentiation in the countryside. While the CACP data can, perhaps, be used to ascertain the incomes from agriculture for big capitalist farmers and landlords, they are misleading in respect of the incomes of peasants, particularly tenant-cultivators. It follows that minimum support prices recommended on the basis of the CACP estimates will not ensure an adequate return to all cultivators.

Annexure 1
COST CONCEPTS

We have referred to two cost concepts, Cost A1 and Cost A2, as defined by the Comprehensive Scheme for the Study of Cost of Cultivation of Principal Crops. The components of **Cost A1** are:

(a)   Value of hired human labour.
(b)   Value of hired and owned bullock labour.
(c)   Value of owned machine labour.
(d)   Value of hired machine charges.
(e)   Value of seed (both farm-produced and purchased).
(f)   Value of insecticides and pesticides.
(g)   Value of manure (owned and purchased).
(h)   Value of fertilisers.
(i)   Irrigation charges.
(j)   Depreciation of implements and farm buildings.
(k)   Land revenue, cesses and other taxes.
(l)   Interest on working capital.
(m)   Other miscellaneous expenses.

Cost A2 = Cost A1 + Rent paid for leased-in land (GOI 1996, cited in Surjit 2008).

Annexure 2

Table A *Gross cropped area (GCA) by crop and season, Ananthavaram village, 2005–06*

Crop	Crop season	Gross cropped area (ha)	% of GCA that is Irrigated	Unirrigated	GCA as % of column total
Paddy	Kharif	462.8	93	7	47.5
Other kharif crops	Kharif	12.7	39	61	1.3
Maize	Rabi	268.3	93	7	27.6
Black gram	Rabi	121.8	18	82	12.5
Black gram with mustard	Rabi	17	0	100	1.7
Sesamum	Rabi	15.7	0	100	1.6
Other rabi crops	Rabi	13.7	29	71	1.4
Millet	Rabi	10.3	100	0	1.1
Sugarcane	Annual	38.4	100	0	3.9
Betel leaves	Annual	12.9	100	0	1.3
All crops		973.5	79	21	100

Note: (i) Other rabi crops include jowar, green gram, sunflower, fodder crops, groundnut, mesta, and so on.

(ii) Other kharif crops include red gram, mesta, turmeric, fodder crops, green gram, lady's finger, millet, chilli, and so on.

Source: Survey data.

Table B *Gross cropped area (GCA) by crop and season, Bukkacherla village, 2005–06*

Crop	Crop season	Gross cropped area (ha)	% of GCA that is Irrigated	Unirrigated	GCA as % of column total
Groundnut (intercropped)	Kharif	506.7	0	100	74.2
Groundnut	Kharif	31.9	19	81	4.7
Paddy	Kharif	35.6	97	3	5.2
Other kharif crops	Kharif	26.5	88	12	3.9
Paddy	Rabi	40.5	97	3	5.9
Groundnut	Rabi	12.6	0	100	1.8
Groundnut (intercropped)	Rabi	12	0	100	1.8
Muskmelon	Rabi	10.8	33	67	1.6
Watermelon	Rabi	6	77	23	0.9
All crops		682.7	9	91	100

Note: (i) Groundnut is intercropped with red gram, cowpea, green gram, sweet lime, bajra, jowar, beans and sesame.

(ii) Other kharif crops include fodder crops, tomato, jowar, red gram, green gram, millet, sesame, onion, chilli, brinjal, cluster bean, drumstick, lady's finger, wheat, chilli, and so on.

Source: Survey data.

Table C *Gross cropped area (GCA) by crop and season, Kothapalle village, 2005–06*

Crop	Crop season	Gross cropped area (hectare)	% of GCA that is Irrigated	% of GCA that is Unirrigated	GCA as % of column total
Maize	Kharif	38.5	37	63	17.4
Maize with red gram	Kharif	17.8	0	100	8
Paddy	Kharif	34	100	0	15.3
Fodder crops	Kharif	19.9	0	100	9
Cotton	Kharif	17.2	59	41	7.7
Groundnut	Kharif	4	0	100	1.8
Cow pea	Kharif	3.8	32	68	1.7
Red gram	Kharif	3.8	34	66	1.7
Cucumber	Kharif	3.2	100	0	1.4
Oilseed	Kharif	3.2	100	0	1.4
Pulses	Kharif	2.4	0	100	1
Green gram	Kharif	2.3	0	100	1
Other kharif crops	Kharif	1.7	100	0	0.8
Paddy	Rabi	38.3	96	4	17.3
Maize	Rabi	16.9	90	10	8
Cowpea	Rabi	4.7	38	62	2
Groundnut	Rabi	2.9	100	0	1.3
Groundnut with red gram	Rabi	2.3	0	100	1
Other rabi crops	Rabi	1.1	100	0	0.5
Mango	NA	3.8	100	0	1.7
All crops		221.6	65	35	100

Note: (i) Other kharif crops include chilli, lady's finger, brinjal, tomato.

(ii) Other rabi crops include green gram, sesame, brinjal, onion, tomato.

Source: Survey data.

7

Some Features of the Employment
of Manual Workers

This chapter deals, first, with the number of days of paid employment tasks received by members of hired manual worker households. Secondly, it deals with wage rates for the tasks at which these workers are employed; and, thirdly, it deals with their earnings from wages at such tasks.

Before presenting the results of our detailed analysis, we need to qualify its scope. First, the analysis in this chapter applies only to manual worker households, that is, to households whose major income comes from paid hired manual work outside the house. Manual workers are not, of course, the only class whose members are employed at such tasks. In fact, our survey data indicate that, of all the days of hired manual work performed in Ananthavaram, only 52 per cent was performed by members of manual worker households, while 48 per cent was performed by members of households of other classes (mostly poor peasant and lower-middle peasant households). The corresponding figures were 56 per cent (manual worker households) and 44 per cent (other households) for Bukka-cherla, and 84 per cent (manual worker households) and 16 per cent (other households) for Kothapalle.

Secondly, the data refer only to the number of days of employment in paid labour outside the home, not the total number of days of all types of work, including work at self-employed tasks. Manual worker households can and do have multiple sources of livelihood (see chapter 5). These may include small operational holdings of land, livestock and other animal resources, small businesses and toddy-tapping. This chapter deals only with the time and earnings of members of such households who are engaged in paid work outside the home.

Thirdly, the main body of this chapter deals with work at daily-rated and piece-rated tasks. Workers employed on annual wages are dealt with separately.

Despite these qualifications, the chapter addresses what we believe to be a very relevant question: What is the volume of paid employment available to workers in households that have to depend on manual work as the main means of their livelihood?

MANUAL WORKER HOUSEHOLDS

The class of hired manual workers constituted 20 per cent of all households in Bukkacherla, 25 per cent in Ananthavaram and 42 per cent in Kothapalle (Table 1). The main sources of income in these households are earnings from labour, both wage labour and self-employment, at agricultural and non-agricultural tasks.

On average, there were around two workers per household in all three villages (ranging from 1.9 in Kothapalle to 2.2 in Ananthavaram). The class of manual worker households is caste-heterogenous. At the same time, the representation of Dalit and Adivasi households in the class of manual workers was much higher than their representation in the population (Table 2). In Bukkacherla, Dalit households constituted 19 per cent of all households and 45 per cent of manual worker households. In Ananthavaram, Dalit households constituted 43 per cent of all households and 59 per cent of manual worker households. Similarly, in Ananthavaram, Adivasi households constituted only 6 per cent of all households but accounted for 19 per cent of manual worker households.

The obverse was that, in Ananthavaram, Other Castes comprised 28 per cent of all households and 2 per cent of manual worker households. The same pattern occurred in Ananthavaram and Bukkacherla in respect of households belonging to Backward Classes. In Kothapalle, however, the proportion of households from Backward Class households in the class of manual workers was higher than their proportion in the population (Table 2).

Table 1 *Number of hired manual worker households and workers, by sex, study villages, May 2006*

Village	No. of households	% of all households	Male	Workers Female	Persons	No. of workers per household
Ananthavaram	164	25	218	136	354	2.2
Bukkacherla	59	20	54	62	116	2.0
Kothapalle	155	42	108	182	290	1.9

Source: Survey data.

Table 2 *Manual worker households as proportion of all households and all manual worker households, by caste, study villages, May 2006* (%)

Social group	Ananathavaram		Bukkacherla		Kothapalle	
	As proportion of all households	As proportion of all manual worker households	As proportion of all households	As proportion of all manual worker households	As proportion of all households	As proportion of all manual worker households
Dalit households	43	59	19	45	33	35
Adivasi households	6	19	0	0	1	3
Muslim households	4	12	2	NA	1	NA
Backward Class households	19	8	35	25	42	54
Other Caste households	28	2	44	30	23	8
All households	100	100	100	100	100	100

Note: NA = Not applicable.
Source: Survey data.

The proportion of manual workers among Adivasi and Dalit households was substantially higher than among other social groups (Table 3). In Kothapalle, for example, 99 per cent of Adivasi households were hired manual workers; the corresponding proportion was 80 per cent in Ananthavaram. Between 34 to 48 per cent of Dalit households in the three villages belonged to the class of manual workers. The contrast with Other Caste households is apparent: between 2 and 14 per cent of Other Caste households in the three villages belonged to the class of hired manual workers. The pattern was similar among members of Backward Class households in Ananthavaram and Bukkacherla, though not in Kothapalle, where 54 per cent of Backward Class households were in the class of manual workers.

To sum up, while hired manual workers as a class had members from all castes, we still find a high concentration of Dalit and Adivasi households in the class.[1]

---

[1] This of course reflects the unequal distribution of productive assets like land and other resources between underprivileged social groups and upper-caste households (Shah, Mander, Thorat, Deshpande and Baviskar 2006).

Table 3 *Proportion of manual worker households, by caste, study villages, May 2006* (%)

Social group	Ananthavaram	Bukkacherla	Kothapalle
Dalit households	34	48	46
Adivasi households	80	NA	99
Muslim households	82	NA	NA
Backward Class households	9	15	54
Other Caste households	2	14	14
All households	25	20	42

Note: NA = not applicable.
Source: Survey data.

Agricultural and Non-Agricultural Work

Hired manual workers are employed at both agricultural and non-agricultural tasks. In Ananthavaram, 80 per cent of all workers (100 per cent among women and 68 per cent among men) worked exclusively at agricultural operations (Table 4). The proportion was lower, 74 per cent, in Bukkacherla and Kothapalle.

In all the study villages, women worked predominantly in agriculture. There was more diversification out of agriculture among male workers than among female workers. The highest degree of diversification was in Kothapalle, where 45 per cent of male workers worked only at agricultural tasks, 33 per cent only at non-agricultural tasks and 22 per cent at both.

Table 4 *Proportion of workers employed in agricultural and non-agricultural wage labour, by sex, study villages, 2005– 06* (%)

Village	Sex	Agriculture	Non-agriculture	Both
Ananthavaram	Male	68	14	18
	Female	100	0	0
	All workers	80	9	11
Bukkacherla	Male	56	6	38
	Female	90	0	10
	All workers	74	3	23
Kothapalle	Male	45	33	22
	Female	91	4	5
	All workers	74	15	11

Source: Survey data.

Days of Employment

In the tables that follow, all labour days have been standardised to 8-hour days, and the days of labour of long-term workers have been excluded from the calculation of days of employment. All data pertain to the agricultural year 2005–06.

The data on the number of days of employment per worker confirm the very low levels of employment among workers, male and female, from manual worker households (Table 5). The average number of days of paid work was between 90 to 100 days per worker, that is, around three months of employment. The average number of days of employment was the highest in Bukkacherla (104 days).

Labour absorption per hectare of gross cropped area (irrespective of the crop grown and land type) is 275 days in Ananthavaram and 70 days in Bukkacherla. It may seem paradoxical in this context that the average number of days of employment in agriculture for women (and female wage earnings from agriculture) are higher in Bukkacherla than in Ananthavaram. The reasons, however, are clear. Ananthavaram is a densely populated village where landlessness is high and the pressure of population on the existing means of employment greater than in the other two villages. In Bukkacherla, the supply of labour is restricted by the fact that 84 per cent of manual worker households have operational holdings of land, on which they must expend family labour.

Male workers received more days of employment than female workers in Ananthavaram (106 days and 65 days, respectively) and Bukkacherla (132 days and 80 days respectively). The pattern was reversed in Kothapalle, where women workers received 93 days and men 83 days of paid employment in the year (Table 5).

In 1974, the "average number of days of employment available to men and

Table 5 *Average number of days of paid employment per worker, by sex, study villages, 2005–06*

Gender	Ananthavaram	Bukkacherla	Kothapalle
Male	106	132	83
Female	65	80	93
All workers	90	104	89

Source: Survey data.

women from agricultural labour families" in Ananthavaram was 150 days and 75 days, respectively (Sundarayya 1977). According to our survey data, employment levels were much lower among both male and female workers from manual worker households in 2005–06.

There were also significant variations across workers (Table 6). Almost 45 per cent of workers in Ananthavaram and Kothapalle obtained employment for less than two months. On the other hand, some 12 per cent of workers received more than 180 days of employment in a year in all three villages. The majority of workers were thus employed for less than six months in a year. We reiterate that the data here are a measure of the days of paid employment outside the house received by members of manual worker households. These households gain income from other sources, particularly forms of self-employment, and may also receive incomes from small remittances and pensions (see chapter 5).

Agriculture provided around 65 days of employment for males and females in Ananthavaram, and around 80 days of employment in Bukkacherla (Table 7). In Ananthavaram and Bukkacherla, on an average, agriculture provided more days of employment than non-agricultural activities to hired manual workers. In fact, women workers in Ananthavaram and Bukkacherla received either no work or a negligible volume of work at non-agricultural tasks.

In Kothapalle, however, the situation was different. First, in the case of male workers, the average number of days of employment in non-agricultural work

Table 6 *Distribution of hired manual workers, by size-class of number of days of employment, study villages, 2005–06*

Size-class of number of days of employment	Ananthavaram		Bukkacherla		Kothapalle	
	No. of workers	As a % of all workers	No. of workers	As a % of all workers	No. of workers	As a % of all workers
1 to 30 days	89	25	15	13	71	25
31 to 60 days	70	20	21	18	63	22
61 to 90 days	58	16	18	16	44	15
91 to 120 days	43	12	30	26	16	5
121 to 150 days	28	8	12	10	48	17
151 to 180 days	23	7	6	5	12	4
More than 180 days	43	12	15	12	36	12
All workers	354	100	116	100	290	100

Source: Survey data.

Table 7 *Average number of days of employment in agricultural and non-agricultural sector, by sex, study villages, 2005–06*

Gender	Ananthavaram		Bukkacherla		Kothapalle	
	Agricultural work	Non-agricultural work	Agricultural work	Non-agricultural work	Agricultural work	Non-agricultural work
Male	65	41	80	52	21	62
Female	65	0	79	1	73	20
All workers	65	25	80	24	54	36

Source: Survey data.

exceeded the average number of days of employment in agricultural work. The average female worker, however, continued to obtain more days of work in farm activity than in non-farm activity, but also received some days of employment in non-farm activity. The higher aggregate days of employment among women workers in Kothapalle can probably be explained by the fact that they received work at both farm and non-farm tasks.

Agricultural Work

Our first conclusion from these data is that the major crops in terms of scale of employment generation were paddy, maize, betel leaf and sugarcane in Ananthavaram; groundnut intercropped with various pulses and paddy in Bukkacherla; and paddy and maize in Kothapalle.

In Ananthavaram, kharif paddy provided almost one-half of the total employment in agriculture for both male and female workers. During rabi, women were employed on maize fields, while men worked more at high-value crops such as betel leaf and turmeric (grouped under spices and condiments in Table 8).

In Bukkacherla, paddy was significant, but groundnut intercropped with various pulses provided an almost equal number of days of employment. Male workers were also employed in the cultivation of fruit and vegetables, and obtained 28 days of employment a year, on average, for such tasks (Table 9).

In Kothapalle, on an average, male workers were engaged for only 21 days a year in agricultural tasks, of which 16 days were in paddy cultivation. Female workers, however, obtained an average of 43 days of employment in paddy cultivation, on average, followed by 20 days in maize production.

Table 8 *Average number of days of agricultural employment per worker, by crop and sex, Ananthavaram village, 2005–06*

Crop	Male workers		Female workers		All workers	
	Days of employment	As % of column total	Days of employment	As % of column total	Days of employment	As % of column total
Paddy	32	50	29	44	31	48
Maize	6	9	23	36	12	19
Spices and condiments	18	28	10	16	15	23
Sugarcane	5	7	0	0	3	5
Other crops	4	6	3	4	3	5
All crops	65	100	65	100	65	100

Source: Survey data.

Table 9 *Average number of days of agricultural employment per worker, by crop, and sex, Bukkacherla village, 2005–06*

Crops	Male workers		Female workers		All workers	
	Days of employment	As % of column total	Days of employment	As % of column total	Days of employment	As % of column total
Paddy	23	29	34	43	29	36
Groundnut	21	26	33	41	28	35
Fruit and vegetables	28	35	3	4	15	18
Other crops	8	10	10	12	9	11
All crops	80	100	79	100	80	100

Source: Survey data.

Table 10 *Average number of days of agricultural employment per worker, by crop and sex, Kothapalle village, 2005–06*

Crops	Male workers		Female workers		All workers.	
	Days of employment	As % of column total	Days of employment	As % of column total	Days of employment	As % of column total
Paddy	16	76	43	59	33	62
Maize	5	23	20	27	14	26
Cotton	0	0	5	6	3	6
Groundnut	0	0	2	3	1	2
Other crops	0	1	3	5	2	4
All crops	21	100	73	100	54	100

Source: Survey data.

Non-Agricultural Work

As already noted, female participation in non-agricultural tasks was virtually absent, except in Kothapalle. In the case of men, work in construction predominated in the non-agricultural employment available to them (Table 11).

In Bukkacherla, construction and related activities were the only sources of non-agricultural employment. The National Rural Employment Guarantee Scheme (NREGS) had just begun in Anantapur district at the time of our survey, and we do not have data to monitor the impact of NREGS on total employment. In Kothapalle, in addition to construction, an important non-agricultural activity was animal-rearing (as shown in the chapter on incomes, sheep-rearing is an important activity in this village). In Ananthavaram, construction, technical services and animal-rearing were the three main types of non-agricultural employment.

It is clear that the non-agricultural work available to workers from manual worker households is not very diverse. The main sources of employment were construction and animal-rearing. Other than Ananthavaram, where some new opportunities for skilled and/or technical services related to the mechanisation of agriculture have emerged, non-agricultural tasks generally provide unskilled and low-paying jobs.

Table 11 *Distribution of number days of non-agricultural employment, by type of activity, male workers, study villages, 2005–06* (%)

Type of activity	Ananthavaram	Bukkacherla	Kothapalle
Construction and related activity	36	97	39
Factory work	0.2	0	0
Painting and related work	0	0	18
Shop attendant	8	0	0
Tasks related to toddy-tapping	3	0	0
Technical services (motor mechanic, welder, plumber, etc.)	30	0	5
Transport-related work	3.8	3	8
Animal-rearing and related work	19	0	30
All non-agricultural employment	100	100	100

Source: Survey data.

WAGE RATES

Wage rates in agriculture vary by crop and crop operation, season, type of contract and gender. There are two major forms of wage contracts, contracts based on time-rates (daily wages or annual wages) and on piece-rates (typically, tasks paid for by the acre or per unit of output).

The following are our major observations from these data (Tables 12 to 14).

First, daily-rated contracts were the norm for all major crop operations in Bukkacherla and Kothapalle. In Ananthavaram, however, piece-rates are widespread, and cover transplanting, harvesting and threshing paddy, and sowing and harvesting maize.[2]

Secondly, wages were completely monetised in Ananthavaram. In Bukkacherla and Kothapalle, however, there were several operations that were paid in kind, such as harvesting paddy and groundnut (Bukkacherla), and harvesting and threshing paddy (Kothapalle). In Ananthavaram, even harvesting and threshing paddy, operations traditionally paid in kind (documented in Sundarayya 1977), were piece-rated operations and workers received *all* wages in cash.[3]

---

[2] On the spread of piece-rate contracts in Andhra Pradesh, see Revathi (2008) and Nirmala and Nalini (2008).

[3] On the shift from wages in kind to wages in cash, see Rao and Subrahmanyam (2002).

Thirdly, in Bukkacherla, cooked food was an integral part of the wages paid to wage workers (and also to long-term workers.) For almost all crop operations, food was provided to both male and female workers, workers being given boiled rice or roti, sambar and pickle at the work-site. In the other two villages, cooked food was no longer a component of the wage.

Fourthly, in the case of almost all daily-rated cash-paid operations, female wage rates were lower than male wage rates. Wage discrimination is generally mediated by the gender division of labour, that is, tasks in which female labour predominate are remunerated at lower wages than tasks in which male labour predominates. There are also cases, however, where men and women are paid differently for essentially the same operation. For example, for weeding paddy fields, in Ananthavaram, the female wage rate was Rs 30–35 and the male wage rate was Rs 50–70 (Table 12). In Kothapalle, the female wage rate for threshing maize was Rs 25–40 and the corresponding male wage rate was Rs 70 (Table 14).

The only operation for which men and women were paid equally in our data was paddy harvesting in Bukkacherla, where men and women were both paid 10 kilograms of paddy and a meal per day.

Table 12 *Wage rates, by form of payment, crop operation, and sex, Ananthavaram village, 2005–06*

Crop operation	Male		Female	
	Cash	Kind	Cash	Kind
Daily-rated				
Paddy: Weeding	Rs 50–70	NA	Rs 30–35	NA
Top dressing	Rs 50–70	NA	NA	NA
All other operations	Rs. 50–80	NA	Rs 30–50	NA
Piece-rated				
Paddy: Transplanting	Rs 400–600 per acre	NA	Rs 400–600 per acre	NA
Harvesting	Rs 450–600 per acre	NA	NA	NA
Threshing	Rs 600–800 per acre	NA	NA	NA
Maize: Sowing in dry land	Rs 500 per acre	NA	NA	NA
Harvesting	Rs 700–800 per acre	NA	NA	NA

Note: NA = Not applicable.
Source: Survey data.

Table 13 *Wage rates, by form of payment, crop operation, and sex, Bukkacherla village, 2005–06*

Crop operation	Male		Female	
	Cash	Kind	Cash	Kind
Daily-rated				
Paddy: Land preparation	Rs 50–100	1 meal	NA	NA
Transplanting	Rs 40–50	1 meal	Rs 30–50	1 meal
Weeding	NA	NA	Rs 30–50	1 meal
Harvest and post-				
harvest operations	Rs 50–100	1 meal	Rs 50–65	1 meal
	NA	10 kg paddy + 1 meal	NA	10 kg paddy + 1 meal
Groundnut: Land				
preparation	Rs 50–100	1 meal	NA	NA
Sowing	Rs 40–50	1 meal	Rs 40–70	NA
Weeding	Rs 40–50	1 meal	Rs 30–50	NA
Harvesting	Rs 70–100	1 meal or 3 kg groundnut	Rs 50–100	1 meal or 3 kg groundnut
Threshing	Rs 50–100	1 meal		

Note: NA = Not applicable.
Source: Survey data.

Table 14 *Wage rates, by form of payment, crop operation, and sex, Kothapalle village, 2005–06*

Crop operation	Male		Female	
	Cash	Kind	Cash	Kind
Daily-rated				
Paddy: Transplanting	NA	NA	Rs 30	NA
Weeding	NA	NA	Rs 30	NA
Harvesting	NA	NA	NA	15 kg paddy
Threshing	NA	NA	NA	20 kg paddy
Maize: Ploughing	Rs 50–70	NA	NA	NA
Sowing	Rs 60	NA	Rs 25–40	NA
Weeding	NA	NA	Rs 25–40	NA
Harvesting	Rs 30–75	NA	Rs 25–40	NA
Threshing	Rs 70	NA	Rs 25–40	NA

Note: NA = Not applicable.
Source: Survey data.

WAGE EARNINGS

The discussion on wages in this section is based on total earnings of all workers in a household. Wage payments received in kind (including meals) have been given a cash value and added to the total wage earnings. The daily wage level is derived by adding up all earnings from wages — time-rated, piece-rated, agricultural and non-agricultural — and dividing the total by the days of employment at all tasks; again including time- and piece-rated work, and agricultural and non-agricultural work.

The average daily wage earnings among male workers from hired manual worker households was Rs 64 in Kothapalle, Rs 73 in Bukkacherla and Rs 88 in Ananthavaram (Table 15). Among female workers, the corresponding average daily earnings were Rs 33 in Kothapalle, Rs 41 in Ananthavaram and Rs 51 in Bukkacherla. Daily earnings for women varied more than for men across the three villages. It is also of note that daily wage earnings for women were higher in Bukkacherla than in Ananthavaram.

With the exception of male wages in Ananthavaram, all wages in all three villages were below the official minimum wage of Rs 80 per day (GOI).[4]

There was a wide gender difference in wages in all three villages. The ratio of female to male wages was the lowest in Ananthavaram, where women's wages were only 47 per cent of male wages. The corresponding ratios were 52 per cent in Kothapalle and 70 per cent in Bukkacherla (Table 15). In Ananthavaram, the average daily wage earning of women in piece-rated work was only 45 per cent of that of men, indicating that, with respect to piece-rated work, women tend to be employed in operations that have lower rates than operations in which men are employed.

Women's wages were lower than men's wages even in operations that were traditionally female-specific tasks. For example, in paddy transplanting, female wages were 71 per cent of male wages in Ananthavaram and only 51 per cent of male wages in Kothapalle.[5]

---

[4] This was the stated wage for agricultural labourers (Rs/day) in Andhra Pradesh in 2005–06, according to the Government of India.

[5] The payment of different wages for the same task — for instance, for transplanting and threshing paddy or harvesting maize — often reflects an on-field gender division of labour, with specific sub-tasks, generally associated with loading, carrying and "heavy" work, allocated to men.

Table 15 *Average wage earnings in study villages, by type of wage contract and sex, 2005–06* (Rs/day)

Village	Type of wage	Male	Female	Ratio of female wage to male wage
Ananthavaram	Daily-rated	69	36	0.52
Ananthavaram	Piece-rated	128	57	0.45
Ananthavaram	All	88	41	0.47
Bukkacherla	All	73	51	0.7
Kothapalle	All	64	33	0.52

Note: As there were very few piece-rated contracts in Bukkacherla and Kothapalle, we have not reported the data separately for daily-rated and piece-rated wages in these villages.
Source: Survey data.

Piece-Rate Contracts and Changes in the Gender Division of Labour

The major agricultural tasks in paddy cultivation are land preparation, transplanting, intercultural operations (irrigation, applying fertilisers and plant protection chemicals, and weeding), and harvest and post-harvest operations. The traditional gender division of labour was such that land preparation was done mainly by male workers. Intercultural operations, and harvest and post-harvest operations, were done by both male and female workers. Transplanting and weeding, while open to male workers, were dominated by female workers.

In Ananthavaram, changes in wage contracts, specifically, a shift from daily-rated casual work to piece-rated work by groups of workers, appear to have altered the gender division of labour. The practice of hiring workers on a piece-rate basis seems to have led to an increase in male workers relative to female workers in operations that were traditionally female-dominated tasks.

In Table 16, for each operation in paddy cultivation, we have examined the share of female employment in total employment separately for daily-rated contracts and piece-rated contracts. Land preparation was almost exclusively a male task, the exception being female employment in basal manuring and field-bund construction in Kothapalle.

Interesting differences emerge in the case of transplanting. In Bukkacherla and Kothapalle, where transplanting is a daily-rated task, female employment dominated (88 and 92 per cent of total employment on this task). However, in Ananthavaram, 67 per cent of the days of work at transplanting were contracted

Table 16 *Female employment as a proportion of total employment, by agricultural operation and form of wage payment, study villages, 2005–06* (%)

Agricultural operations in paddy cultivation	Ananthavaram		Bukkacherla		Kothapalle	
	Daily-rated tasks	Piece-rated tasks	Daily-rated tasks	Piece-rated tasks	Daily-rated tasks	Piece-rated tasks
Land preparation	0	0	2	0	27*	0
Transplanting	49	55	88	0	92	0
Intercultural operations	62	0	86	0	95	0
Harvest and post-harvest operations	15	34	71	44	80	0

Note: *The work was mainly in field operations, such as basal manuring, and the construction and maintenance of bunds.

Source: Survey data.

out on a piece-rate basis, and the share of female employment in total employment was much lower than in the other two villages. By the time of our survey, a task that was traditionally associated with women employed men and women almost equally.

Most intercultural operations were paid on a daily-rated basis. In these the share of women in total employment remained high, especially in Bukkacherla and Kothapalle. In harvest and post-harvest operations, in Bukkacherla, female employment was 44 per cent of total employment where payment was by piece-rate, and 71 per cent of total employment where payment was on daily rates (Table 16).

In Ananthavaram, harvest and post-harvest operations are mechanised, and almost 35 per cent of the employment in these operations is contracted out on a piece-rate basis. The female share of harvest and post-harvest operations was relatively low, 34 per cent for piece-rated operations and 15 per cent for daily-rated operations. These findings suggest that increased occurrence of piece-rated contracts, accompanied in some cases by mechanisation, has tended to displace female workers from crop operations in which women traditionally worked (or dominated).

WAGE EARNINGS AND INCOME POVERTY

If households from the class of manual workers were to depend entirely on their earnings from wage labour, then, on average, a household's earnings would fall far short of the official poverty line.

Given our estimates of average days of employment per worker and daily wage earnings per worker, and assuming that an average manual worker household has two workers (one male, one female), the annual wage earnings of a manual worker household would have been Rs 14,235 in Bukkacherla, Rs 11,132 in Ananthavaram and Rs 7,887 in Kothapalle. The annual household income corresponding to the revised official poverty line for Andhra Pradesh is approximately Rs 22,000 a year. On average, the wage earnings of a manual worker household in Ananthavaram would have been one-half of the poverty line.

It is clear that both wages and days of employment need to increase substantially in order for a wage labour household to reach the poverty-line level of income. If we assume no change in wages, we estimate that the days of employment per household would need to jump to 335 days in Bukkacherla, 349 days in Ananthavaram and 507 days in Kothapalle.[6] The 100 days of employment per household offered by the National Rural Employment Guarantee Scheme will provide substantial relief, but is not enough to meet even this target.

CONCLUDING REMARKS

This chapter examined the days of employment and the wages of workers belonging to the class of hired manual workers. This class constituted 20 per cent of all households in Bukkacherla; the corresponding proportions were 25 per cent in Ananthavaram and 42 per cent in Kothapalle (Table 1).

Manual workers, as a class, are caste-heterogeneous. At the same time, the association between caste and class persists. The proportion of Dalit and Adivasi households among manual workers is significantly higher than their proportion in the village population.

The average number of days of employment per worker was extremely low in all three villages: about 90 days in Ananthavaram and Kothapalle, and 104 days in Bukkacherla — that is, around three months a year (Table 5). Other than in

---

[6] The biggest increase is in Kothapalle, as it is the village with the lowest wage levels.

Kothapalle, the days of employment gained by a woman worker were lower than the days of employment gained by a male worker (Table 7). A small proportion of workers (12 per cent in all the villages) obtained more than six months of employment a year (Table 6). In 1974, P. Sundarayya reported that an agricultural labourer family received, on average, 247 days of employment in a year. Our survey data showed that manual worker households in Ananthavaram obtained 195 days of employment in 2005–06. The corresponding days of employment per household were 203 in Bukkacherla and 167 in Kothapalle.

Agricultural labour was the main activity of female workers in all the study villages. All male workers, however, gained some employment at non-agricultural tasks (Table 7). In Kothapalle, a village with better transport and hence connectivity to the urban economy, more days of employment were obtained in non-farm employment than in agriculture by male workers.

Wage rates were diverse, varying by village, crop operation and gender. In Ananthavaram, relatively advanced in respect of paddy cultivation, wages were completely monetised (Table 12). On the other hand, in Bukkacherla, from the dry region of Anantapur, several operations were paid in kind, and all workers received a cooked meal with their wages (Table 13).

On average, the level of wages was very low. The average daily earnings from wage labour were less than the official minimum wage of Rs 80 a day for all workers other than male workers in Ananthavaram. In all the villages, a gender gap in wages persisted. The largest gap was in Ananthavaram village, where women's wages were only 47 per cent of men's wages (Tables 12 to 15).

High levels of unemployment, combined with low levels of wages, made it very difficult for a hired manual worker household to earn even the poverty-line level of income solely by means of wage labour. A quick calculation shows that if wages were to remain unchanged, the days of employment per household would need to increase substantially — to 335 days per household in Bukkacherla, 349 days in Ananthavaram and 507 days in Kothapalle — in order to reach even the poverty-line level of income.

There appear to be two noteworthy trends with regard to the gender composition of the labour force, both of which have important implications for women's employment in agriculture and for the mobilisation of women in agricultural workers' organisations. The first occurs in situations where men are able to take greater advantage than women of the opportunities for non-agricultural labour, confining women to the drudgery of agricultural tasks. Here, there is a feminisation of the labour force in three senses: first, the absolute number of female agricultural workers is higher than the number of male agricultural workers; secondly, the share of agricultural labour predominates over the share of non-agricultural labour in women's work profiles; and, thirdly, of the aggregate number of labour days worked by manual workers in agriculture, the major part is female labour. This is a trend that is consistent with the data from Bukkacherla and Kothapalle (Table 7).

The second trend is when, as more and more time-rated tasks are converted to piece-rates, and as piece-rates are monetised, crop operations are performed by large groups of workers among whom men predominate. Large groups of male contract-workers take over even those tasks, such as transplanting and harvesting, in which women predominated earlier. In this case, men outnumber women in the labour force, and male labour predominates in the aggregate number of days worked by all manual workers in agriculture. This hypothesis needs further study and confirmation, but is consistent with our data from the southern coastal village of Ananthavaram.

There is an important and self-evident policy conclusion that emerges from the data on unemployment. It is that whether the village is one that is characterised by relatively advanced agriculture, such as Ananthavaram, or by drought-prone conditions, state-financed schemes that create employment in a range of productive tasks, farm and non-farm, are essential if the long periods of joblessness in a working person's year are to be filled.

Some Long-Term Workers

There were eight long-term workers in Ananthavaram and twelve long-term workers in Kothapalle in the class of hired manual workers. These workers were all employed as annual farm servants by big landowners, and all of them were from Dalit households.

Kothapalle

Elkathurthi Chandrayya, aged 35, belongs to the Madiga caste. His household neither owned nor operated any land, nor did he own any other productive assets. Elkathurthi Laxmi, his wife, aged 30, worked as a casual agricultural worker. There were four persons in this household: two workers and two dependent children. Elkathurthi Chandrayya was employed as a long-term worker for a local landowner (who owned 6 acres of cultivable land and also livestock). His main tasks were to work in all field operations and at tasks related to animal husbandry. The length of his working day was usually nine hours.

The contract between the landowner and the long-term worker was oral. The annual wage was fixed at Rs 16,000 (this is equivalent to a daily wage of Rs 45), and the payment was made in cash. A total of twelve days of paid leave was part of the contract.

Lingampalli Bikshapathi, aged 35, from the Madiga caste, is also a landless annual worker. Bikshapathi is a recent migrant to the village: he came from Devuninermeta in Nangunur taluk in 2005. His father is also a long-term farm servant in Devuninermeta. His household had five members: two workers and three minor dependents. At the time of our survey, his children were all enrolled in school.

Lingampalli Bikshapathi and his wife Kanakalakshmi were both employed by the same landowner as long-term workers. The main task assigned to Bikshapathi was to work in the mango orchards of the landowner (who was reported to own 10 acres of land). According to the oral contract, both workers had to perform any task that the employer assigned them. For no additional remuneration, Lingampalli Bikshapathi also had to go to the shops to buy consumer goods and agricultural inputs for the employer, and work at domestic tasks in the landowner's house. Kanakalakshmi also worked in the landowner's house, where her tasks included cleaning and child care.

The annual payment was Rs 18,000 for both workers together. This amounted to merely Rs 25 per day. The contract was renewable after a year. In our survey year, the landowner deducted Rs 1,680 from their annual wage because they did not work for 24 days in the contract period.

Ananthavaram

Golla Francis (35) and his son, Golla Raj Kumar (18), of the Mala caste, live in a two-member household. Francis owned 0.33 acres of land, which he cultivated during the survey year, and his son worked as a long-term worker.

Golla Raj Kumar started work as a child, and has been in employment as a long-term worker for seven years. His employer is an absentee upper-caste landowner, now resident in Vijayawada. Raj Kumar's main task is animal-rearing: he takes care of all tasks related to the maintenance of ten buffalo — cleaning, feeding and milking the animals, cleaning the cattle shed, and so on.

Raj Kumar is employed on an annual contract, and is paid Rs 8,000 and two sets of clothes annually. The daily equivalent of the cash wage is Rs 22. He also receives cooked food from the employer's house three times a day.

8

Rural Indebtedness

This chapter analyses indebtedness among rural households in Andhra Pradesh using data from secondary sources and primary data from our three village surveys.

The main sources of secondary data on household indebtedness are the All India Debt and Investment Surveys (AIDIS). There have been six rounds of surveys in the AIDIS series till date. The first survey was conducted in 1951–52 by the Reserve Bank of India (RBI), and the most recent one in 2002–03 by the NSSO.

There is a detailed literature that attempts to evaluate the quality of AIDIS as a source of information. A major finding is that the incidence of indebtedness as reported in the AIDIS is underestimated, a criticism that applies to state-level AIDIS data on Andhra Pradesh as well. This is corroborated by evidence from the primary village surveys.

The need to improve the quality of data in AIDIS was highlighted by the Committee on Informal Financial Statistics in 2001. The Committee recommended that the estimates of Central and state samples be pooled, and that the size of the AIDIS sample be increased in order to improve the quality of estimates.

SECONDARY DATA:
SOME MAJOR FINDINGS ON ANDHRA PRADESH

First, the proportion of indebted households in rural areas in Andhra Pradesh was found to be among the highest in the country. In 2002, about 42 per cent of rural households in the state were indebted, while the corresponding figure was 27 per cent for rural India as a whole.

Table 1 *Proportion of indebted rural households, Andhra Pradesh and India, 1991 and 2002* (%)

State	1991	2002
Andhra Pradesh	35	42
India	23	27

Source: AIDIS, various rounds.

Table 2 *Average levels of debt outstanding, Andhra Pradesh and India, 2002* (rupees)

State	Cultivator households	Non-cultivator households	All rural households
Andhra Pradesh	16,154	6,401	10,590
India	9,261	4,991	7,539
Debt in Andhra as a proportion of all-India debt (%)	174	128	141

Source: NSSO (2005).

Secondly, the gap in incidence of debt between India and Andhra Pradesh widened between 1991 and 2002.

Thirdly, the average amount of debt per rural household was also among the highest in Andhra Pradesh. The average level of rural debt in Andhra Pradesh was Rs 10,590, which was about 141 per cent of the national average of Rs 7,539 (Table 2).

Fourthly, the debt–asset ratio for Andhra Pradesh was also among the highest in the country. In 2002, when the debt–asset ratio for India was 2.8 per cent, it was 7.8 per cent in Andhra Pradesh, almost three times the all-India level (Tables 3 and 4). While the debt–asset ratio for Andhra Pradesh has been consistently higher than for India in all the years of AIDIS surveys, its rise was particularly sharp after 1991. Moreover, the debt–asset ratio for asset-poor households was considerably higher for Andhra Pradesh than for India as a whole. Rural households in Andhra Pradesh owning assets of an average value of up to Rs 30,000 had a debt–asset ratio of 31.3 per cent. The corresponding national ratio was 12.2 per cent (Table 4). In other words, debt as a burden on assets was greater for asset-poor households in rural Andhra Pradesh than for asset-poor households in the rest of India.

Table 3 *Debt–asset ratio, Andhra Pradesh and India, 1991 and 2002* (%)

Year	Andhra Pradesh	India
1991	4.5	1.8
2002	7.8	2.8

Source: AIDIS, various rounds.

Table 4 *Debt–asset ratio, by asset holding classes, Andhra Pradesh and India, 2002* (%)

Asset holding class (Rs)	Andhra Pradesh	India
<30,000	31.3	12.2
30,000–1,00,000	12.2	6.1
1,00,000–2,00,000	10.2	3.8
2,00,000–4,50,000	6.5	2.8
>4,50,000	4.1	2.2
All households	7.8	2.8

Source: AIDIS, various rounds.

Table 5 *Percentage share of debt from formal sources, Andhra Pradesh and India, 1991 and 2002* (%)

Year	Andhra Pradesh	India
1991	31	64
2002	27	57

Source: AIDIS, various rounds.

Fifthly, informal sources had a relatively strong grip on rural households in the state. The percentage of debt taken from formal sources in 2002 was only 27 per cent in Andhra Pradesh, less than half the corresponding national figure of 57 per cent (Table 5).

The decline in the percentage of debt from formal sources in the country between 1991 and 2002, the period of liberalisation of the banking sector, has been discussed extensively in the literature. In Andhra Pradesh, the period of liberalisation further weakened an already inadequate formal credit system in the rural areas. There was a fall in the proportion of debt from formal sources of credit in rural Andhra Pradesh from 31 per cent to 27 per cent between 1991 and 2002 (Table

6).[1] As in the rest of country, in Andhra Pradesh too, the decline in the share of formal sources was mainly on account of the weakening of commercial banks.

Sixthly, between 1991 and 2002, the fall in the percentage of debt taken from formal sources in general, and from commercial banks in particular, was particularly significant for Dalit households in rural Andhra Pradesh (Table 7).

Table 6 *Proportion of debt outstanding, by source, Andhra Pradesh, 1991 and 2002*

Source	1991	2002
Formal sources	**31**	**27**
Government	3	1
Cooperative	12	12
Commercial bank	15	13
Other	1	2
Informal sources	**69**	**73**
Landlord	15	3
Moneylender	36	57
Trader	5	7
Other	5	5
Unspecified	8	–
All sources	**100**	**100**

Source: AIDIS, various rounds.

Table 7 *Distribution of debt outstanding by source and social group, 1991 and 2002, Andhra Pradesh* (%)

Social group	1991		2002	
	All formal sources	Commercial banks	All formal sources	Commercial banks
Dalit households	36	18	16	9
Adivasi households	22	12	31	16
BC households	–	–	25	11
Other households	–	–	37	18
BC and other households	31	15	31	15
All households	31	15	27	13

Note: BC = Backward Class.
Source: AIDIS, various rounds.

[1] It is noteworthy that the decline in the share of formal sources of credit in Andhra Pradesh had set in much before 1991.

Table 8 *Proportion of debt outstanding by interest type and interest rate (r) categories, 1991 and 2002, Andhra Pradesh (%)*

Interest type	Interest-rate	Andhra Pradesh		India	
		1991	2002	1991	2002
Interest free	Total	3.0	2.1	8.4	8.4
Simple	r<6	3.9	0.4	2.5	1.6
	6<r<10	2.3	0.5	2.2	1.6
	10<r<15	11.3	13.4	25.9	22.1
	15<r<20	10.1	9.5	10.4	15.5
	20<r	52.6	64.6	20.7	27.8
	Total	80.2	88.4	61.7	68.6
Compound	r<6	0.4	0	0.3	0.4
	6<r<10	0.2	0	0.6	0.4
	10<r<15	2.0	2.3	11.0	10.1
	15<r<20	2.6	1.1	5.2	5.2
	20<r	3.5	5.9	3.6	4.7
	Total	8.7	9.3	20.7	20.8
Concessional	Total	1.2	0.1	4.2	1.8
Not specified	Total	6.4	0	3.7	0
All	Interest free	3.0	2.1	8.4	8.4
	r<6	4.3	0.4	3.2	2.1
	6<r<10	2.5	0.6	3.1	2.5
	10<r<15	14.5	15.7	39.8	33.1
	15<r<20	12.7	10.7	15.8	20.8
	20<r	56.2	70.4	24.4	32.6
	Not specified	6.7	0.1	5.3	0.4
	Total	100.0	100.0	100.0	100.0

Source: AIDIS, various rounds.

Finally, the share of debt contracted at high rates of interest was larger in Andhra Pradesh than in India as a whole. In 2002, only 32.6 per cent of the total debt was taken at rates above 20 per cent per annum in India as a whole; the corresponding share in Andhra Pradesh was about 70.4 per cent (Table 8). Further, about 6 per cent of the total debt in 1991 was borrowed at compound rates of interest exceeding 15 per cent per annum. The share rose to 7 per cent in 2002.

To summarise, the trends in rural indebtedness from the AIDIS after 1991 in Andhra Pradesh are disturbing. The share of indebted households is high and increasing, as is the burden of debt on rural households. The share of the informal sector in the total principal borrowed by rural households increased, and the share of loans borrowed at high rates of interest is very high indeed.

RESULTS FROM THE VILLAGE SURVEYS

Incidence of Debt

The proportion of households indebted was 67 per cent in Ananthavaram village, 88 per cent in Bukkacherla village and 80 per cent in Kothapalle village (Table 9).

Incidence of debt was high for almost all socio-economic classes of households in Bukkacherla and Kothapalle (Table 9). In all three villages, all artisan households were in debt. In Bukkacherla and Kothapalle, all poor peasant households were in debt. In Bukkacherla, all lower-middle peasant households were in

Table 9 *Share of indebted households, by class, study villages, May 2006* (%)

Socio-economic class	Share of indebted households		
	Ananthavaram	Bukkacherla	Kothapalle
Landlord/Big capitalist farmer	42	100	61
Capitalist farmer/Rich peasant	92	91	82
Peasant: upper-middle	43	93	83
Peasant: lower-middle	76	100	71
Peasant: poor	71	100	100
Hired manual worker	84	85	78
Artisan work and work at traditional caste calling	100	100	100
Business activity/self-employed	53	100	100
Rents/Moneylending	60	75	0
Salaried person/s	51	83	90
Remittances/pensions	21	38	39
Unclassified	100	0	0
Total	67	88	80

Source: Survey data.

Table 10 *Proportion of indebted households, by social group, study villages, May 2006* (%)

| Social group | Share of indebted households in | | |
	Ananthavaram	Bukkacherla	Kothapalle
Muslim	67	100	0
Backward Class	80	92	83
Other Castes	51	84	88
Dalit	72	89	78
Adivasi	82	0	100
Total	67	88	80

Source: Survey data.

debt. In Ananthavaram, which had the lowest level of overall incidence of debt among the three villages, the incidence was particularly high for capitalist farmer/ rich peasant households, hired manual worker households, artisan households and lower-middle peasant households.

Caste-wise data on the incidence of debt is presented in Table 10. In the two villages in which overall levels of incidence of debts were high in 2006, Bukkacherla and Kothapalle, almost all caste groups were heavily indebted. All Muslim households in Bukkacherla and all Adivasi households in Kothapalle were in debt.

Average Debt Outstanding

Among the three villages surveyed, the average level of debt outstanding in 2006 was the highest in Bukkacherla: the average debt per household was Rs 61,162. In Kothapalle the average debt outstanding was Rs 37,200 per household, and in Ananthavaram the average debt outstanding was Rs 25,310 per household (see Table 11).

In Ananthavaram, it was the capitalist farmer/rich peasant households that owed the highest average levels of debt outstanding (Rs 2,50,879). In Bukkacherla, it was the landlord/big capitalist farmer households that owed the highest average levels of debt outstanding (Rs 2,63,067 per household). In Kothapalle, it was the upper-middle peasant households that owed the highest average levels of debt outstanding (Rs 1,09,304).

In Bukkacherla, the village with the highest levels of incidence, the debt burden of poor peasant households was most severe, with average levels of debt outstanding of Rs 89,032, which was considerably higher than the village average

DEBT–ASSET RATIOS

Debt–asset ratio is the simplest measure of the burden of debt on households. It shows the extent to which the value of assets (through their sale) can finance loan repayment in extreme situations of default.

The data in Table B1 are from the census-type survey of households in the three villages conducted in December 2005 (the data in the main chapter are from the sample survey of May 2006).

They show, in each village, a great burden of debt on the relatively poor. Debt–asset ratios are the highest for landless households in all three villages. Among landless households, the burden of debt was the highest in Kothapalle, followed by Bukkacherla and Ananthavaram. Generally, as the extent of land owned increased, the debt–asset ratio decreased. In general, debt–asset ratios were the lowest for households with more than 25 acres of land.

Between the three villages, Kothapalle had the highest debt–asset ratio — a whopping 112.4 per cent (Table B1). In other words, even after selling all its assets, an average household in Kothapalle would not have been able to repay the full amount of loan in an extreme situation.

Table B1 *Average debt–asset ratio among households belonging to different size classes of operational holdings of land, study villages, December 2005 (%)*

Size-class of operational holdings	Ananthavaram	Bukkacherla	Kothapalle
Landless	53.5	169.6	206.5
<3 acres	45.7	98.0	26.8
>=3 acres and <5 acres	21.5	35.6	20.2
>=5 acres and <10 acres	12.6	46.8	19.4
>=10 acres < 25 acres	16.2	26.9	11.1
>=25 acres	11.4	17.9	6.6
All households	45.8	23	112.4

Source: Survey data.

Table 11 *Average amount of loan outstanding among all households, by class, study villages, May 2006* (Rs/household)

Socio-economic class	Ananthavaram	Bukkacherla	Kothapalle
Landlord/Big capitalist farmer	1,08,934	2,63,067	1,05,431
Capitalist farmer/Rich peasant	2,50,879	99,074	88,977
Peasant: upper-middle	24,725	51,288	1,09,304
Peasant: lower-middle	35,256	53,992	20,807
Peasant: poor	8,572	89,032	38,193
Hired manual worker	12,142	18,761	19,050
Artisan work and work at traditional caste calling	14,618	1,40,271	6,509
Business activity/Self-employed	52,587	40,651	25,050
Rents/Moneylending	64,593	1,11,533	0
Salaried person/s	6,380	38,130	49,456
Remittances/pensions	1,818	8,146	25,447
All households	25,310	61,162	37,200

Source: Survey data.

itself (Table 11). Artisan households in Bukkacherla were also heavily indebted (Rs 1,40,271 per household). Another important feature of Bukkacherla was the high level of debt outstanding for almost all classes of households, except for hired manual worker households. Hired manual worker households in Bukkacherla, on average, had outstanding debt of Rs 18,761, which was only a third of the village average. In Ananthavaram and Kothapalle, the average debt outstanding of hired manual worker households was up to one-half of the village average.

Sources of Debt

In none of the three villages surveyed was the share of the number of loans from the formal sector above 50 per cent. If 47 per cent of loans were taken from the formal sector in Bukkacherla, only 19 per cent of loans were taken from the formal sector in Kothapalle (Table 12). However, what is more important from the peasants' perspective is the share of principal borrowed from the formal sector in total principal borrowed. In terms of the amount of debt, the share from the formal sector in Bukkacherla was only 37 per cent. The corresponding

Table 12 *Number of loans borrowed from the formal sector as a proportion of all loans, by class, study villages, May 2006* (%)

Socio-economic class	Share of number of loans from the formal sector		
	Ananthavaram	Bukkacherla	Kothapalle
Landlord/Big capitalist farmer	53	59	63
Capitalist farmer/Rich peasant	58	47	32
Peasant: upper-middle	56	75	21
Peasant: lower-middle	37	45	–
Peasant: poor	17	39	13
Hired manual worker	17	26	10
Artisan work and work at traditional caste calling	–	50	–
Business activity/self-employed	59	20	24
Rents/Moneylending	32	80	–
Salaried person/s	61	42	31
Remittances/pensions	33	50	62
Total	29	47	19

Source: Survey data.

share in Ananthavaram and Kothapalle were 31 per cent and 23 per cent respectively (Table 13). In other words, not more than about one-third of the amount of debt came from formal sources in any of the three villages surveyed.

Let us now consider class-wise data on the share of amount of debt from formal sources. In Bukkacherla, the village where 100 per cent of the poor peasant households were indebted, only 19 per cent of the amount of debt came from the formal sector and 80 per cent came from the informal sector. For lower-middle peasant households, who were also 100 per cent indebted, only about 35 per cent of the amount of debt came from the formal sector (Table 15).

In Kothapalle, all poor peasant households and all artisan households were indebted. However, only 17 per cent of the amount of debt of poor peasant households came from the formal sector, compared to the village average of 23 per cent (Table 13). Among artisan households, all loans were taken from the informal sector alone (Table 16).

Table 13 *Share of formal sector in the total outstanding debt of households, by class, study villages, May 2006* (%)

Socio-economic class	Share of amount of debt from the formal sector		
	Ananthavaram	Bukkacherla	Kothapalle
Landlord/Big capitalist farmer	43	31	76
Capitalist farmer/Rich peasant	31	39	24
Peasant: upper-middle	26	67	14
Peasant: lower-middle	31	35	–
Peasant: poor	28	19	17
Hired manual worker	12	39	8
Artisan work and work at traditional caste calling	–	23	–
Business activity/self-employed	66	30	36
Rents/Moneylending	13	43	–
Salaried person/s	51	50	33
Remittances/pensions	53	50	84
Total	31	37	23

Source: Survey data.

Hired manual worker households accounted for 44 per cent of all households in Kothapalle in 2007. Among these households, 78 per cent were indebted (Table 9). Yet only 10 per cent of the number of loans and 8 per cent of the amount of debt came from the formal sector (Tables 12 and 13). Similarly, in Ananthavaram, hired manual worker households accounted for 25 per cent of all households; 84 per cent of these households were indebted, and only 17 per cent of the number of loans and 12 per cent of the amount of debt came from the formal sector (Tables 12 and 13).

Thus the access to formal credit for poor peasant households, hired manual worker households and artisan households was severely restricted in the villages surveyed.

More detailed class-wise information on the share of debt from different sources of credit in the three villages is presented in Tables 14, 15 and 16. In Bukkacherla, the most important informal source of credit for poor peasant households and lower-middle peasant households was the "small and medium

Table 14 Distribution of debt outstanding by class, source, Ananthavaram, May 2006 (%)

Socio-economic class	All formal	Com-mercial banks	Co-op banks	All in-formal	Friends, relatives	Land-lord/ Rich peasant	Money-lender	Private finance company/ chit fund	Salaried person	Small and medium peasant	Trader/ busi-nessman	SHG	Total
Landlord/Big capitalist farmer	43	43	–	57	–	4	32	–	–	21	–	–	100
Capitalist farmer/Rich peasant/Peasant: upper	31	31	–	69	–	–	2	–	–	6	60	–	100
Peasant: upper middle	26	26	–	74	–	–	19	–	32	–	23	–	100
Peasant: lower middle	31	31	–	67	3	14	6	–	17	24	4	1	100
Peasant: poor	28	28	–	69	7	9	11	10	–	26	6	1	100
Hired manual worker	12	12	–	73	10	–	27	20	2	13	–	2	100
Artisan work and work at traditional caste calling	–	–	–	84	–	60	–	–	–	16	8	–	100
Business activity/ Self-employed	66	39	26	34	–	10	–	–	–	20	–	–	100
Rents/Moneylending	13	13	–	87	9	2	32	–	–	2	41	–	100
Salaried person/s	51	51	–	45	12	–	–	10	–	23	–	4	100
Remittances/Pensions	53	53	–	47	–	–	–	–	–	47	–	–	100
All classes	31	28	3	66	4	6	13	3	5	15	19	1	100

Note: "Others and unspecified sources" are not represented separately in the table.
Source: Survey data.

Table 15 *Distribution of debt outstanding by class, source, Bukkacherla village, May 2006 (%)*

Socio-economic class	All formal	Com-mercial bank	Coop bank	All in-formal	Friend, relative	Land lord/ Rich peasant	Money-lender	Private finance company/ chit fund	Salaried person	Artisan	Small and medium peasant	Trader/ busi-nessman	SHG	Total
Landlord/Big capitalist farmer	31	5	26	69	-	23	23	-	15	-	6	2	-	100
Capitalist farmer/ Rich peasant/														
Peasant: upper	39	7	32	58	-	21	26	-	-	-	11	-	-	100
Peasant: upper middle	67	12	55	33	-	20	-	-	-	-	13	-	-	100
Peasant: lower middle	35	-	35	60	-	11	3	-	5	2	38	-	1	100
Peasant: poor	19	-	19	80	-	27	-	-	20	-	30	3	1	100
Hired manual worker	39	-	39	60	-	2	13	12	-	-	33	-	2	100
Artisan work and work at traditional caste calling	23	-	23	77	-	28	-	-	-	-	49	-	-	100
Business activity/														
Self-employed	30	-	30	41	-	18	-	-	-	-	23	-	-	100
Rents/Moneylending	43	6	37	57	-	-	-	-	-	-	4	52	-	100
Salaried person/s	50	-	38	50	-	16	5	-	-	-	21	9	4	100
Remittances/Pensions	50	-	50	50	-	49	-	-	-	-	2	-	-	100
All classes	37	4	33	61	-	19	9	1	7	-	20	5	1	100

Note: "Others and unspecified sources" are not represented separately in the table.
Source: Survey data.

Table 16 *Distribution of debt outstanding by class, source, Kothapalle village, May 2006, (%)*

Class	All formal banks	Com-mercial banks	Co-op banks	All in-formal	Friend, relative	Land-lord/Rich peasant	Money-lender	Private finance company/chit fund	Salaried person	Agri/non-agri labourers	Small and medium peasant	Trader/busi-nessman	SHG	Total
Landlord/Big capitalist farmer	76	76	–	24	–	20	–	–	–	–	4	–	–	100
Rich peasant/ Capitalist farmer/														
Peasant: upper	24	19	–	76	–	42	7	–	–	2	21	–	1	100
Peasant: upper middle	14	14	1	77	–	8	24	–	25	–	15	2	1	100
Peasant: lower middle	–	–	–	91	–	14	62	–	4	–	10	–	–	100
Peasant: poor	17	12	–	83	13	20	1	–	10	14	24	–	–	100
Hired manual worker	8	8	–	90	1	4	3	12	2	6	74	–	2	100
Artisan work and work at traditional caste calling	–	–	–	100	–	–	–	–	–	–	100	–	–	100
Business activity/ Self-employed	36	34	–	50	–	–	11	–	2	–	16	17	1	100
Rents/Moneylending	–	–	–	–	–	–	–	–	–	–	–	–	–	100
Salaried person/s	33	32	–	67	–	–	18	–	18	–	29	2	–	100
Remittances/Pensions	84	81	–	16	–	–	–	–	8	–	7	–	–	100
All classes	23	21	–	74	1	14	13	1	9	2	31	2	1	100

Note: "Others and unspecified sources" are not represented separately in the table.
Source: Survey data.

peasant", followed by the landlord/rich peasant class. In Kothapalle, the most important source of debt for poor peasant households was, again, the "small and medium peasant" class, followed by the landlord/rich peasant class. For hired manual worker households and artisan households in Kothapalle, the most important source of debt was the "small and medium peasant" class.

In Ananthavaram, most of the debt of hired manual worker households came from moneylenders, private finance companies or chit funds (Table 14). The moneylender in Ananthavaram was a major source of debt for households in other classes too. Traders were also an important source of credit for households in Ananthavaram in 2006.

Among the formal sources of credit, cooperatives were a major source of credit in only one village – Bukkacherla. Almost all of the formal credit supplied in Bukkacherla was from cooperatives. In Ananthavaram and Kothapalle, commercial banks were the most important source of formal credit.

Purpose of Borrowing

Among the three villages, Ananthavaram had the highest share of debt incurred for productive purposes (productive purposes include expenses on working capital and medium/long-term investments in agriculture, animal husbandry, business and trade). About 62 per cent of the debt in Ananthavaram was for productive purposes (Table 17), while in Bukkacherla about 47 per cent of debt was incurred for productive purposes. The share was the lowest in Kothapalle, at 20 per cent. Thus in Kothapalle, poor development of the formal sector went hand in hand with poor flow of credit into production.

Class-wise data on the share of debt incurred for productive purposes in the three villages is given in Tables 18, 19 and 20. In Ananthavaram, almost all the debt incurred by landlord/big capitalist farmer households was to finance mortgaging-in land. For lower-middle peasant households and poor peasant households, debt for consumption requirements were mainly loans to meet day-to-day domestic requirements and to repay old loans. For hired manual worker households, consumption debts were mainly loans taken to meet expenses on day-to-day domestic requirements and ceremonies.

In Bukkacherla, while the major part of consumption credit was incurred to meet expenses on ceremonies, poor peasant households and hired manual worker households took loans also to meet medical expenses. For example, 53 per cent

Table 17 *Share of amount of debt incurred for productive purposes in total debt, by class, study villages, May 2006 (%)*

Socio-economic class	Ananthavaram	Bukkacherla	Kothapalle
Landlord/Big capitalist farmer	50	31	57
Capitalist farmer/Rich peasant	93	66	25
Peasant: upper middle	79	55	14
Peasant: lower middle	47	43	18
Peasant: poor	45	34	35
Hired manual worker	8	30	14
Artisan work and work at traditional caste calling	40	23	–
Business activity/self-employed	91	100	53
Rents/Moneylending	79	66	–
Salaried person/s	33	50	5
Remittances/pensions	53	–	19
Total	62	47	20

Source: Survey data.

out of the 58 per cent share of consumption credit taken by poor peasant households in Bukkacherla was to meet medical expenses.

In Kothapalle, too, while the major part of consumption credit was incurred to meet expenses on ceremonies, upper-middle peasant households and hired manual worker households also borrowed heavily for house construction purposes.

A feature of the debt portfolios of households in Bukkacherla and Kothapalle was credit taken for purposes that could not be classified specifically as either production-related or consumption-related. In Bukkacherla, a large section of hired manual worker households operated land, which explains the high share of debt they incurred for multipurpose activities, including production. In Kothapalle, many households combined production in land and toddy-tapping activities with hired manual work, which explains the high share of debt they incurred for multipurpose activities, including production.

Table 18 *Distribution of debt outstanding by class and purpose of loan, Ananthavaram village, May 2006 (%)*

Socio-economic class	Production related	Agricultural expenses	Animal husbandry	Business and trade	Consumption related	Day-to-day expenses	Education	Ceremonies	Medical	On domestic durable assets	On house	To mortgage in land	Repay old loans	Total
Landlord/Big capitalist farmer/ Capitalist farmer/Rich peasant/	50	50	–	–	46	–	5	–	–	–	9	32	–	100
Peasant: upper	93	93	–	–	6	3	3	–	–	–	–	–	–	100
Peasant: upper middle	79	79	–	–	18	–	1	–	–	–	–	–	18	100
Peasant: lower middle	47	42	4	–	34	14	–	6	–	–	–	–	18	100
Peasant: poor	45	41	4	–	37	16	–	–	3	2	–	–	5	100
Hired manual worker	8	2	6	–	91	30	–	28	7	–	14	–	3	100
Artisan work and work at traditional caste calling	40	40	–	–	60	–	–	60	–	–	–	–	–	100
Business activity/ Self-employed	91	46	–	45	4	4	–	–	–	–	–	–	–	100
Rents/Moneylending	79	79	–	–	15	5	–	–	1	–	–	–	–	100
Salaried person/s	33	31	2	–	55	11	18	–	–	–	23	–	–	100
Remittances/Pensions	53	53	–	–	47	–	–	47	–	–	–	–	–	100
All classes	62	55	2	6	31	9	2	5	1	–	3	3	5	100

Source: Survey data.

Table 19 *Distribution of debt outstanding by class and purpose of loan, Bukkacheria village, May 2006 (%)*

Socio-economic class	Production related	Agricultural expenses	Animal husbandry	Business and trade	Consumption related	Day-to-day expenses	Cere-monies	Medical	On domestic durable assets	On house	Repay old loans	Multi-purpose production, consumption	Land purchase	Total
Landlord/Big capitalist farmer	31	31	–	–	23	–	23	–	–	–	–	41	6	100
Capitalist farmer/Rich peasant/Peasant: upper	66	55	1	–	32	–	14	2	–	–	–	2	–	100
Peasant: upper middle	55	55	–	–	25	–	9	16	–	–	–	20	–	100
Peasant: lower middle	43	39	5	–	4	1	–	3	–	–	–	48	–	100
Peasant: poor	34	19	3	2	58	2	–	53	–	–	2	6	2	100
Hired manual worker	30	30	–	–	39	3	19	11	–	1	–	18	–	100
Artisan work and work at traditional caste calling	23	22	1	–	77	–	77	–	–	–	–	–	–	100
Business activity/Self-employed	100	29	12	59	–	–	–	–	–	–	–	–	–	100
Rents/Moneylending	66	64	1	–	22	11	–	2	–	–	–	12	–	100
Salaried person/s	50	50	–	–	37	11	–	14	–	11	–	13	–	100
Remittances/Pensions	–	–	–	–	50	2	–	49	–	–	–	50	–	100
All classes	47	39	2	2	32	2	10	15	–	1	–	19	1	100

Source: Survey data.

Table 20 *Distribution of debt outstanding by class and purpose of loan, Kothapalle village, May 2006* (%)

Socio-economic class	Production related	Agricultural expenses	Animal husbandry	Business and trade	On productive durable assets	Consumption related	Day-to-day expenses	Education	Ceremonies	Medical	On domestic durable assets	On house	Repay old loans	Multi-purpose (production, consumption)	Land purchase	Total
Landlord/Big capitalist farmer	57	26	31	–	–	43	20	–	–	–	–	23	–	–	–	100
Capitalist farmer/Rich peasant/Peasant: upper	25	17	9	–	–	56	–	–	38	7	2	–	–	16	–	100
Peasant: upper middle	14	14	1	–	–	72	1	4	–	1	–	53	14	11	–	100
Peasant: lower middle	18	12	5	–	–	28	2	–	15	9	–	–	–	54	–	100
Peasant: poor	35	14	8	–	12	52	5	3	24	17	–	3	–	13	–	100
Hired manual worker	14	1	6	7	–	85	13	–	13	9	–	42	2	–	–	100
Artisan work and work at traditional caste calling	0	–	–	–	–	100	–	–	–	–	–	100	–	–	–	100
Business activity/Self-employed	53	41	–	12	–	46	1	–	11	18	16	–	–	2	–	100
Salaried person/s	5	4	–	2	–	69	15	10	25	–	–	3	–	–	26	100
Remittances/Pensions	19	11	–	–	8	81	12	–	–	–	–	68	–	–	–	100
All classes	20	12	5	3	1	66	7	2	17	6	1	23	3	9	4	100

Source: Survey data.

Rates of Interest

In general, the share of the total number of loans contracted at more than 24 per cent per annum was 10 per cent in Ananthavaram, 2 per cent in Bukkacherla and 10 per cent in Kothapalle (Tables 21, 22 and 23). The classes of households that had a significant share of loans at interest rates above 24 per cent included poor peasant households and artisan households in Ananthavaram; business households in Bukkacherla; and hired manual worker households and upper peasant households in Kothapalle. The lower share of loans at more than 24 per cent interest in Bukkacherla was evidently due to the spread of the formal credit sector in the village.

Loans taken at more than 15 per cent but less than 24 per cent per annum indicate the reliance on high-interest loans, as most crop loans are available at less than 15 per cent per annum. The share of number of loans borrowed at between

Table 21 *Distribution of number of loans by class and interest rates, Ananthavaram village, May 2006* (%)

Socio-economic class	Share of number of loans taken at annual interest rate					
	0 per cent	0–10 per cent	10–15 per cent	15–24 per cent	> 24 per cent	All loans
Landlord/Big capitalist farmer	0	0	60	40	0	100
Capitalist farmer/Rich peasant/Peasant: upper	0	0	50	50	0	100
Peasant: upper-middle	0	0	36	64	0	100
Peasant: lower-middle	6	0	42	48	3	100
Peasant: poor	14	0	19	42	25	100
Hired manual worker	38	5	10	40	8	100
Artisan work and work at traditional caste calling	0	0	0	86	14	100
Business activity/Self-employed	32	0	36	32	0	100
Rents/Moneylending	0	0	39	61	0	100
Salaried person/s	18	0	55	27	0	100
Remittances/Pensions	0	0	0	33	67	100
All classes	17	1	27	45	10	100

Source: Survey data.

Table 22 *Distribution of number of loans by class and interest rates, Bukkacherla village, May 2006* (%)

Socio-economic class	Share of number of loans taken at annual interest rate classes of					
	0 per cent	0–10 per cent	10–15 per cent	15–24 per cent	> 24 per cent	All loans
Landlord/Big capitalist farmer	0	0	81	19	0	100
Capitalist farmer/Rich peasant/Peasant: upper	0	0	67	33	0	100
Peasant: upper-middle	4	0	77	19	0	100
Peasant: lower-middle	0	0	55	45	0	100
Peasant: poor	0	0	52	44	4	100
Hired manual worker	13	0	38	46	4	100
Artisan work and work at traditional caste calling	0	0	50	50	0	100
Business activity/Self-employed	0	0	57	29	14	100
Rents/Moneylending	0	0	67	33	0	100
Salaried person/s	10	0	60	30	0	100
Remittances/Pensions	33	0	33	33	0	100
All classes	4	0	57	36	2	100

Source: Survey data.

Table 23 *Distribution of number of loans by class and interest rates, Kothapalle village, May 2006* (%)

Socio-economic class	Share of number of loans taken at annual interest rate					
	0 per cent	0–10 per cent	10–15 per cent	15–24 per cent	> 24 per cent	All loans
Landlord/Big capitalist farmer	0	0	100	0	0	100
Capitalist farmer/Rich peasant/Peasant: upper	4	0	35	48	13	100
Peasant: upper middle	0	0	64	36	0	100
Peasant: lower middle	14	0	14	71	0	100
Peasant: poor	0	0	17	83	0	100
Hired manual worker	2	0	25	61	11	100
Artisan work and work at traditional caste calling	100	0	0	0	0	100
Business activity/Self-employed	9	0	18	64	9	100
Rents/Moneylending	0	0	0	0	0	–
Salaried person/s	0	0	31	46	23	100
Remittances/Pensions	20	0	60	20	0	100
All classes	5	0	29	56	10	100

Source: Survey data.

15 and 24 per cent per annum was 45 per cent in Ananthavaram, 36 per cent in Bukkacherla and 56 per cent in Kothapalle. In other words, about half the number of loans in Ananthavaram and Kothapalle and about one-third of the number of loans in Bukkacherla were contracted at an above-normal rate of interest in 2006. Across classes, such reliance was generally higher among poor peasant households as well as manual worker and artisan households. Our data indicate a heavy interest burden on peasant and manual worker households in the villages surveyed.

CONCLUSIONS

Scholars have pointed out the underestimation of the incidence of debt in the AIDIS data. Data from AIDIS, however, continue to be used uncritically while arguing for major shifts in policy. For example, AIDIS figures have been used in the context of the debate on the policy measures required to address agrarian distress:

> There is a widespread perception that unbearable burden of debt and increased competition from imports are symptomatic of a crisis in Indian agriculture . . . Suicides [should not] be interpreted to mean that the Indian peasantry, in general and everywhere, is suffering from an unbearable burden of debt. In 2002, less than 30 per cent of rural households in the country had outstanding debt and this constituted barely 2–3 per cent of the total value of assets held by them . . . *The burden of debt is neither crushing nor of crisis-making proportions.* (Vaidyanathan 2006)

Data from our study villages, and indeed from village surveys in different parts of India, offer a sobering counter-example.

1. Data on the incidence of indebtedness from AIDIS, which is the most important secondary data source on rural credit, are significant underestimates owing to problems in its sampling methodology and large-scale under-reporting.

2. The estimates of incidence of indebtedness in AIDIS are consistently lower than the corresponding figures estimated from primary village surveys.

3. Given these problems, AIDIS data should not be used uncritically, especially while arguing for major shifts in official agricultural policy.

4. Even cautious use of data from AIDIS shows that the trends in rural

indebtedness from AIDIS after 1991 in Andhra Pradesh are disturbing. The official data indicate that indebtedness is high and increasing, and that the burden of debt on rural households continues to increase. The informal sector has a powerful hold on rural credit markets, resulting in burdensome interest rate obligations. It is noteworthy that, according to AIDIS, the share of debt taken by rural households at interest rates above 20 per cent was as high as 70.4 per cent in Andhra Pradesh, while the corresponding all-India figure was 32.6 per cent.

5. Levels of incidence of indebtedness in all the villages surveyed in Andhra Pradesh were significantly higher than the incidence figures in AIDIS.

6. The incidence of indebtedness was particularly high among poor peasant households, lower-middle peasant households, artisan households and hired manual worker households in the villages.

7. Average levels of debt per household in the three villages were in the range of Rs 25,310 to Rs 61,162. The highest level of average debt per household was in Bukkacherla and the lowest was in Ananthavaram.

8. In no village surveyed did the share of amount of debt from formal sources account for more than 37 per cent of the total debt of households. The rest of the amount of debt came from informal sources, at higher rates of interest. For hired manual worker households in Ananthavaram and Kothapalle, the share of amount of debt from formal sources was less than 12 per cent (Table 13). For poor peasant households and lower-middle peasant households, the share of debt from formal sources was lower than the village average in all three villages. No artisan household in Anantha-varam and Kothapalle had debt outstanding to a formal credit source in 2006; in other words, the entire principal borrowed was from informal sources (Tables 14 and 16).

9. Among poor peasant households, lower-middle peasant households and hired manual worker households, a considerable share of the debt was taken for consumption purposes. These purposes mainly included ceremonies at home, medical expenses and repayment of old loans (Tables 18, 19 and 20).

10. Across the villages surveyed, about 2 to 10 per cent of the loans were taken at rates of interest above 24 per cent per annum (Tables 21, 22 and 23). More importantly, about half the number of loans in Ananthavaram and Kothapalle and about one-third of the number of loans in Bukkacherla

were taken at interest rates below 24 per cent but above 15 per cent per annum. Among poor peasant households in Ananthavaram, 25 per cent of the numbers of loans were taken at an interest rate of more than 24 per cent per annum. Similarly, 14 per cent of the numbers of loans of artisan households were taken at an interest rate of more than 24 per cent per annum. In Kothapalle, 11 per cent of the numbers of loans taken by hired manual worker households were at an interest rate of more than 24 per cent per annum.

9

Literacy and Schooling

Universal schooling — that is, ten years of schooling for every person in a society — is of intrinsic importance; it is also a necessary condition for basic social, economic and political transformation and development. Commenting in 1980 on the low levels of literacy and school education achievement in rural India, P. Sundarayya made the incisive observation that "under the present system, even for the next 50 years, we shall not be able to provide every child in our country with 10 years of continuous education." [1]

Thirty years later, literacy and educational achievement in rural Andhra Pradesh remain inadequate and deeply unequal, fractured along lines of class, caste and gender. Andhra Pradesh is a state rich in natural resources, but abysmally poor in its record of providing free and universal school education to the children of its villages.

LITERACY

In each study village, of the population above 7 years, one-third of all males and almost half of all females were illiterate. Our data also indicate that the Census of India 2001 over-reports literacy (and, correspondingly, under-reports illiteracy). Despite our surveys having been conducted about six years after the Census of India, and despite similarities of definition, the rates of literacy at the surveys were generally below the rates reported in the Census.[2]

[1] Ramachandran (1990: 185).
[2] All individuals in the survey were classified into one of the following categories: (i) cannot read or write, (ii) can only sign name, (iii) can read but not write, and (iv) can read and write. Only category (iv) was marked as being literate.

With respect to regional disparities in literacy, Census of India data suggest that Guntur district records a higher achievement than the other districts covered by our surveys, and that a substantial increase in literacy was recorded in the 1990s (though levels still fell far short of being universal). Census of India data also suggest that literacy levels in Anantapur and Karimnagar districts lagged behind the state average in 2001.

As Table 1 shows, the gender gap in literacy achievement is very great, ranging from 13 percentage points in Ananthavaram to 23 percentage points in Bukkacherla. Looking at the data class-wise, it is clear that literacy levels among manual workers is lower than for the rest of the population in the survey villages (Table 2).

The literacy rate among members of manual worker households was consistently lower than that among members of all other households in the three villages. The gap was the largest in Bukkacherla (18 percentage points) and the smallest in Kothapalle (9 percentage points). A gap in literacy rates was also observed among males and females. To take the case of Ananthavaram, only 39 percent of females of manual worker households were literate as compared to 60 percent of females in all other classes.

Social discrimination and deprivation are most evident when the data are disaggregated by caste and other social groups (Tables 3, 4, 5).

Table 1 *Literate persons as a proportion of the population, sex-wise, study villages, December 2005* (%)

| Village | Sex | Proportion of literates | |
		Survey data	Census of India 2001
Ananthavaram	Male	67	86
	Female	54	77
	Persons	60	82
Bukkacherla	Male	66	72
	Female	43	46
	Persons	55	59
Kothapalle	Male	67	67
	Female	45	44
	Persons	55	55

Note: Data are for persons above the age of 7 years.
Sources: Survey data and Census of India 2001.

Table 2 *Literate persons as a proportion of the population, by manual workers and others, sex-wise, study villages, December 2005* (%)

	Ananthavaram		Bukkacherla		Kothapalle	
	Manual workers	Other households	Manual workers	Other households	Manual workers	Other households
Males	56	71	50	68	59	72
Females	39	60	30	45	42	46
Persons	48	65	39	57	50	59

Note: Data are for persons above the age of 7 years.
Source: Survey data.

Table 3 *Literate persons as a proportion of the population, by social group and sex, Ananthavaram village, December 2005* (%)

Social group	Proportion of literates		
	Males	Females	Persons
Adivasi households	44	24	33
Dalit households	61	44	53
BC households	68	53	60
Other Caste households	81	78	80
All households	67	54	60

Notes: (i) Data are for persons above the age of 7 years.
　　　(ii) BC = Backward Class.
Source: Survey data.

Table 4 *Literate persons as a proportion of the population, by sex and social group, Bukkacherla village, December 2005* (%)

Social group	Males	Females	Persons
Dalit households	43	28	36
BC households	61	37	49
Other Caste households	77	53	66
All households	66	43	55

Notes: (i) Data are for persons above the age of 7 years.
　　　(ii) BC = Backward Class.
Source: Survey data.

Table 5 *Literate persons as a proportion of the population, by sex and caste–religion, Kothapalle village, December 2005* (%)

Social group	Persons	Males	Females
Adivasi households	29	36	22
Dalit households	52	58	46
BC households	53	65	42
Muslim households	56	73	40
Other Caste households	68	84	52
All households	55	67	45

Notes: (i) Data are for persons above the age of 7 years.
(ii) BC = Backward Class.
Source: Survey data.

The extreme level of educational deprivation among Adivasi and Dalit households, particularly women, is the most glaring feature of these tables. In the two villages with a tribal population, 76 per cent and 78 per cent of women and 56 per cent and 64 per cent of men were illiterate. Of Dalit females above the age of 7 years in the three villages, 56 per cent in Ananthavaram, 63 per cent in Bukkacherla and 54 per cent in Kothapalle were illiterate. Of Dalit males, 39 per cent in Ananthavaram, 39 per cent in Bukkacherla and 42 per cent in Kothapalle were illiterate. Households classified as Backward Class, though characterised by higher levels of literacy than Adivasi and Dalit households, scored consistently lower than Other Caste households, and (other than in the case of males in Ananthavaram) lower than village averages.

YEARS OF SCHOOLING

A useful measure of adult achievement with respect to school education is the median of years of schooling in a group.[3] We have measured the median of years of schooling for all persons aged 16 years and above in each of the study villages.

[3] Put simply, the median of years of schooling for a group is the number of years of schooling completed by the 50th person in a group of 100. For example, if all members of a group of 251 people are ranked by the number of years of schooling that they have completed, the number of years completed by the 126th person (the half-way mark) is the median of years of schooling. If the median of years of schooling for a group is, say, 0, then at least 50 per cent of all members of that group have had no schooling at all.

Table 6 *Median of years of schooling for persons aged 16 years and above, by sex, study villages, December 2005*

Village	Median of years of schooling completed		
	Males	Females	Persons
Ananthavaram	6	3	5
Bukkacherla	6	0	3
Kothapalle	6	0	0

Source: Survey data.

Measured in this way, achievement with respect to school education is as dismal as achievement with respect to literacy.

The data show that, in all three villages, the median of years of schooling among men was only 6. The median of years of schooling among women was 3 in Ananthavaram and 0 in the two other villages (Table 6).

Once again, disaggregation by social groups gives us, in stark relief, a picture of social deprivation and inequality with respect to school education (see Tables 7, 8 and 9).

In all the villages, schooling among Adivasis and Dalit adults was lower than among Backward Class adults, and much lower than among Other Castes. In the two villages with an Adivasi population, the median of years of schooling among Adivasi men and women was 0. In all the villages, the same index for women was again 0.

Once again, there is a clear picture of low achievement *plus* great social inequality in educational achievement along lines of gender and caste.

SCHOOL ATTENDANCE

Ananthavaram

The first school in the village was established in 1915 by the Lutheran church. At the time of our survey, this school functioned as a government primary school. There are four schools in the village today: three primary schools and a high school. All have *pucca* buildings. All three primary schools were managed by the local Mandal Parishad, were co-educational with instruction in the Telugu medium, and covered Grades 1 to 5. Although the pupil–teacher ratio in each school was 30 or less, not one school had a regular head teacher at the time of the survey.

CLASS DIFFERENCES IN EDUCATIONAL ACCESS

Table B1 shows differences in educational access between individuals from manual worker households and individuals from all other households. An interesting feature of the data is that in the case of the number of years of schooling, disparities with respect to *class*, between manual workers and other classes in the villages, are not as sharp as disparities with respect to gender and caste.

Table B1 *Median of years of schooling for persons aged 16 years and above, manual workers and other households, study villages, December 2005* (in years)

Village	Males		Females	
	Manual worker households	Other households	Manual worker households	Other households
Ananthavaram (Guntur district)	6	6	2	3
Bukkacherla (Anantapur district)	6	6	0	0
Kothapalle (Karimnagar district)	6	6	0	0

Source: Survey data.

There are several schemes in operation in the village schools, including the Sarva Shiksha Abhiyan (SSA) and the mid-day meal programme.

When collecting data, we attempted specifically to identify children who attended school regularly, distinguishing them from children who were not enrolled in school and from children enrolled in but not regularly attending school. The data in the tables that follow represent children in the first category, that is, children enrolled and attending school regularly.

From Table 10, it is clear that all children do *not* attend school regularly. The proportion attending school was around 84 per cent in the age group 6 to 9 years and 84 per cent in the age group 10 to 14 years. This proportion fell sharply — to 49 per cent — in the age group 15 to 16 years.

Thus, two notable features of the data are, first, that school attendance is not

Table 7 *Median of years of schooling for persons aged 16 years and above, by social group and sex, Ananthavaram village, Guntur district, December 2005*

Social group	Males	Females	Persons
Adivasi households	0	0	0
Dalit households	5	0	2
BC households	5	2	4
Other Caste households	9	7	7

Note: BC = Backward Class.
Source: Survey data.

Table 8 *Median of years of schooling for persons aged 16 years and above, by social group and sex, Bukkacherla village, Anantapur district, December 2005*

Social group	Males	Females	Persons
Dalit households	0	0	0
BC households	5	0	0
Other Caste households	7	0	5

Note: BC = Backward Class.
Source: Survey data.

Table 9 *Median of years of schooling for persons aged 16 years and above, by social group and sex, Kothapalle village, Karimnagar district, December 2005*

Social group	Males	Females	Persons
Dalit households	4	0	2
Adivasi households	0	0	0
BC households	6	0	0
Muslim households	7	0	0
Other Caste households	10	0	7

Note: BC = Backward Class.
Source: Survey data.

Table 10 *Proportion of children attending school, by age group and sex, Ananthavaram village, 2005* (%)

Age group	Boys	Girls	All children
6 to 9 years	87	81	84
10 to 14 years	86	79	83
6 to 14 years	87	80	83
15 to 16 years	48	50	49
6 to 16 years	79	74	76

Source: Survey data.

universal in the age group 6 to 14 years; and, secondly, that the drop-out rate rises sharply after the age of 14 years. Despite the fact that every residential quarter in the village had a school, school attendance was not universal. Thirdly, there was a systematic gender difference in school attendance. Among 6 to 14-year-old children, 87 per cent of boys attended school, while the corresponding rate among girls was 80 per cent. Fourthly, as shown in Tables 11, 12 and 13, there were important inequalities across caste groups.

We have disaggregated the data into four caste groups: Dalits, Adivasis, Backward Class and all others. Among young children aged 6 to 9 years, the lowest attendance rate was among Adivasis, followed by Dalits. The attendance rate was similar among the Backward Class and Other Caste groups (86 per cent). In the next age group, 10 to 14 years, the lowest attendance rate was among Dalits (75 per cent), followed by Adivasis (78 per cent). The attendance rate among children in Backward Class households in this age group fell below that of children from Other Caste households.

Among children in the age group 15 to 16 years, the attendance rate fell very sharply for all caste groups other than Other Castes. Only 25 per cent of Adivasi children and 41 per cent of Dalit children aged 15 to 16 attended school. The figure was a little higher for children from Backward Class households (48 per cent) and the highest for children from Other Caste households (81 per cent).

With regard to gender differences within castes, the most striking feature of the data is that the fall in attendance rates as children grow older was higher among boys, and that school attendance among girls fell sharply when the children turned 15.

One of the reasons for low attendance rates is that children are in the work force. In Table 14, all children aged 6 to 14 are categorised according to those attending school and those not attending school. Within each of these groups, we

Table 11 *Proportion of children attending school, by caste group, Ananthavaram village, 2005* (%)

Age group	Adivasi households	Dalit households	BC households	Other Caste households
6 to 9 years	74	85	86	86
10 to 14 years	78	75	87	95
6 to 14 years	75	78	87	93
15 to 16 years	25	41	48	81
6 to 16 years	69	70	78	91

Note: BC = Backward Class.
Source: Survey data.

Table 12 *Proportion of boys attending school, by caste group, Ananthavaram village, 2005* (%)

Age group	Adivasi households	Dalit households	BC households	Other Caste households
6 to 9 years	83	90	81	100 *
10 to 14 years	71	85	80	97
6 to 14 years	79	87	81	97
15 to 16 years	50	36	60	71
6 to 16 years	76	75	77	93

Note: (i) BC = Backward Class.
             (ii) * There were seven boys in this age group.
Source: Survey data.

Table 13 *Proportion of girls attending school by caste group, Ananthavaram village, 2005* (%)

Age group	Adivasi households	Dalit households	BC households	Other Caste households
6 to 9 years	57	81	93	79
10 to 14 years	100 *	64	95	94
6 to 14 years	67	71	94	89
15 to 16 years	0 **	46	36	89
6 to 16 years	55	66	80	89

Note: (i) BC = Backward Class.
             (ii) * There were two girls in this age group.
             (iii) ** There was one girl in this age group.
Source: Survey data.

Table 14 *School attendance among children aged 6 to 14 years, by sex and work status, Ananthavaram village, December 2005 (%)*

Children	Attending		Not Attending	
	Working	Not working	Working	Not working
Boys	–	87	5	8
Girls	5	75	8	12
Total	2	81	7	10

Source: Survey data.

then identified those engaged in some work (including work outside the home and unpaid domestic work).

The last row of the table should be read as follows: 81 per cent of children aged 6 to 14 years attended school and did not work; 2 per cent attended school but also participated in work. Of all children, 7 per cent did not attend school and were working, while 10 per cent did not attend school but were reported to be not working either. The main point to note from these data is that 7 per cent of children (5 per cent of boys and 8 per cent of girls) in the age group 6 to 14 years were in the labour force. This represents a high incidence of child labour. Many scholars argue that all children not attending school should be regarded as being in some form of work. If we were to make that assumption, the incidence of child labour would be 10 per cent (8 per cent for boys and 12 per cent for girls).

Where do these children work? As Table 15 shows, in Ananthavaram, most of the children who are not in school are engaged in some form of agricultural work.

To further understand child labour, we examined school attendance rates by the occupation of the head of each household (Table 16).[4]

The data show that school attendance was over 90 per cent for children from families where the head was engaged in business activity or was an owner-cultivator. However, only 67 per cent of boys and girls of households where the head reported tenant cultivation as the main occupation attended schools. This is indeed a low attendance rate. The attendance rate was low for girls from households engaged in manual work.

[4] The socio-economic stratification used in previous chapters is not used here, since this chapter is based on the census-type survey of December 2005.

Table 15 *Distribution of working children (6 to 14 years) by occupation, Ananthavram village, December 2005*

Occupational category	Boys	Girls	Persons
Agriculture and related activity	58	65	63
Housework	17	35	29
Business activity	8	–	3
Manual work other than agriculture	17	–	6

Source: Survey data.

Table 16 *Proportion of children (6 to 14 years) attending school by occupation of household head, Ananthavaram village, December 2005*

Primary occupation of head of household	Attending		
	Boys	Girls	Persons
Owner-cultivator	95	95	95
Business activity	100	85	91
Salaried employment	82	88	83
Tenant cultivator	67	67	67
Transport workers (self-employed and salaried)	91	79	74
Manual work	82	66	75

Source: Survey data.

As explained in chapter 4 (see also Rawal and Osmani 2009), tenancy is an important feature of agrarian relations in Ananthavaram. Tenants comprise 71 per cent of cultivating households, and 67 per cent of the extent of operational holdings of land is under tenancy arrangements. Among landless households or households with small holdings of owned land, many leased land in for paddy cultivation on a fixed-rent basis. The rent on this type of contract was a punishing 78 per cent of the average yield of paddy. In the kharif season, agriculture was loss-making for these tenants. Some income could be gained where a rabi crop was sown.

It is evident that tenant households, in an oppressive rent regime with very narrow margins and under pressure to maintain livestock, draw upon child labour to contribute to their labour needs on operational holdings.

Bukkacherla

Bukkacherla has only one upper primary school (Classes 1 to 7). The school, which was opened in 1978, is in a state of disrepair. Children from the village attend high school in the neighbouring village of Gandlaparthy, 6 km away.

School attendance rates for boys and girls in Bukkacherla are shown in Table 17. First, the aggregate attendance rate for children aged 6 to 14 years was 92 per cent (higher than the attendance rate in Ananthavaram). Secondly — and very significantly — there was hardly any difference in attendance rates between boys and girls. In fact, the attendance rate was slightly higher among girls. From age 15 onwards, however, the male–female differences widened, with a sharp drop in attendance among girls. In other words, for children up to the age of 14, the gender gap had been closed in Bukkacherla, but it re-emerged sharply among older children.

Turning to caste, attendance rates by caste groups are shown in Tables 18, 19 and 20, for all children, boys and girls, respectively.

Taking the age group of 6 to 14 years, the attendance rate was 93 per cent among children from Dalit households, 94 per cent among children from Backward Class households and 91 per cent among children from Other Caste households. There were thus no big variations by caste.

However, if we include older children and take the age group 6 to 16 years, attendance rates were 84 per cent among Dalit children, 88 per cent among children from Backward Class households and 89 per cent among children from Other Caste households. Traditional caste disparities emerge. These data show that there was a big drop in the attendance rate at ages 15 to 16 years, especially among girls from Dalit and Backward Class households: 80 per cent of Dalit boys aged 15 to 16 years were in school as compared to 93 per cent of boys from Other Castes. It is worth pointing out that the attendance rate is the same for all ages among persons of Other Castes (93 per cent).

Not surprisingly, in Bukkacherla, the incidence of child labour was lower than in Ananthavaram: around 8 per cent of children aged 6 to 14 years were not attending school, and half of them (4 per cent) reported that they were engaged in some work. To identify the class of households to which these children belong, we examined the rate of school attendance by the occupation of the head of the household (Table 21).

There is not much difference in school attendance rates among children from

Table 17 *Proportion of children attending school by age group and sex, Bukkacherla village, December 2005*

Age group	Boys	Girls	Persons
6 to 9 years	95	95	95
10 to 14 years	90	92	91
6 to 14 years	92	93	92
15 to 16 years	88	50	69
6 to 16 years	91	84	88

Source: Survey data.

Table 18 *Proportion of children attending school by caste and age group, Bukkacherla village, December 2005*

Age group	Dalit households	BC households	Other Caste households
6 to 9 years	94	96	94
10 to 14 years	92	94	89
6 to 14 years	93	94	91
15 to 16 years	54	57	83
6 to 16 years	84	88	89

Note: BC = Backward Class.
Source: Survey data.

Table 19 *Proportion of boys (6 to 16 years) attending school by caste and age group, Bukkacherla village, December 2005*

Age group	Dalit households	BC households	Other Caste households
6 to 9 years	100 *	92	94
10 to 14 years	78	91	93
6 to 14 years	88	91	93
15 to 16 years	80	83	93
6 to 16 years	86	90	93

Notes: (i) BC = Backward Class.
         (ii) * There were only 8 boys in this category.
Source: Survey data.

Table 20 *Proportion of girls (6 to 16 years) attending school by caste and age group, Bukkacherla village, December 2005*(%)

Age group	Dalit households	BC households	Other Caste households
6 to 9 years	89	100 *	95
10 to 14 years	100 **	96	83
6 to 14 years	96	97	88
15 to 16 years	37	38	70
6 to 16 years	82	86	85

Notes: (i) BC = Backward Class.
　　　(ii) * There were 9 girls in this category.
　　　(iii) ** There were 16 girls in this category.
Source: Survey data.

Table 21 *Proportion of children (6 to 14 years) not attending school by occupation of head of household, Bukkacherla village, December 2005*(%)

Occupation of head of household	Not attending school		
	Boys	Girls	Persons
Manual work	29	17	23
Business activity	0	43	16
Small cultivator	12	13	12
Tenant peasant-cum-agricultural labour	7	16	12
Large and medium cultivator	10	15	12
Pensions, remittances and others	0	0	0
Salaried	0	0	0

Source: Survey data.

large, medium, small and tenant-cultivator households (about 12 per cent). As we know, agriculture in Bukkacherla is mainly rain-fed and it is rare to have a second crop. The demand for labour in agriculture is thus not very high. Among children of manual workers, however, as many as 29 per cent of boys and 17 per cent of girls did not attend school, a very high rate of non-attendance. Our survey indicated that when both parents were engaged in manual work, children were withdrawn from school either to attend to domestic tasks or to participate in the labour force. Among households engaged in petty trade, four out of five girls aged 14 were out of school. One of them was engaged in agricultural labour and the rest were engaged in housework. Another reason stated for the withdrawal of girls from school was that they had to travel 6 km outside the village in order to get to high school.

Kothapalle

There were two primary schools and one upper primary school in Kothapalle, the latter established as recently as 2001. However, because of its location and good transport facilities, children from the village attended the high school at Nustlapur as well as schools in Karimnagar.

The school attendance rate for children aged 6 to 14 years was 93 per cent, the highest among the three villages surveyed (Table 22).

In the age group 6 to 9 years, there was a small gender gap, but there was no gender gap among 10 to 14-year-old children. In general, we found that up to the age of 14, the attendance rate among girls was almost the same as attendance among boys. However, as in Bukkacherla, a serious gender gap emerged among older children: 86 per cent of boys and 63 per cent of girls aged 15 to 16 attended school.

The attendance rate in the age group 6 to 14 years was only 50 per cent among Adivasi children (who accounted for 4.5 per cent of all children in this age group). This extremely low rate of school attendance is of serious concern.

It is worth noting that there was universal school attendance among Dalit boys in the age group 6 to 14 years in Kothapalle, an achievement not observed among any Other Caste group. By contrast, among Adivasis, there was 100 per cent attendance up to the age of 9, but all three boys aged 10 to 14 years were out of

Table 22 *Proportion of children (6 to 16 years) attending school by sex and age group, Kothapalle, December 2005* (%)

Age group	Boys	Girls	Persons
6 to 9 years	96	92	94
10 to 14 years	93	93	93
6 to 14 years	95	93	93
15 to 16 years	86	63	73
6 to 16 years	93	87	90

Source: Survey data.

Table 23 *Proportion of children attending school by caste group, Kothapalle village, December 2005* (%)

Age group	Adivasi households	Dalit households	BC households	Other Caste households
6 to 9 years	80	100 *	93	91
10 to 14 years	29	98	97	91
6 to 14 years	50	99	95	91
15 to 16 years	0	73	64	100
6 to 16 years	46	93	90	93

Notes: (i) BC = Backward Class.
(ii) * There were 36 boys in this group.
Source: Survey data.

Table 24 *Proportion of boys attending school by caste, Kothapalle village, December 2005*

Age group	Adivasi households	Dalit households	BC households	Other Caste households
6 to 9 years	100 (3)	100 (20)	91	100 (11)
10 to 14 years	0 (3)	100 (20)	97	95
6 to 14 years	50	100 (40)	94	97
15 to 16 years	N.A.	72.7	92	100 (5)
6 to 16 years	50	94.1	94	97

Notes: (i) BC = Backward Class.
(ii) Numbers in parentheses represent the absolute number of children in this age and caste group.
(ii) N.A. = Not Available
Source: Survey data

Table 25 *Proportion of girls attending school by caste, Kothapalle village, December 2005*

Age group	Adivasi households	Dalit households	BC households	Other Caste households
6 to 9 years	50 (1)	100 (16)	94	83
10 to 14 years	50	97	97	88
6 to 14 years	50	98	96	86
15 to 16 years	0 (1)	73	30	100 (6)
6 to 16 years	43	92	87	88

Note: Numbers in parentheses represent the absolute number of children.
Source: Survey data.

Table 26 *Proportion of children (6 to 14 years) not attending school by occupation of head of household, Kothapalle village, December 2005*

Occupation of head of household	Not attending school		
	Boys	Girls	Total
Animal husbandry	67	20	38
Salaried	12	21	17
Manual work	10	15	13
Toddy tappers	15	9	13
Transport (self-employed and salaried)	0	33	11
Small peasant and tenant peasant	5	16	11
Business activity	13	0	8
Large and medium landowner	0	0	0

Note: Occupations are listed in descending order of non-attendance.
Source: Survey data.

school. In this age group, the attendance rate was worse for Adivasi boys than for Adivasi girls.

Another interesting observation is that among households from Other Castes, *all* children (boys and girls) aged 15 to 16 years were in school.

To sum up, though the overall attendance rates are high in Kothapalle, there are noticeable differences across castes, with Adivasi children lagging far behind others. Dalit children aged 6 to 14 years attended school, but the drop-out rate was high when children reached the age of 15.

Corresponding to the higher attendance rates, the proportion of children not attending school or engaged in regular work was lower in Kothapalle than in the other villages. Thirty eight per cent of all children from households whose heads were engaged in animal husbandry were not in school and were child workers. The numbers in this group were small but the underlying problem is important. In Kothapalle, the Adivasi community includes persons of the Yerukala tribe. These families are nomadic, and reported that their children, particularly boys, were sent to graze animals rather than to school.

CONCLUSIONS

Literacy in rural Andhra Pradesh is far from being universal, and appears, in fact, to be distinctly lower than even the Census of India results suggest. In Ananthavaram, our surveys found a literacy rate of 60 per cent (the Census of India reported a literacy rate of 82 per cent). In both Bukkacherla and Kothapalle, our surveys reported a literacy rate of 55 per cent.

Corresponding to the low literacy rates are very low rates of achievement with respect to school education, measured in this chapter by the median of years of completed schooling among the adult population. Not only is performance with respect to school education poor, it is also, like literacy, deeply unequal as between males and females, socio-economic classes and castes.

For example, the median of years of completed schooling for the population above 15 years was 5 years, 3 years and 0 years, respectively, in Ananthavaram, Bukkacherla and Kothapalle. The median of years of schooling for women was 3, 0 and 0 in the three villages. The corresponding figure was 0 for women from Dalit households in all three villages. Among Adivasi households, the corresponding figure was 0 years for men and women in all villages.

With respect to school attendance today, differences across the three villages do not necessarily correspond to differences in aggregate incomes or natural resources, or even to the level of school education recorded in the surveys. Although Guntur and the neighbouring districts are known not only for highly fertile tracts of high-yielding paddy cultivation, but also for a long history with respect to institutions of secondary and higher education, Ananthavaram did not perform better than the other villages with respect to school attendance, particularly among the educationally deprived. If we take girls aged 6 to 14, the school attendance rates were 67 per cent among Adivasi households and 71 per cent among Dalit households.

Although gender disparities in school attendance in the early years of schooling are less than before, inequality sets in because girls are more likely to have to leave school ("drop out") earlier than boys. Disparities become particularly apparent after children reach the age of 14 years, when the rates of enrolment between boys and girls begin to vary sharply.

Caste deprivation with respect to school attendance endures. In Kothapalle, for instance, only 50 per cent of 6 to 14-year-old children from Adivasi households attended school regularly, and it is evident that, without direct and specifically targeted interventions, deprivation will continue to exist among Dalit and Adivasi children.

This chapter began by noting that school education is a necessary condition for basic social, economic and political transformation and development. Universal school education can be achieved only through programmes of public action: governments must, *inter alia*, pass appropriate compulsory education laws and allocate enough money for universal school education, and people must be mobilised politically for the establishment of universal compulsory school education. The evidence shows that the state has failed the people of rural Andhra Pradesh in respect of the public provision of ten years of school education.

10

Selected Household Amenities

Basic housing and household amenities are essential to human development. Housing, electrification, sanitation, and the provision of safe water to drink and for domestic use are essential to human health and dignity, to economic growth, and to the prevention of environmental pollution. A pervasive feature of Indian society is the large-scale absence of access to these basic amenities. A substantial section of our society is denied access to adequate housing, electricity, sanitation and safe water; consequently, a large part of our society is denied access to health, self-dignity, economic progress and an unpolluted environment. Further, the absence of specific civic amenities affects different people differently: the absence of lavatories and consequent defecation in the open creates special problems for women; the drudgery of drawing and carrying water for domestic use falls on women; the absence of electricity affects education; the absence of sanitation affects the people of particular castes in particular ways, and so on.

In addition to deprivation, there is *discrimination* in access to basic amenities. Such discrimination is associated historically with the systematic denial of social equality — including equal conditions of social dignity — to individuals and social groups.

This chapter reports on the state of household amenities and the access to selected facilities of modern life available to households in rural Andhra Pradesh. Specifically, it deals with housing, electricity, lavatories and drinking water in the survey villages.

We illustrate class and caste inequalities in access to these amenities by comparing, first, the access of Dalit households and Other Caste households to the amenities selected; and, secondly, the access of households from selected socio-economic classes — landlords, rich peasants, poor peasants and hired manual workers — to the same selected amenities.[1] The populations of Adivasis and Muslims in the villages are small, and data on them are in information boxes provided later in the chapter.

HOUSING

Home Ownership

In all the villages studied, a high proportion of households owned their dwelling places. This is not uncommon in rural areas. In all three villages, the proportion of Dalit households owning their homes was higher than the proportion of Other Caste households owning their homes (this phenomenon also shows up in data from the Census of India). For example, in Ananthavaram, 87 per cent of Dalits owned their homes as compared to 80 per cent among Other Castes and 72 per cent of Muslims. Similarly, in Bukkacherla, 93 per cent of Dalits owned their homes as compared to 80 per cent of Other Castes (Table 1). These results reflect, in the first place, the *spatial separateness* of Dalit settlements in the villages. Second, they reflect the fact that Dalit households have little access to rented accommodation in the villages.[2]

Inequality in ownership between socio-economic *classes*, however, were more sharp (Table 2). In Ananthavaram and Bukkacherla, for example, while all households from among big landlords owned their homes, only 70 to 74 per cent of manual labour households did so.

Table 1 *Proportion of households owning their own houses, study villages, Dalit and Other Caste households, December 2005* (%)

Villages	Dalit	Other Castes
Ananthavaram	87	80
Bukkacherla	93	80
Kothapalle	88	81

Source: Survey data.

[1] Data on socio-economic classes are from the samples collected in May 2006. In this chapter, Other Caste includes all households other than Dalit, Adivasi and Muslim households.

[2] As Thorat (2009) has pointed out, the fact that a higher proportion of SC households own their homes in rural areas reflects, perhaps, their lack of access to rented housing.

Table 2 *Proportion of households owning their own houses, by selected socio-economic class, study villages, May 2006 (%)*

Socio-economic class	Ananthavaram	Bukkacherla	Kothapalle
Landlord/Big capitalist farmer	100	100	100
Capitalist farmer/Rich peasant			
Peasant: upper	66	91	100
Peasant: poor	87	77	100
Hired manual worker	74	70	76
All households	82	84	84

Source: Survey data.

Housing Quality

As early as 1961, the International Labour Office (ILO) made a "Recommendation on Workers' Housing" in which it suggested that each country fix appropriate standards for housing. Such standards were to cover, among other things, the minimum space per person or per family; appropriate protection against heat, cold, damp, noise, fire, and disease-carrying animals and insects; adequate sanitary and washing facilities; ventilation, cooking and storage facilities; and a minimum degree of privacy.

Our classification of the quality of houses follows the definition used by the Census of India and the National Sample Survey Organisation (NSSO), in which a house with roof and walls made with permanent or pucca material is defined as a pucca house.[3] If either the roof or wall of a residence is made of temporary material, it is termed a semi-pucca house, and if both are of temporary material, it is called a katcha house. The problem is that not all items in the list of pucca material provide adequate protection, and meet health and safety standards. Nevertheless, we have continued with this definition for the present.

Among the three villages, Kothapalle had the best housing conditions: 90 per cent of the households lived in pucca houses. In the other two villages, around

---

[3] Pucca material includes cement, concrete, oven-burnt bricks, hollow cement or ash bricks, stone, stone blocks, jack-boards (cement-plastered reeds), iron, zinc or other metal sheets, timber, tiles, slate, corrugated iron, asbestos and cement sheets, veneer, plywood, artificial wood of synthetic material and polyvinyl chloride (PVC) material.

one-half of all households lived in *pucca* houses (54 per cent in Ananthavaram and 57 per cent in Bukkacherla).

In terms of caste differences, there was a remarkable contrast between Ananthavaram on the one hand, and Bukkacherla and Kothapalle on the other. In Ananthavaram, only 23 per cent of Dalit households lived in pucca houses and as many as 50 per cent had katcha houses. By contrast, in Bukkacherla and Kothapalle, 90 per cent of Dalit households lived in pucca constructions (Table 3). Among Other Caste households, 87 per cent in Kothapalle had pucca houses; the corresponding figure in Bukkacherla was 48 per cent. In Bukkacherla, the Dalit settlement is at the end of the pucca road from Gandlaparthy to the village (whereas the main village settlement is a little way off, on a katcha road) and most of the houses are newly constructed concrete structures. The houses in the main village settlement are older and many of them are mud-walled.

The contrast across classes is striking: in Ananthavaram all landlord and rich-peasant households lived in pucca homes, whereas over 40 per cent of poor peasant and hired manual worker households lived in katcha homes. The overall quality of housing was much better in Kothapalle and Bukkacherla. In Kothapalle 95 per cent of manual worker households lived in pucca houses; the corresponding figure was 75 per cent in Bukkacherla.

From a health perspective, the separation of the cooking area from the living and/or sleeping areas is very important. Our data show that only 47 per cent of households in Bukkacherla and 32 per cent in Kothapalle lived in houses with separate kitchens.[4]

Table 3 *Proportion of households by type of house, Dalit and Other Caste households, study villages, December 2005* (%)

Villages	Pucca houses		Semi-pucca		Katcha	
	Dalit	Other Castes	Dalit	Other Castes	Dalit	Other Castes
Ananthavaram	23	88	27	3	50	9
Bukkacherla	90	48	5	48	5	4
Kothapalle	90	87	5	11	5	2

Source: Survey data.

[4] This information was not collected for Ananthavaram.

Table 4 *Proportion of households by type of house and selected socio-economic class, study villages, May 2006* (%)

Socio-economic class	Ananthavaram			Bukkacherla			Kothapalle		
	Pucca	Semi-pucca	Katcha	Pucca	Semi-pucca	Katcha	Pucca	Semi-pucca	Katcha
Landlord/Big capitalist farmer	100	0	0	33	67	0	100	0	0
Capitalist farmer/ Rich peasant/ Peasant: upper	100	0	0	36	64	0	94	6	0
Peasant: poor	43	48	9	38	55	7	100	0	0
Hired manual worker	40	17	43	75	20	5	95	2	3
All households	54	15	31	57	39	4	90	7	3

Source: Survey data.

ELECTRICITY PROVISION

Household electricity connections were not universal in any of the villages (Table 5). The three villages, however, differed in the extent of coverage of electricity for domestic use. It is clear that in Bukkacherla and Kothapalle, electricity was more likely to be used in homes, irrespective of socio-economic class. In Ananthavaram, less than 70 per cent of manual worker households had electricity in their homes.

In Ananthavaram, less than 80 per cent of Dalit households had an electricity connection (Table 6). By contrast, in Bukkacherla, as explained later, Dalit families had relatively newly constructed pucca homes with electricity connections.

Problems with obtaining authorised electricity connections were not serious in Ananthavaram and Kothapalle, where 3 and 2 per cent of households reported unauthorised connections, but were serious in Bukkacherla, where 28 per cent of households reported having unauthorised connections.

Table 5 *Proportion of households with electricity connection, by selected socio-economic class, study villages, May 2006* (%)

Socio-economic class	Ananthavaram	Bukkacherla	Kothapalle
Landlord/Big capitalist farmer	100	100	100
Capitalist farmer/Rich peasant/Peasant: upper	100	82	82
Peasant: poor	94	85	100
Hired manual worker	69	90	88
All households	94	90	92

Source: Survey data.

Table 6 *Proportion of households with electricity connection, Dalit and Other Caste households, study villages, December 2005* (%)

Villages	Dalit	Other Castes
Ananthavaram	79	94
Bukkacherla	95	88
Kothapalle	86	94

Source: Survey data.

LAVATORIES

Absence of access to sanitary systems for the disposal of human waste is a serious problem for individual welfare as well as for the well-being of a community. Although the construction of private and public toilets was to have accelerated after the introduction of the Government of India's Total Sanitation Campaign, the condition of sanitary facilities in the study villages is deplorable.

No one in the three villages used a public toilet. Of all households, 53 per cent in Ananthavaram, 78 per cent in Bukkacherla and 56 per cent in Kothapalle did not have lavatories (Table 7). Since there were no public toilets in the villages, those who did not have private lavatories had to defecate in open spaces.

Ananthavaram showed the sharpest inequality with respect to the use of toilets. Among landlord and rich peasant households 100 per cent used lavatories, while among poor peasants and manual workers, the proportions were 30 per cent and 26 per cent respectively (Table 7). Similarly, when disaggregated by broad caste groups, 74 per cent of Dalit households had to resort to open defecation, while the corresponding figure for Other Castes was 24 percent. In Bukkacherla, over-

Table 7 *Proportion of households with own lavatory, by selected socio-economic class, study villages, May 2006* (%)

Socio-economic class	Ananthavaram	Bukkacherla	Kothapalle
Landlord/Big capitalist farmer	100	33	61
Capitalist farmer/Rich peasant/Peasant: upper	100	45	65
Peasant: poor	30	15	40
Hired manual worker	26	15	41
All households	47	22	44

Source: Survey data.

Table 8 *Proportion of households by system of sanitation, Dalit and Other Caste households, study villages, December 2005* (%)

Villages	Using lavatory		Open defecation	
	Dalit	Other Castes	Dalit	Other Castes
Ananthavaram	26	76	74	24
Bukkacherla	21	20	79	80
Kothapalle	35	48	65	52

Source: Survey data.

all achievement was the worst by far among the three study villages — marked though the other villages were by caste and class inequalities.

The majority of households were thus forced into conditions of open defecation. Even public provision of housing is no assurance of access to the basic amenity of a toilet.

Drinking Water

According to the ILO recommendation on workers' housing, workers' dwellings are to be "supplied with safe water in such ample quantities as to provide for all personal and household uses" (ILO 1961). The ILO recommendation thus specifies a norm for the location of the water source, as well as one for the adequacy and quality of water supply.

We did not collect samples and conduct tests on the quality of water in the villages. The statistical tables below use "covered source" as a proxy for a safe source of water. In the Census of India and NSSO, safe drinking water is defined as water from a "covered source", that is, a tap, hand-pump, borewell or tube well. All open sources (wells, tanks, ponds, canals and rivers) are termed "unsafe". This is a somewhat imprecise definition, since there can be open wells with clean water as well as tube wells with water that is unsafe. Large sections of the population of Kerala, for example, drink water drawn from open wells and then boiled.

All households (Dalit and non-Dalit, and of all classes) in Ananthavaram and Bukkacherla had access to a covered source of water (Tables 9 and 10). In Kothapalle, a significant proportion of households drew drinking water from open wells.

In rural areas many households do not have a source of drinking water within their home or homestead, as the system of distribution of water through private taps is uncommon. Thus the overall situation in respect of the availability of water within a house or homestead is poor. Households in Bukkacherla were the

Table 9 *Proportion of households with access to a covered source of drinking water, by selected socio-economic class, study villages, May 2006* (%)

Socio-economic class	Ananthavaram	Bukkacherla	Kothapalle
Landlord/Big capitalist farmer	91 *	100	61
Capitalist farmer/Rich peasant/Peasant: upper	100	100	83
Peasant: poor	100	100	100
Hired manual worker	100	100	85
All households	99	99	81

Note: _ * One household used an open well within the homestead for drinking water.
Source: Survey data.

Table 10 *Proportion of households with access to a covered source of drinking water, Dalit and Other Caste households, study villages, December 2005* (%)

Villages	Dalit	Other Castes
Ananthavaram	100	99
Bukkacherla	100	99
Kothapalle	85	75

Source: Survey data.

Table 11 *Proportion of households with source of drinking water within the homestead, by selected socio-economic class, study villages, May 2006* (%)

Socio-economic class	Ananthavaram	Bukkacherla	Kothapalle
Landlord/Big capitalist farmer	100	0*	61
Capitalist farmer/Rich peasant/Peasant: upper	100	36	65
Peasant: poor	43	0	60
Hired manual worker	24	5	28
All households	54	12	44

Note: * All households rely on street taps.
Source: Survey data.

Table 12 *Proportion of houses with source of drinking water within the homestead, Dalit and Other Caste households, study villages, December 2005* (%)

Villages	Dalit	Other Castes
Ananthavaram	31	77
Bukkacherla	2	20
Kothapalle	48	37

Source: Survey data.

worst off in terms of availability of water within the home (most households relied on hand pumps or taps in the neighbourhood), while class differences in this respect were stark in Ananthavaram (Table 11).

Among Other Caste households, only in Ananthavaram village did a majority report a source of water within the homestead. The proportion of Dalit households with a source of drinking water within the homestead was lower than the proportion of Other Caste households in all villages other than Kothapalle (Table 12). In Bukkacherla, only 2 per cent of Dalit households had water sources within the homestead.

OVERALL QUALITY OF HOUSING

Now we turn to a combined indicator of quality of housing and availability of different amenities. A household living in a pucca structure (whether owned or rented) with a toilet, electricity and its own source of water can be defined as having adequate housing with adequate civic amenities. At the other extreme, a family living in a katcha house with no electricity, no toilet and no water within the homestead can be characterised as having severely deficient housing. In between these two extremes there are several types of substandard housing. As there are many types of substandard housing (katcha house with electricity, semi-pucca house with electricity but no toilets, etc.), we have focused on the two extreme categories, defined as follows:

- When a household lives in a pucca house with electricity, a toilet and a source of drinking water within the homestead, we say that it has "adequate housing".
- When a household lives in a house with no electricity, no toilet and no source of drinking water within the homestead, we say that it has "severely deficient housing".

One-third of all households in Ananthavaram reported adequate housing: this was the highest among the three villages. At the other extreme was Bukkacherla: none of the households had adequate housing. This was mainly on account of the fact that no household had a source of water within the homestead. Only 1 per cent of households in Bukkacherla and Kothapalle had severely deficient housing; the figure was 8 per cent in Ananthavaram (Table 13).

These data on housing show that, first, in aggregate, the state of housing and

Table 13 *Proportion of households by overall quality of housing, selected socio-economic class, study villages, May 2006* (%)

Socio-economic class	Ananthavaram		Bukkacherla		Kothapalle	
	Adequate housing	Severely deficient	Adequate housing	Severely deficient	Adequate housing	Severely deficient
Landlord/Big capitalist farmer	100	0	0	0	61	0
Capitalist farmer/Rich peasant/Peasant: upper	100	0	0	0	41	0
Peasant: poor	18	0	0	8	20	0
Hired manual worker	14	21	0	0	2	2
All households	33	8	0	1	16	1

Source: Survey data.

Table 14 *Proportion of households by overall quality of housing, Dalit and Other Caste households, study villages, December 2005* (%)

Villages	Adequate housing		Severely deficient housing	
	Dalit	Other Caste	Dalit	Other Caste
Ananthavaram	7	86	13	2
Bukkacherla	0	2	0	1
Kothapalle	12	19	2	0

Source: Survey data.

basic amenities is far from satisfactory in the three villages; and secondly, that there are large inequalities across castes and classes, particularly in Ananthavaram and Kothapalle.

In Ananthavaram the overwhelming majority of Other Caste households had adequate housing (Table 14). In the remaining villages housing was substandard for the majority of households irrespective of caste. Thus the overall situation is one where a large majority of households in all the villages have substandard housing. Nevertheless, there is a clear difference between Dalit households and those belonging to Other Castes. It is noteworthy that 0 or, at most, 1–2 per cent of Other Caste households lived in severely deficient housing, that is, katcha homes with no amenities. In other words, while many non-Dalit households lived in substandard housing, very few lived in severely deficient housing. Ananthavaram is a good illustration of inequality in the quality of housing: 86 per cent of Other Caste households had adequate housing while 7 per cent of Dalit households had adequate housing.

HOUSEHOLD AMENITIES AND INCOMES

We have classified all households in the survey villages into three income groups based on net annual household incomes from all sources (Tables 15, 16 and 17). The first and lowest income category consists of households with total incomes that are less than Rs 22,000 a year, which corresponds roughly to the official rural poverty line for Andhra Pradesh in 2005–06 by the current calculation. The second category consists of households with incomes from Rs 22,000 to 100,000, and the third category of household with incomes over Rs 100,000.

The data show that households in a very high-income bracket generally had

DEPRIVATION AMONG ADIVASI AND MUSLIM HOUSEHOLDS

Ananthavaram and Kothapalle have a small Adivasi population (7 and 3 per cent of the population respectively). There is no doubt that Adivasi households are among the worst-off sections of the population in respect of access to basic amenities. For all the indicators examined in this chapter, Adivasi households were worse off than Dalit households.

There were two villages with Scheduled Tribe populations in our surveys: Ananthavaram with 44 Adivasi households and Kothapalle with 11 Adivasi households. Our survey data show that not a single Adivasi home was in the "adequate housing category" and sixteen households (29 per cent) lived in homes that were in the "severely deficient" category.

Table B1 *Housing conditions, Adivasi households, aggregates for Ananthavaram and Kothapalle, December 2005*

	Number	%
All Adivasi households	55	
of which, living in:		
Pucca	8	14
Katcha	40	73
Semi-pucca	7	13
Houses with toilets	3	5
Houses with electricity	36	65
Houses with water sources in homestead	2	4

Source: Survey data.

Of all Adivasi households, 35 per cent lived in homes without electricity, 86 per cent lived in katcha or semi-pucca houses, only 5 per cent had toilets in their homesteads, and only 4 per cent had sources of water for domestic use within their homesteads (Table B1).

Even a casual visitor to Ananthavaram can see that the Adivasi settlement is the worst-off area of the village in respect of housing and basic amenities. The settlement has no street lighting and all the roads within the settlement are katcha roads. The area is low-lying and prone to flooding.

In 2007–08, the Government sanctioned the construction of 23 houses for Scheduled Tribe families under the "Indiramma" rural housing scheme. The scheme envisages assistance in cash and kind (in the form of cement bags) for the construction of a house. However, the payment is on an instalment basis. According to the panchayat office, all four instalments are to be paid in cash and according to the following schedule: Rs 4,000 after construction of the foundation, Rs 12,000 after door-level construction, Rs 6,000 after roof-level construction and Rs 10,000 after completion. In short, each household invests in construction and then is reimbursed as per this schedule of payments.

Since all the Adivasi households are too poor to invest the money themselves, the construction of most of these houses has now (that is, in December 2009) been abandoned at the door-level stage.

Table B2 *Housing conditions, Muslim households, aggregates for the three study villages, December 2005*

	Number	%
All Muslim households	31	
of which, living in:		
Pucca	21	68
Katcha	6	19
Semi-pucca	4	13
Houses with toilets	12	39
Houses with electricity	27	87
Houses with water sources in homestead	11	35

Source: Survey data.

With respect to household amenities, Muslim households in the three villages occupy a position substantially worse-off than Other Caste households.

Table 15 *Proportion of households with specified amenity, by income group, Ananthavaram village, 2006 (%)*

Income group (Rs per annum)	Lavatory	Electricity	Pucca house	Water within homestead
Up to Rs 22,000	37	83	44	35
Rs 22,000 < Rs 1 lakh	44	90	56	55
Rs 1 lakh and above	95	100	89	94
All households	47	94	54	53

Source: Survey data.

Table 16 *Proportion of households with specified amenity, by income group, Bukkacherla village, 2006 (%)*

Income group (Rs per annum)	Lavatory	Electricity	Pucca house	Water within homestead
Up to Rs 22,000	13	87	51	10
Rs 22,000 < Rs1 lakh	21	92	63	8
Rs 1 lakh and above	86	100	100	55
All households	22	90	59	12

Source: Survey data.

Table 17 *Proportion of households with specified amenity, by income group, Kothapalle village, 2006 (%)*

Income group (Rs per annum)	Lavatory	Electricity	Pucca house	Water within homestead
Up to Rs 22,000	38	89	89	38
Rs 22,000 < Rs 1 lakh	49	96	89	51
Rs 1 lakh and above	71	100	100	73
All households	44	92	89	44

Source: Survey data.

greater access to basic amenities than others. At the same time, qualitative differences among households in basic living conditions, as measured by access to these four amenities (housing, drinking water, toilets and electricity), did not correspond solely to differences in incomes. In particular, it did not correspond to a simple criterion of crossing the "poverty line". Our data show that small increases in incomes were neither necessary nor sufficient to ensure adequate amenities.

The presence or absence of governmental or other external intervention is crucial in determining a household's access to basic amenities. We refer here not only to village-level schemes such as programmes for electrification or provision of drinking water, but also to schemes that have benefited specific households. Two types of benefits that were reported in our surveys were support for construction of houses and for construction of toilets. Such assistance was either in cash or in kind, or both (support in kind was in the form of wages for family labour employed in the construction). We have two contrasting cases.

Bukkacherla is a village where 90 per cent of Dalit households lived in pucca houses with electricity connections (Tables 3 and 6). Of all Dalit households, 71 per cent had received financial aid for housing. In addition to government support, Dalit households received financial aid from a local NGO called the Rural Development Trust. The improved housing is very visible: the newly constructed houses are in a settlement close to the pucca road. There is a clear association here between improved housing and specific assistance for house construction.

By contrast, in Ananthavaram only 23 per cent of Dalit households lived in pucca homes and 50 per cent lived in katcha homes (Table 3). Not surprisingly, only 18 per cent of Dalit households in the village reported receiving some form of government benefit. Further, even among households that were assisted, some continued to live in katcha constructions.

CONCLUSIONS

This chapter examined the endowments of households in respect of certain basic household amenities, that is, domestic electricity connections, pucca houses in which to live, safe water sources within households and access to latrines. The general picture was one of inadequate achievement for the majority, and inequality as between classes and castes in the villages.

If electrification is measured (as we have done here) merely by whether or not a household has an electricity connection, and not by any measure of the volume of electricity consumed per household, then electricity is the best distributed of the amenities we have considered here. On average, nearly 90 per cent of households had an electricity connection in all three villages.

Nevertheless, there is still inequality in access to domestic electricity. In Ananthavaram, for example, 79 per cent of Dalit households had electricity connections as compared to 94 per cent of Other Caste households (Table 6).

In general, pucca housing comes with higher incomes. The poor and socially disadvantaged do not have access to pucca housing other than in instances where special schemes for housing among the poor have been implemented. Disparities in this regard are stark in Ananthavaram, where 100 per cent of landlord and rich peasant households, and only 40 per cent of manual worker households, lived in pucca houses, and 88 per cent of Other Caste households and only 23 per cent of Dalit households lived in pucca houses (Table 3). By contrast, where there is direct investment in housing for Dalits some gains can be made, as illustrated by the experience of Bukkacherla, where 90 per cent of Dalit households lived in pucca homes (Table 3) built with assistance from the government and an NGO. Government housing schemes that depend on hefty financial contributions by the poor do not succeed, as the failure of the Indiramma housing scheme among Adivasis in Ananthavaram shows.

Only when water sources are available within homesteads will women be relieved of the drudgery of walking substantial distances from home for water, waiting in queues and carrying it back to their houses. Achievement in this regard has been poor and unequal. To illustrate, in Ananthavaram, 46 per cent of all households and 76 per cent of manual worker households had no source of water in their homes; in Bukkacherla, 88 per cent of all households, 95 per cent of manual worker households and 98 per cent of Dalit households had no source of water in their homes; and in Kothapalle, 56 per cent of all households and 72 per cent of manual worker households had no source of water in their homes (Tables 11 and 12).

Further, the public good nature of safe drinking water and of water sources within homesteads implies that an individual's access depends not just on individual incomes but on common facilities. In the case of piped water, a house can have provision for piped water inside only if there is access to piped water in the neighbourhood (similarly, a household in a distant hamlet can only get electricity if the hamlet itself has provision for electricity connections).

The worst performance of all has been in respect of providing villages and homes with lavatories. The vast majority of the population has to defecate in open spaces, an affront to human dignity and hazard to human health.

The members of 53 per cent of all households in Ananthavaram, 78 per cent of all households in Bukkacherla and 56 per cent of all households in Kothapalle were forced to defecate in open spaces. The members of 74 per cent of manual worker households in Ananthavaram, 85 per cent of manual worker households in Bukkacherla and 59 per cent of manual worker households in Kothapalle were forced to defecate in open spaces (Table 7). Caste differences in this regard were particularly sharp in Ananthavaram, where 76 per cent of Other Caste households and only 26 per cent of Dalit households used lavatories.

Given the performance with respect to individual indicators, it is not surprising that the vast majority of households do not live in "adequate housing", that is, in houses that are pucca, have an electricity connection, and have a source of water and lavatory within the premises. In Bukkacherla, not a single household lived in "adequate housing". In Kothapalle, 84 per cent of households did not live in adequate housing, while the corresponding figure for Ananthavaram was 67 per cent (Table 13). As the detailed data in the chapter show, social inequalities in respect of the overall quality of housing were very great indeed.

Much progress needs to be made with respect to the amenities and living conditions described in this chapter. Deprivation based on centuries of class and caste exploitation cannot be overcome without large-scale public intervention.

Statistical Appendix

CHAPTER 3

Table 3.1 *Asset holdings of households, by class, Ananthavaram village, May 2006 (rupees)*

Socio-economic class	Land and water bodies	Buildings	Animals	Means of production	Means of transport	Domestic durables	Other assets	All assets
Landlord/Big capitalist farmer	45,840,700	9,353,000	108,000	350,500	147,450	902,815	74,900	56,777,365
Capitalist farmer/ Rich peasant	25,599,816	4,401,624	564,944	311,254	148,495	648,068	93,419	31,767,620
Peasant: upper middle	40,110,635	5,299,808	1,079,905	415,549	171,841	687,044	79,914	47,844,696
Peasant: lower middle	15,217,178	4,607,563	949,126	73,183	155,969	797,460	115,087	21,915,567
Peasant: poor	9,857,039	4,070,139	653,244	346,828	124,672	682,178	84,870	15,818,969
Hired manual worker	2,509,280	2,993,241	345,476	119,064	56,029	475,001	34,870	6,532,961
Artisan work and work at traditional caste calling	252,107	300,536	3,866	92,780	83,303	148,837	3,256	884,685
Business activity/ self-employed	10,136,896	11,020,336	1,689,671	1,392,765	234,865	620,613	201,938	25,297,083
Rents/Moneylending	20,404,647	4,657,897	142,251	148,466	5,162,325	783,850	46,625	31,346,062
Salaried person/s	14,899,895	2,969,625	3,182	101,927	272,188	687,883	31,744	18,966,444
Remittances/Pensions	8,447,231	3,520,221	125,101	436,568	424,894	572,325	9,810	13,536,150
Unclassified households	123,999	371,997	8,267	0	4,547	79,483	0	588,293
All households	193,399,423	53,565,986	5,673,031	3,788,884	6,986,578	7,085,558	776,434	271,275,895

Source: Survey data.

Table 3.2 *Asset holdings of households, by class, Bukkacherla village, May 2006* (rupees)

Socio-economic class	Land and water bodies	Buildings	Animals	Means of production	Means of transport	Domestic durables	Other assets	All assets
Landlord/Big capitalist farmer	24,376,486	4,560,104	38,444	693,565	688,714	223,611	108,947	30,689,870
Capitalist farmer/ Rich peasant	14,657,346	4,855,843	220,863	1,067,941	153,814	317,428	113,906	21,387,141
Peasant: upper middle	7,723,179	2,218,431	652,523	1,463,315	372,658	384,714	140,565	12,955,386
Peasant: lower middle	3,153,789	1,539,629	101,405	614,515	212,905	136,651	474,638	6,233,533
Peasant: poor	1,592,098	555,573	184,013	361,375	111,055	127,179	104,528	3,035,821
Hired manual worker	2,497,028	1,357,011	6,562	112,094	10,660	187,398	59,385	4,230,140
Artisan work and work at traditional caste calling	579,031	371,174	0	59,388	118,776	61,318	4,454	1,194,140
Business activity/ self-employed	703,745	296,939	194,495	0	66,811	121,953	15,203	1,399,147
Rents/Moneylending	8,080,824	4,201,587	0	213,796	60,872	178,000	221,992	12,957,171
Salaried person/s	1,607,271	703,745	0	0	1,485	168,335	8,938	2,489,774
Remittances/Pensions	1,248,896	552,307	0	102,444	0	60,947	6,627	1,971,220
All households	66,219,693	21,212,443	1,398,306	4,688,434	1,797,752	1,967,534	1,259,183	98,543,343

Source: Survey data.

Table 3.3 *Asset holdings of households, by class, Kothapalle village, May 2006* (rupees)

Socio-economic class	Land and water bodies	Buildings	Animals	Means of production	Means of transport	Domestic durables	Other assets	All assets
Landlord/Big capitalist farmer	18,818,155	1,627,133	494,286	399,857	515,000	99,959	10,678	21,965,067
Capitalist farmer/ Rich peasant	25,366,930	6,263,123	386,848	578,604	383,368	352,889	215,920	33,547,683
Peasant: upper middle	4,956,478	2,206,801	265,292	164,172	22,603	127,491	68,429	7,811,266
Peasant: lower middle	1,981,429	943,789	309,706	167,078	11,698	90,909	7,475	3,512,085
Peasant: poor	936,453	491,722	293,447	123,525	6,741	93,883	70,844	2,016,615
Hired manual worker	8,537,523	9,318,925	707,842	220,720	72,529	679,853	45,377	19,582,769
Artisan work and work at traditional caste calling	82,482	396,550	2,379	47,586	2,379	25,776	952	558,104
Business activity/ self-employed	2,467,875	1,838,009	34,103	2,229	644,093	291,975	47,947	5,326,231
Rents/Moneylending	95,172	475,860	0	79,310	0	59,958	119	710,419
Salaried person/s	13,607,053	4,712,663	28,247	115,900	26,965	494,610	24,957	19,010,395
Remittances/Pensions	2,820,943	3,126,960	79,863	15,971	28,599	99,431	15,809	6,187,575
All households	79,670,494	31,401,534	2,602,013	1,914,951	1,713,977	2,416,734	508,506	120,228,210

Source: Survey data.

Table 3.4 *Average values of assets in different categories, by class, Ananthavaram village, May 2006* (rupees)

Socio-economic class	Land and water bodies	Buildings	Animals	Means of production	Means of transport	Domestic durables	Other assets	All assets
Landlord/Big capitalist farmer	4,167,336	850,273	9,818	31,864	13,405	82,074	6,809	5,161,579
Capitalist farmer/ Rich peasant	2,130,531	366,323	47,017	25,904	12,358	53,935	7,775	2,643,843
Peasant: upper middle	1,637,276	216,333	44,081	16,962	7,014	28,044	3,262	1,952,972
Peasant: lower middle	164,423	49,735	10,255	791	1,685	8,617	1,244	236,800
Peasant: poor	75,081	31,002	4,976	2,642	950	5,196	646	120,493
Hired manual worker	15,315	18,268	2,109	727	342	2,899	213	39,872
Artisan work and work at traditional caste calling	9,156	10,915	140	3,370	3,025	5,406	118	32,130
Business activity/ self-employed	257,070	279,474	42,850	35,320	5,956	15,739	5,121	641,530
Rents/Moneylending	590,852	134,877	4,119	4,299	149,484	22,698	1,350	907,679
Salaried person/s	244,952	48,820	52	1,676	4,475	11,309	522	311,805
Remittances/Pensions	145,116	60,474	2,149	7,500	7,299	9,832	169	232,539
Unclassified households	15,000	45,000	1,000	0	550	9,615	0	71,165
All households	291,264	80,572	8,544	5,706	10,522	10,671	1,169	408,547

Source: Survey data.

Table 3.5 *Average values of assets in different categories, by class, Bukkacherla village, May 2006 (rupees)*

Socio-economic class	Land and water bodies	Building	Animals	Means of production	Means of transport	Domestic durables	Other assets	All assets
Landlord/Big capitalist farmer	2,460,241	460,237	3,880	69,999	69,510	22,568	10,996	3,097,431
Capitalist farmer/ Rich peasant	448,741	148,664	6,762	32,695	4,709	9,718	3,487	654,776
Peasant: upper middle	173,395	49,807	14,650	32,853	8,367	8,637	3,156	290,865
Peasant: lower middle	81,700	39,885	2,627	15,919	5,515	3,540	12,296	161,482
Peasant: poor	41,244	14,392	4,767	9,362	2,877	3,295	2,708	78,644
Hired manual worker	42,046	22,850	111	1,888	180	3,156	1,000	71,229
Artisan work and work at traditional caste calling	195,000	125,000	0	20,000	40,000	20,650	1,500	402,150
Business activity/ self-employed	59,250	25,000	16,375	0	5,625	10,268	1,280	117,798
Rents/Moneylending	680,344	353,750	0	18,000	5,125	14,986	18,690	1,090,895
Salaried person/s	90,213	39,500	0	0	83	9,448	502	139,747
Remittances/Pensions	60,084	26,571	0	4,929	0	2,932	319	94,835
All households	229,109	73,392	4,838	16,221	6,220	6,807	4,357	340,944

Source: Survey data.

Table 3.6 *Average values of assets in different categories, by class, Kothapalle village, May 2006 (rupees)*

Socio-economic class	Land and water bodies	Buildings	Animals	Means of production	Means of transport	Domestic durables	Other assets	All assets
Landlord/Big capitalist farmer	3,991,802	345,156	104,850	84,820	109,244	21,204	2,265	4,659,341
Capitalist farmer/ Rich peasant	772,741	190,791	11,784	17,626	11,678	10,750	6,577	1,021,948
Peasant: upper middle	208,317	92,750	11,150	6,900	950	5,358	2,876	328,301
Peasant: lower middle	71,381	34,600	11,157	6,019	421	3,275	269	126,523
Peasant: poor	47,230	24,800	14,800	6,230	340	4,735	3,573	101,708
Hired manual worker	52,511	57,317	4,354	1,358	446	4,182	279	120,446
Artisan work and work at traditional caste calling	20,800	100,000	600	12,000	600	6,500	240	140,740
Business activity/ self-employed	83,330	62,062	1,152	75	21,748	9,859	1,619	179,845
Rents/Moneylending	24,000	120,000	0	20,000	0	15,120	30	179,150
Salaried person/s	327,785	113,525	680	2,792	650	11,915	601	457,948
Remittances/Pensions	144,101	159,733	4,080	816	1,461	5,079	808	316,076
All households	215,244	84,837	7,030	5,174	4,631	6,529	1,374	324,818

Source: Survey data.

Table 3.7 *Assets in each category as a proportion of all assets, by class, Ananthavaram village, May 2006 (%)*

Socio-economic class	Land and water bodies	Buildings	Animals	Means of production	Means of transport	Domestic durables	Other assets	All assets
Landlord/Big capitalist farmer	80.7	16.5	0.2	0.6	0.3	1.6	0.1	100
Capitalist farmer/ Rich peasant	80.6	13.9	1.8	1	0.4	2	0.3	100
Peasant: upper middle	83.8	11.1	2.3	0.9	0.4	1.3	0.2	100
Peasant: lower middle	69.4	21	4.3	0.4	0.8	3.6	0.5	100
Peasant: poor	62.3	25.7	4.1	2.2	0.9	4.3	0.5	100
Hired manual worker	38.4	45.8	5.3	1.8	0.9	7.3	0.5	100
Artisan work and work at traditional caste calling	28.5	34	0.4	10.5	9.4	16.8	0.4	100
Business activity/ self-employed	40.1	43.6	6.7	5.5	0.9	2.4	0.8	100
Rents/Moneylending	65.1	14.9	0.5	0.5	16.5	2.4	0.1	100
Salaried person/s	78.6	15.7	0	0.5	1.4	3.6	0.2	100
Remittances/Pensions	62.4	26	0.9	3.2	3.2	4.2	0.1	100
Unclassified households	21.1	63.2	1.4	0	0.8	13.5	0	100
All households	71.3	19.7	2.1	1.4	2.6	2.6	0.3	100

Source: Survey data.

Table 3.8 *Assets in each category as a proportion of all assets, by class, Bukkacberla village, May 2006 (%)*

Socio-economic class	Land and water bodies	Buildings	Animals	Means of production	Means of transport	Domestic durables	Other assets	All assets
Landlord/Big capitalist farmer	79.4	14.9	0.1	2.3	2.2	0.7	0.4	100
Capitalist farmer/ Rich peasant	68.5	22.7	1	5	0.8	1.5	0.5	100
Peasant: upper middle	59.6	17.1	5	11.3	2.9	3	1.1	100
Peasant: lower middle	50.6	24.7	1.6	9.9	3.4	2.2	7.6	100
Peasant: poor	52.4	18.3	6.1	11.9	3.7	4.2	3.4	100
Hired manual worker	59	32.1	0.2	2.6	0.3	4.4	1.4	100
Artisan work and work at traditional caste calling	48.5	31.1	0	5	9.9	5.1	0.4	100
Business activity/self-employed	50.3	21.2	13.9	0	4.8	8.7	1.1	100
Rents/Moneylending	62.4	32.4	0	1.7	0.5	1.4	1.6	100
Salaried person/s	64.6	28.3	0	0	0.1	6.7	0.3	100
Remittances/Pensions	63.4	28	0	5.2	0	3.1	0.3	100
All households	67.2	21.5	1.4	4.8	1.8	2	1.3	100

Source: Survey data.

Table 3.9 *Assets in each category as a proportion of all assets, by class, Kothapalle village, May 2006 (%)*

Socio-economic class	Land and water bodies	Buildings	Animals	Means of production	Means of transport	Domestic durables	Other assets	All assets
Landlord/Big capitalist farmer	85.7	7.4	2.3	1.8	2.3	0.5	0	100
Capitalist farmer/ Rich peasant	75.6	18.7	1.2	1.7	1.1	1.1	0.6	100
Peasant: upper middle	63.5	28.3	3.4	2.1	0.3	1.6	0.8	100
Peasant: lower middle	56.4	26.9	8.8	4.8	0.3	2.6	0.2	100
Peasant: poor	46.4	24.4	14.6	6.1	0.3	4.7	3.5	100
Hired manual worker	43.6	47.6	3.6	1.1	0.4	3.5	0.2	100
Artisan work and work at traditional caste calling	14.8	71.1	0.4	8.5	0.4	4.6	0.2	100
Business activity/self-employed	46.3	34.5	0.6	0.1	12.1	5.5	0.9	100
Rents/Moneylending	13.4	67	0	11.2	0	8.4	0	100
Salaried person/s	71.6	24.8	0.1	0.6	0.2	2.6	0.1	100
Remittances/Pensions	45.6	50.5	1.3	0.3	0.5	1.5	0.3	100
All households	66.3	26.1	2.2	1.6	1.4	2	0.4	100

Source: Survey data.

Table 3.10 *Proportion of different types of assets owned, by class, Ananthavaram village, May 2006* (%)

Socio-economic class	Land and water bodies	Buildings	Animals	Means of production	Means of transport	Domestic durables	Other assets	All assets
Landlord/Big capitalist farmer	23.7	17.5	1.9	9.3	2.1	12.7	9.7	20.9
Capitalist farmer/ Rich peasant	13.2	8.2	10	8.2	2.1	9.1	12	11.8
Peasant: upper middle	20.7	9.9	19	11	2.5	9.7	10.3	17.6
Peasant: lower middle	7.9	8.5	16.7	1.9	2.2	11.3	14.8	8.1
Peasant: poor	5.1	7.5	11.5	9.2	1.8	9.6	10.9	5.8
Hired manual worker	1.3	5.5	6.1	3.1	0.8	6.7	4.5	2.4
Artisan work and work at traditional caste calling	0.1	0.5	0.1	2.4	1.2	2.1	0.4	0.3
Business activity/ self-employed	5.2	20.5	29.8	36.8	3.4	8.8	26	9.3
Rents/Moneylending	10.6	8.7	2.5	3.9	73.9	11.1	6	11.6
Salaried person/s	7.7	5.5	0.1	2.7	3.8	9.7	4.1	7
Remittances/Pensions	4.4	6.5	2.2	11.5	6.1	8.1	1.3	5
Unclassified households	0.1	0.7	0.1	0	0.1	1.1	0	0.2
All households	100	100	100	100	100	100	100	100

Source: Survey data.

Table 3.11 *Proportion of different types of assets owned, by class, Bukkacherla village, May 2006 (%)*

Socio-economic class	Land and water bodies	Buildings	Animals	Means of production	Means of transport	Domestic durables	Other assets	All assets
Landlord/Big capitalist farmer	36.8	21.5	2.7	14.8	38.3	11.4	8.7	31.2
Capitalist farmer/ Rich peasant	22.1	22.9	15.8	22.8	8.6	16.1	9	21.7
Peasant: upper middle	11.7	10.5	46.7	31.2	20.7	19.6	11.2	13.2
Peasant: lower middle	4.8	7.3	7.3	13.1	11.8	6.9	37.7	6.3
Peasant: poor	2.4	2.6	13.2	7.7	6.2	6.5	8.3	3.1
Hired manual worker	3.8	6.4	0.5	2.4	0.6	9.5	4.7	4.3
Artisan work and work at traditional caste calling	0.9	1.7	0	1.3	6.6	3.1	0.4	1.2
Business activity/ self-employed	1.1	1.4	13.8	0	3.7	6.2	1.2	1.4
Rents/Moneylending	12.1	19.8	0	4.5	3.4	9	17.6	13.1
Salaried person/s	2.4	3.3	0	0	0.1	8.6	0.7	2.5
Remittances/Pensions	1.9	2.6	0	2.2	0	3.1	0.5	2
All households	100	100	100	100	100	100	100	100

Source: Survey data.

Table 3.12 *Proportion of different types of assets owned, by class, Kothapalle village, May 2006 (%)*

Socio-economic class	Land and water bodies	Buildings	Animals	Means of production	Means of transport	Domestic durables	Other assets	All assets
Landlord/Big capitalist farmer	23.6	5.2	19	20.9	30	4.1	2.1	18.3
Capitalist farmer/ Rich peasant	31.8	19.9	14.9	30.2	22.4	14.6	42.5	27.9
Peasant: upper middle	6.3	7	10.2	8.6	1.3	5.3	13.5	6.5
Peasant: lower middle	2.5	3	11.9	8.7	0.7	3.8	1.5	2.9
Peasant: poor	1.2	1.6	11.3	6.5	0.4	3.9	13.9	1.7
Hired manual worker	10.7	29.6	27.2	11.5	4.2	28.1	8.9	16.3
Artisan work and work at traditional caste calling	0.1	1.3	0.1	2.5	0.1	1.1	0.2	0.5
Business activity/ self-employed	3.1	5.9	1.2	0.1	37.6	12.1	9.4	4.4
Rents/Moneylending	0.1	1.5	0	4.1	0	2.5	0	0.6
Salaried person/s	17.1	15	1.1	6.1	1.6	20.4	4.9	15.8
Remittances/Pensions	3.5	10	3.1	0.8	1.7	4.1	3.1	5.1
All households	100	100	100	100	100	100	100	100

Source: Survey data.

Table 3.13 *Asset holdings of households, by social group, Ananthavaram village, December 2005 (rupees)*

Social group	Land and water bodies	Buildings	Animals	Means of production	Means of transport	Domestic durables	Other assets	All assets
Dalit households	7,534,885	7,381,750	1,271,912	233,020	457,270	1,320,735	101,913	18,301,485
Adivasi households	258,100	450,100	46,680	1,500	7,300	90,165	1,693	855,538
Muslim households	158,800	381,400	33,000	60,000	117,050	90,670	9,835	850,755
BC households	20,246,220	6,922,250	631,290	423,706	439,410	1,146,545	132,656	29,942,077
Other Caste households	193,060,812	40,366,100	2,419,950	3,453,280	2,282,920	4,980,361	594,224	247,157,647
All households	221,258,817	55,501,600	4,402,832	4,171,506	3,303,950	7,628,476	840,321	297,107,502

Source: Survey data.

Table 3.14 *Asset holdings of households, by social group, Bukkacherla village, December 2005 (rupees)*

Social group	Land and water bodies	Buildings	Animals	Means of production	Means of transport	Domestic durables	Other assets	All assets
Dalit households	1,857,490	1,366,000	11,650	142,250	69,130	169,020	176,511	3,792,051
Muslim households	324,700	455,500	150	24,700	110,800	93,450	4,465	1,013,765
BC households	7,912,885	3,896,500	584,340	1,394,250	458,750	505,095	214,627	14,966,447
Other Caste households	44,469,498	12,509,930	1,526,900	4,655,650	1,426,300	1,185,203	697,745	66,471,226
All households	54,564,573	18,227,930	2,123,040	6,216,850	2,064,980	1,952,768	1,093,348	86,243,489

Source: Survey data.

Table 3.15 *Asset holdings of households, by social group, Kothapalle village, December 2005 (rupees)*

Social group	Land and water bodies	Buildings	Animals	Means of production	Means of transport	Domestic durables	Other assets	All assets
Dalit households	6,723,630	4,420,200	505,520	223,880	208,820	510,175	88,978	12,681,203
Adivasi households	95,000	138,300	25,630	5,200	14,850	17,475	1,169	298,124
Muslim households	591,000	180,300	0	5,400	7,200	33,195	993	817,788
BC households	14,570,008	10,579,467	667,520	1,105,588	246,440	751,542	139,781	28,060,346
Other Caste households	51,171,650	12,985,000	1,234,900	1,701,350	1,064,540	1,052,110	264,308	69,473,858
All households	73,151,288	28,303,467	2,433,570	3,041,418	1,541,850	2,364,497	495,229	111,331,319

Source: Survey data.

Table 3.16 *Average values of assets in different categories, by social group, Ananthavaram village, December 2005 (rupees)*

Social group	Land and water bodies	Buildings	Animals	Means of production	Means of transport	Domestic durables	Other assets	All assets
Dalit households	26,625	26,064	4,494	823	1,616	4,667	360	64,670
Adivasi households	5,866	10,230	1,061	34	166	2,049	38	19,444
Muslim households	8,822	21,189	1,833	3,333	6,503	5,037	546	47,264
BC households	154,551	52,842	4,819	3,234	3,354	8,752	1,013	228,565
Other Caste households	1,016,110	212,453	12,737	18,175	12,015	26,212	3,127	1,300,830
All households	332,220	83,236	6,611	6,264	4,961	11,454	1,262	446,107

Source: Survey data.

Table 3.17 *Average values of assets in different categories, by social group, Bukkacherla village, December 2005* (rupees)

Social group	Land and water bodies	Buildings	Animals	Means of production	Means of transport	Domestic durables	Other assets	All assets
Dalit households	32,026	23,552	201	2,453	1,192	2,914	3,043	65,380
Muslim households	40,588	56,938	19	3,088	13,850	11,681	558	126,721
BC households	81,576	40,170	6,024	14,374	4,729	5,207	2,213	154,293
Other Caste households	347,418	97,734	11,929	36,372	11,143	9,259	5,451	519,306
All households	187,507	62,639	7,296	21,364	7,096	6,711	3,757	296,369

Source: Survey data.

Table 3.18 *Average values of assets in different categories, by social group, Kothapalle village, December 2005* (rupees)

Social group	Land and water bodies	Buildings	Animals	Means of production	Means of transport	Domestic durables	Other assets	All assets
Dalit households	56,980	37,459	4,284	1,897	1,770	4,324	754	107,468
Adivasi households	8,636	12,618	2,330	473	1,350	1,589	106	27,102
Muslim households	118,200	36,000	0	1,080	1,440	6,639	199	163,558
BC households	97,133	70,530	4,450	7,371	1,643	5,010	932	187,069
Other Caste households	588,180	149,253	14,194	19,556	12,236	12,093	3,038	798,550
All households	197,173	76,290	6,559	8,198	4,156	6,373	1,335	300,084

Source: Survey data.

Table 3.19 *Assets in each category as a proportion of all assets, by social group, Ananthavaram village, December 2005 (%)*

Social group	Land and water bodies	Buildings	Animals	Means of production	Means of transport	Domestic durables	Other assets	All assets
Dalit households	41.2	40.3	6.9	1.3	2.5	7.2	0.6	100
Adivasi households	30.2	52.6	5.5	0.2	0.9	10.4	0.2	100
Muslim households	18.7	44.8	3.9	7.1	13.8	10.6	1.1	100
BC households	67.6	23.1	2.1	1.4	1.6	3.8	0.4	100
Other Caste households	78.1	16.3	1.1	1.4	0.9	2	0.2	100
All households	74.5	18.7	1.5	1.4	1.1	2.5	0.3	100

Source: Survey data.

Table 3.20 *Assets in each category as a proportion of all assets, by social group, Bukkacherla village, December 2005 (%)*

Social group	Land and water bodies	Buildings	Animals	Means of production	Means of transport	Domestic durables	Other assets	All assets
Dalit households	49.0	36.0	0.3	3.8	1.8	4.5	4.6	100
Muslim households	32.1	44.9	0.0	2.5	10.9	9.2	0.4	100
BC households	52.9	26	3.9	9.3	3.1	3.4	1.4	100
Other Caste households	66.9	18.8	2.3	7.1	2.1	1.8	1.0	100
All households	63.3	21.1	2.5	7.2	2.3	2.3	1.3	100

Source: Survey data.

Table 3.21 *Assets in each category as a proportion of all assets, by social group, Kothapalle village, December 2005 (%)*

Social group	Land and water bodies	Buildings	Animals	Means of production	Means of transport	Domestic durables	Other assets	All assets
Dalit households	53.0	34.9	4.0	1.8	1.6	4.0	0.7	100
Adivasi households	31.9	46.6	8.6	1.7	5.0	5.9	0.3	100
Muslim households	72.3	22.0	0	0.7	0.8	4.1	0.1	100
BC households	51.9	37.7	2.4	3.9	0.9	2.7	0.5	100
Other Caste households	73.7	18.7	1.8	2.4	1.5	1.5	0.4	100
All households	65.7	25.4	2.2	2.7	1.4	2.2	0.4	100

Source: Survey data.

Table 3.22 *Proportion of different types of assets owned, by social group, Ananthavaram village, December 2005 (%)*

Social group	Land and water bodies	Buildings	Animals	Means of production	Means of transport	Domestic durables	Other assets	All assets
Dalit households	3.3	13.3	28.9	5.6	13.8	17.3	12.1	6.1
Adivasi households	0.1	0.8	1.1	0	0.2	1.2	0.2	0.3
Muslim households	0.1	0.7	0.7	1.4	3.5	1.2	1.2	0.3
BC households	9.2	12.5	14.3	10.2	13.3	15	15.8	10.1
Other Caste households	87.3	72.7	55	82.8	69.2	65.3	70.7	83.2
All households	100	100	100	100	100	100	100	100

Source: Survey data.

Table 3.23 *Proportion of different types of assets owned, by social group, Bukkacherla village, December 2005* (%)

Social group	Land and water bodies	Buildings	Animals	Means of production	Means of transport	Domestic durables	Other assets	All assets
Dalit households	3.4	7.5	0.5	2.3	3.3	8.7	16.1	4.4
Muslim households	0.6	2.5	0.0	0.4	5.4	4.8	0.4	1.2
BC households	14.5	21.4	27.5	22.4	22.2	25.9	19.6	17.4
Other Caste households	81.5	68.6	71.9	74.9	69.1	60.7	63.8	77.1
All households	100	100	100	100	100	100	100	100

Source: Survey data.

Table 3.24 *Proportion of different types of assets owned, by social group, Kothapalle village, December 2005* (%)

Social group	Land and water bodies	Buildings	Animals	Means of production	Means of transport	Domestic durables	Other assets	All assets
Dalit households	9.2	15.6	20.8	7.4	13.5	21.6	18.0	11.4
Adivasi households	0.1	0.5	1.1	0.2	1.0	0.7	0.2	0.3
Muslim households	0.8	0.6	0.0	0.2	0.5	1.4	0.2	0.7
BC households	19.9	37.4	27.4	36.4	16.0	31.8	28.2	25.2
Other Caste households	70.0	45.9	50.7	55.9	69.0	44.5	53.4	62.4
All households	100	100	100	100	100	100	100	100

Source: Survey data.

Table 3.25 *Access indices for different categories of assets, by class, Ananthavaram village, May 2006*

Socio-economic class	Land and water bodies	Buildings	Animals	Means of production	Means of transport	Domestic durables	Other assets	All assets
Landlord/Big capitalist farmer	14.31	10.54	1.15	5.58	1.27	7.69	5.82	12.63
Capitalist farmer/Rich peasant	7.31	4.54	5.50	4.54	1.17	5.05	6.65	6.47
Peasant: upper middle	5.62	2.68	5.16	2.97	0.67	2.63	2.79	4.78
Peasant: lower middle	0.56	0.62	1.20	0.14	0.16	0.81	1.06	0.58
Peasant: poor	0.26	0.38	0.58	0.46	0.09	0.49	0.55	0.29
Hired manual worker	0.05	0.23	0.25	0.13	0.03	0.27	0.18	0.10
Artisan work and work at traditional caste calling	0.03	0.14	0.02	0.59	0.29	0.51	0.10	0.08
Business activity/self-employed	0.88	3.46	5.02	6.19	0.57	1.47	4.38	1.57
Rents/Moneylending	2.03	1.67	0.48	0.75	14.21	2.13	1.15	2.22
Salaried person/s	0.84	0.61	0.01	0.29	0.43	1.06	0.45	0.76
Remittances/Pensions	0.50	0.75	0.25	1.31	0.69	0.92	0.14	0.57

Note: (i) Access index for a socio-economic class is defined as share of the class in total assets for a particular category divided by share of the class in total number of households.

(ii) Access index values less than 1 represent disproportionately poor access to the asset while access index values more than 1 represent disproportionately favourable access to the asset for a social group.

Source: Survey data.

Table 3.26 *Access indices for different categories of assets, by class, Bukkacherla village, May 2006*

Socio-economic class	Land and water bodies	Buildings	Animals	Means of production	Means of transport	Domestic durables	Other assets	All assets
Landlord/Big capitalist farmer	10.74	6.27	0.80	4.32	11.18	3.32	2.52	9.08
Capitalist farmer/Rich peasant	1.96	2.03	1.40	2.02	0.76	1.43	0.80	1.92
Peasant: upper middle	0.76	0.68	3.03	2.03	1.35	1.27	0.72	0.85
Peasant: lower middle	0.36	0.54	0.54	0.98	0.89	0.52	2.82	0.47
Peasant: poor	0.18	0.20	0.99	0.58	0.46	0.48	0.62	0.23
Hired manual worker	0.18	0.31	0.02	0.12	0.03	0.46	0.23	0.21
Artisan work and work at traditional caste calling	0.85	1.70	0.00	1.23	6.43	3.03	0.34	1.18
Business activity/self-employed	0.26	0.34	3.38	0.00	0.90	1.51	0.29	0.35
Rents/Moneylending	2.97	4.82	0.00	1.11	0.82	2.20	4.29	3.20
Salaried person/s	0.39	0.54	0.00	0.00	0.01	1.39	0.12	0.41
Remittances/Pensions	0.26	0.36	0.00	0.30	0.00	0.43	0.07	0.28

Note: (i) Access index for a socio-economic class is defined as share of the class in total assets for a particular category divided by share of the class in total number of households.

(ii) Access index values less than 1 represent disproportionately poor access to the asset while access index values more than 1 represent disproportionately favourable access to the asset for a social group.

Source: Survey data.

Table 3.27 Access indices for different categories of assets, by class, Kothapalle village, May 2006

Socio-economic class	Land and water bodies	Buildings	Animals	Means of production	Means of transport	Domestic durables	Other assets	All assets
Landlord/Big capitalist farmer	18.55	4.07	14.92	16.39	23.59	3.25	1.65	14.34
Capitalist farmer/Rich peasant	3.59	2.25	1.68	3.41	2.52	1.65	4.79	3.15
Peasant: upper middle	0.97	1.09	1.59	1.33	0.21	0.82	2.09	1.01
Peasant: lower middle	0.33	0.40	1.59	1.16	0.09	0.50	0.20	0.39
Peasant: poor	0.22	0.29	2.11	1.20	0.07	0.73	2.60	0.31
Hired manual worker	0.24	0.68	0.62	0.26	0.10	0.64	0.20	0.37
Artisan work and work at traditional caste calling	0.10	1.18	0.09	2.32	0.13	1.00	0.17	0.43
Business activity/self-employed	0.39	0.73	0.16	0.01	4.70	1.51	1.18	0.55
Rents/Moneylending	0.11	1.41	0.00	3.87	0.00	2.32	0.02	0.55
Salaried person/s	1.52	1.34	0.10	0.54	0.14	1.82	0.44	1.41
Remittances/Pensions	0.67	1.88	0.58	0.16	0.32	0.78	0.59	0.97

Note: (i) Access index for a socio-economic class is defined as share of the class in total assets for a particular category divided by share of the class in total number of households.

(ii) Access index values less than 1 represent disproportionately poor access to the asset while access index values more than 1 represent disproportionately favourable access to the asset for a social group.

Source: Survey data.

Table 3.28 *Access indices for different categories of assets, by social group, Ananthavaram village, December 2005*

Social group	Land and water bodies	Houses and other buildings	Animals	Other means of production	Means of transport	Other domestic durable goods	Other assets	All assets
Dalit households	0.08	0.31	0.68	0.13	0.33	0.41	0.29	0.14
Adivasi households	0.02	0.12	0.16	0.01	0.03	0.18	0.03	0.04
Muslim households	0.03	0.25	0.28	0.53	1.31	0.44	0.43	0.11
BC households	0.46	0.63	0.73	0.52	0.68	0.76	0.8	0.51
Other Caste households	3.05	2.55	1.93	2.9	2.43	2.28	2.48	2.91

Note: (i) Access index for a social group is defined as share of the social group in total assets for a particular category divided by share of the social group in total number of households.

(ii) Access index values less than 1 represent disproportionately poor access to the asset while access index values more than 1 represent disproportionately favourable access to the asset for a social group.

Source: Survey data.

Table 3.29 *Access indices for different categories of assets, by social group, Bukkacherla village, December 2005*

Social group	Land and water bodies	Houses and other buildings	Animals	Other means of production	Means of transport	Other domestic durable goods	Other assets	All assets
Dalit households	0.17	0.38	0.03	0.11	0.17	0.43	0.81	0.22
Muslim households	0.22	0.91	0	0.14	1.95	1.74	0.15	0.43
BC households	0.44	0.64	0.83	0.67	0.67	0.78	0.59	0.52
Other Caste households	1.85	1.56	1.64	1.7	1.57	1.38	1.45	1.75

Note: (i) Access index for a social group is defined as share of the social group in total assets for a particular category divided by share of the social group in total number of households.

(ii) Access index values less than 1 represent disproportionately poor access to the asset while access index values more than 1 represent disproportionately favourable access to the asset for a social group.

Source: Survey data.

Table 3.30 *Access indices for different categories of assets, by social group, Kothapalle village, December 2005*

Social group	Land and water bodies	Houses and other buildings	Animals	Other means of production	Means of transport	Other domestic durable goods	Other assets	All assets
Dalit households	0.29	0.49	0.65	0.23	0.42	0.67	0.57	0.36
Adivasi households	0.04	0.17	0.36	0.06	0.32	0.24	0.08	0.09
Muslim households	0.6	0.47	0	0.13	0.34	1.02	0.15	0.55
BC households	0.49	0.93	0.68	0.9	0.39	0.77	0.7	0.62
Other Caste households	2.99	1.96	2.17	2.39	2.91	1.86	2.28	2.67

Note: (i) Access index for a social group is defined as share of the social group in total assets for a particular category divided by share of the social group in total number of households.
(ii) Access index values less than 1 represent disproportionately poor access to the asset while access index values more than 1 represent disproportionately favourable access to the asset for a social group.
Source: Survey data.

Table 3.31 *Distribution of household wealth across deciles of households, by study villages, December 2005* (%)

Decile of households	Ananthavaram	Bukkacherla	Kothapalle
Decile 1	0.1	0.4	0.2
Decile 2	0.3	1	0.9
Decile 3	0.4	2	2
Decile 4	0.7	3	3
Decile 5	1	4	3
Decile 6	2	5	4
Decile 7	3	7	6
Decile 8	5	10	8
Decile 9	13	13	14
Decile 10	75	54	58
All households	100	100	100
Decile 10/Decile1 (ratio)	877	146	314
Decile 10/Decile 9 (ratio)	6	4	4

Source: Survey data.

Table 3.32 *Index of access to assets, by class, study villages, May 2006*

Socio-economic class	Ananthavaram	Bukkacherla	Kothapalle
Landlord/Big capitalist farmer	12.63	9.08	14.34
Capitalist farmer/Rich peasant	6.47	1.92	3.15
Peasant: upper middle	4.78	0.85	1.01
Peasant: lower middle	0.58	0.47	0.39
Peasant: poor	0.29	0.23	0.31
Hired manual worker	0.10	0.21	0.37
Artisan work and work at traditional caste calling	0.08	1.18	0.43
Business activity/self-employed	1.57	0.35	0.55
Rents/Moneylending	2.22	3.20	0.55
Salaried person/s	0.76	0.41	1.41
Remittances/Pensions	0.57	0.28	0.97

Note: (i) Based on data for sample households.

(ii) Access index for a social group is defined as share of the social group in total assets divided by share of the social group in total number of households.

Source: Survey data.

Table 3.33 *Index of access to assets, by social group, study villages, December 2005*

Social group	Ananthavaram	Bukkacherla	Kothapalle
Dalit households	0.14	0.22	0.36
Adivasi households	0.04		0.09
Muslim households	0.11	0.43	0.55
BC households	0.51	0.52	0.62
Other Caste households	2.91	1.75	2.67

Note: Access index for a social group is defined as share of the social group in total assets divided by share of the social group in total number of households.
Source: Survey data.

Table 3.34 *Average size of ownership and operational holding, by class, study villages, May 2006* (acres)

Socio-economic class	Ananthavaram		Bukkacherla		Kothapalle	
	Owner-ship holding	Opera-tional holding	Owner-ship holding	Opera-tional holding	Owner-ship holding	Opera-tional holding
Landlord/Big capitalist farmer	16.3	10.9	51.8	31.8	19.8	14.1
Capitalist farmer/ Rich peasant	9.5	19.4	13.1	12.4	4.6	5.2
Peasant: upper middle	5.7	7.4	8.3	10.4	1.8	2.3
Peasant: lower middle	0.6	2.6	5	6.9	0.8	1.6
Peasant: poor	0.2	1.6	4.3	7.5	0.5	2.6
Hired manual worker	0	0.1	3.5	2.7	0.4	0.4
Non-agricultural classes	0.8	1.3	6.4	1.7	1.1	0.8
Unclassified households	0	1.3				
All households	1.1	1.9	7.9	6.9	1.3	1.5

Source: Survey data.

Table 3.35 *Extent of land leased in as a proportion of total land operated and the share of different classes in total land leased in, May 2006* (%)

Socio-economic class	Share in total extent of land leased			Area leased in as a proportion of total land operated		
	Anantha-varam	Bukka-cherla	Kotha-palle	Anantha-varam	Bukka-cherla	Kotha-palle
Landlord/Big capitalist farmer	1	9	0	4	9	0
Capitalist farmer/ Rich peasant	21	0	29	77	0	21
Peasant: upper middle	5	29	10	25	20	22
Peasant: lower middle	21	23	19	76	28	51
Peasant: poor	21	39	34	85	43	81
Hired manual worker	1	0	0	54	0	0
Non-agricultural classes	30	0	8	92	0	12
Unclassified households	1	–	–	100	–	–

Note: Various non-agricultural classes together account for 33 per cent of households in Ananthavaram, 23 per cent of households in Bukkacherla and 27 per cent of households in Kothapalle.

Source: Survey data.

Table 3.36 *Proportion of households that own different types of buildings and share of different types of buildings in total value of buildings, study villages, December 2005* (%)

Type of asset	Proportion of households that own different types of buildings			Share of different types of buildings in total value		
	Anantha-varam	Bukka-cherla	Kotha-palle	Anantha-varam	Bukka-cherla	Kotha-palle
Houses	83	84	85	93	93	97
Cattle-sheds	26	28	10	2	6	1
Shops and other commercial establishments	4	3	4	4	1	2
Other buildings	1	0.3	0.3	1	0	0
All	100	100	100	100	100	100

Note: Sum of proportion of households exceeds 100 because some households own more than one type of building.

Source: Survey data.

CHAPTER 5

Table 5.1 *Average income from different sources, in rupees and in percentage of total income, by class, Ananthavaram village, 2005–06*

Socio-economic class	Crop pro-duction	Rental income from agricul-tural land	Animal res-ources	Agri cultural labour earnings	Ear-nings from long term labour	Toddy tapping	Pri-mary sector	Non agricul-tural casual labour earnings
Landlord/Big capitalist farmer	51,613 (32)	52,318 (33)	20,778 (13)	0 (0)	0 (0)	0 (0)	124,709 (78)	0 (0)
Capitalist farmer/ Rich peasant	551,854 (85)	33,068 (5)	44,209 (7)	0 (0)	0 (0)	0 (0)	629,131 (97)	0 (0)
Peasant: upper middle	59,235 (52)	1,633 (1)	48,266 (42)	951 (1)	0 (0)	0 (0)	110,085 (96)	0 (0)
Peasant: lower middle	6,273 (11)	100 (0)	36,619 (62)	6,643 (11)	2,005 (3)	0 (0)	51,640 (87)	3,166 (5)
Peasant: poor	−2,142 (−13)	60 (0)	7,624 (45)	6,725 (40)	0 (0)	0 (0)	12,267 (72)	2,976 (18)
Hired manual worker	94 (0)	51 (0)	1,275 (6)	12,560 (64)	584 (3)	0 (0)	14,565 (74)	2,605 (13)
Artisan work and work at traditional caste calling	227 (2)	0 (0)	−28 (0)	130 (1)	0 (0)	0 (0)	329 (3)	0 (0)
Business activity/ self-employed	1,200 (1)	0 (0)	100,031 (65)	0 (0)	0 (0)	0 (0)	101,231 (66)	2,348 (2)
Rents/Moneylending	574 (1)	21,537 (30)	9,539 (13)	0 (0)	0 (0)	0 (0)	31,650 (43)	201 (0)
Salaried person/s	1,498 (2)	4,459 (7)	1,621 (2)	1,858 (3)	0 (0)	0 (0)	9,436 (14)	0 (0)
Remittances/pensions	210 (0)	1,958 (5)	−1,184 (−3)	197 (0)	0 (0)	0 (0)	1,181 (3)	0 (0)
All households	14,506 (25)	3,264 (6)	16,331 (28)	5,583 (9)	424 (1)	0 (0)	40,107 (68)	1,822 (3)

Note: Figures in parentheses represent shares of different sources in per cent.
Source: Survey data.

Government salaried jobs	Private salaried jobs	Business and trade earnings	Rental income from machinery	Secondary and tertiary sector	Pensions scholarships and insurance claims	Remittances	Rental income from other assets	Other sources	Total income
3,164	0	11,091	0	14,255	0	19,273	873	0	159,109
(2)	(0)	(7)	(0)	(9)	(0)	(12)	(1)	(0)	(100)
0	0	406	424	831	832	4,161	0	13,784	648,740
(0)	(0)	(0)	(0)	(0)	(0)	(1)	(0)	(2)	(100)
0	0	2,105	0	2,105	265	0	0	1,633	114,087
(0)	(0)	(2)	(0)	(2)	(0)	(0)	(0)	(1)	(100)
823	1,841	439	0	6,269	0	632	4	832	59,377
(1)	(3)	(1)	(0)	(11)	(0)	(1)	(0)	(1)	(100)
0	1,350	141	0	4,468	77	0	0	174	16,985
(0)	(8)	(1)	(0)	(26)	(0)	(0)	(0)	(1)	(100)
0	1,404	834	0	4,843	123	142	0	35	19,707
(0)	(7)	(4)	(0)	(25)	(1)	(1)	(0)	(0)	(100)
0	0	180	0	180	0	0	0	10,603	11,393
(0)	(0)	(2)	(0)	(2)	(0)	(0)	(0)	(93)	(100)
0	0	38,989	11,071	52,408	255	0	0	0	153,894
(0)	(0)	(25)	(7)	(34)	(0)	(0)	(0)	(0)	(100)
1,853	0	12,125	0	14,180	2,320	0	0	24,644	72,793
(3)	(0)	(17)	(0)	(19)	(3)	(0)	(0)	(34)	(100)
31,714	17,610	1,119	0	50,442	4,282	1,617	157	1,852	67,786
(47)	(26)	(2)	(0)	(74)	(6)	(2)	(0)	(3)	(100)
0	0	886	0	886	17,242	23,406	0	0	42,715
(0)	(0)	(2)	(0)	(2)	(40)	(55)	(0)	(0)	(100)
3,169	2,483	3,697	665	11,837	2,110	2,718	29	2,360	59,173
(5)	(4)	(6)	(1)	(20)	(4)	(5)	(0)	(4)	(100)

Table 5.2 *Average income from different sources, in rupees and as percentage of total income, by class, Bukkacherla village, 2005–06*

Socio-economic class	Crop production	Rental income from agricultural land	Animal resources	Agricultural labour earnings	Earnings from long term labour	Toddy tapping	Primary sector	Non agricultural casual labour earnings
Landlord/Big capitalist farmer	12,820 (6)	26,708 (13)	10,718 (5)	0 (0)	0 (0)	0 (0)	50,246 (24)	0 (0)
Capitalist farmer/ Rich peasant	28,952 (55)	3,653 (7)	12,206 (23)	0 (0)	0 (0)	0 (0)	44,811 (85)	0 (0)
Peasant: upper middle	15,512 (40)	0 (0)	13,593 (35)	3,843 (10)	0 (0)	5,187 (13)	38,135 (99)	0 (0)
Peasant: lower middle	6,060 (25)	0 (0)	8,188 (34)	2,715 (11)	0 (0)	0 (0)	16,963 (70)	3,008 (12)
Peasant: poor	2,695 (15)	0 (0)	5,636 (30)	4,329 (23)	631 (3)	0 (0)	13,291 (72)	317 (2)
Hired manual worker	3,429 (15)	718 (3)	610 (3)	9,941 (43)	0 (0)	0 (0)	14,697 (63)	4,473 (19)
Artisan work and work at traditional caste calling	0 (0)	1,568 (2)	0 (0)	0 (0)	0 (0)	0 (0)	1,568 (2)	0 (0)
Business activity/ self-employed	0 (0)	1,640 (7)	8,831 (35)	0 (0)	0 (0)	0 (0)	10,471 (42)	0 (0)
Rents/Moneylending	–3,061 (–7)	30,785 (72)	0 (0)	240 (1)	0 (0)	0 (0)	27,963 (66)	0 (0)
Salaried person/s	–136 (0)	2,020 (6)	0 (0)	268 (1)	0 (0)	0 (0)	2,152 (6)	0 (0)
Remittances/pensions	947 (6)	1,823 (12)	0 (0)	0 (0)	0 (0)	0 (0)	2,770 (18)	48 (0)
All households	7,839 (21)	3,067 (8)	6,113 (17)	3,565 (10)	83 (0)	791 (2)	21,459 (59)	1,353 (4)

Note: Figures in parentheses represent shares of different sources in per cent.
Source: Survey data.

Government salaried jobs	Private salaried jobs	Business and trade earnings	Rental income from machinery	Secondary and tertiary sector	Pensions scholarships and insurance claims	Remittances	Rental income from other assets	Other sources	Total income
90,634	0	28,446	13,275	132,354	0	0	28,446	0	211,046
(43)	(0)	(13)	(6)	(63)	(0)	(0)	(13)	(0)	(100)
8,182	0	0	0	8,182	0	0	0	0	52,993
(15)	(0)	(0)	(0)	(15)	(0)	(0)	(0)	(0)	(100)
0	0	0	113	113	173	0	0	0	38,422
(0)	(0)	(0)	(0)	(0)	(0)	(0)	(0)	(0)	(100)
0	0	2,462	42	5,512	1,673	0	0	0	24,162
(0)	(0)	(10)	(0)	(23)	(7)	(0)	(0)	(0)	(100)
0	0	4,762	154	5,232	0	0	0	0	18,523
(0)	(0)	(26)	(1)	(28)	(0)	(0)	(0)	(0)	(100)
1,800	1,080	0	0	7,353	200	900	0	90	23,241
(8)	(5)	(0)	(0)	(32)	(1)	(4)	(0)	(0)	(100)
0	0	72,000	0	72,000	0	0	0	30,000	103,568
(0)	(0)	(70)	(0)	(70)	(0)	(0)	(0)	(29)	(100)
0	0	14,160	0	14,160	375	0	0	0	25,006
(0)	(0)	(57)	(0)	(57)	(1)	(0)	(0)	(0)	(100)
0	0	1,667	0	1,667	0	75	0	12,900	42,605
(0)	(0)	(4)	(0)	(4)	(0)	(0)	(0)	(30)	(100)
30,377	2,400	1,200	0	33,977	0	0	0	0	36,129
(84)	(7)	(3)	(0)	(94)	(0)	(0)	(0)	(0)	(100)
0	0	0	0	48	488	12,000	0	0	15,305
(0)	(0)	(0)	(0)	(0)	(3)	(78)	(0)	(0)	(100)
6,210	366	3,369	494	11,792	343	1,162	965	848	36,572
(17)	(1)	(9)	(1)	(32)	(1)	(3)	(3)	(2)	(100)

Table 5.3 *Average income from different sources, in rupees and as percentage of total income, by class, Kothapalle village, 2005–06*

Socio-economic class	Crop produc-tion	Rental income from agricul-tural land	Animal res-ources	Agricul-tural labour earnings	Earn-ings from long term labour	Toddy tapp-ing	Pri-mary sector	Non agricul-tural casual labour earnings
Landlord/Big capitalist farmer	11,451 (2)	50,260 (9)	50,749 (9)	0 (0)	0 (0)	0 (0)	112,459 (20)	0 (0)
Capitalist farmer/ Rich peasant	13,663 (46)	620 (2)	11,084 (37)	272 (1)	0 (0)	695 (2)	26,334 (88)	18 (0)
Peasant: upper middle	2,986 (13)	0 (0)	9,258 (40)	1,213 (5)	0 (0)	2,681 (11)	16,138 (69)	3,000 (13)
Peasant: lower middle	−349 (−2)	0 (0)	13,939 (72)	1,924 (10)	0 (0)	2,237 (12)	17,751 (92)	57 (0)
Peasant: poor	10,557 (26)	0 (0)	20,807 (51)	1,185 (3)	0 (0)	0 (0)	32,549 (79)	3,776 (9)
Hired manual worker	291 (1)	0 (0)	2,878 (13)	4,632 (21)	1,032 (5)	4,147 (19)	12,981 (58)	3,482 (16)
Artisan work and work at traditional caste calling	0 (0)	0 (0)	9,210 (23)	7,335 (18)	0 (0)	0 (0)	16,545 (41)	0 (0)
Business activity/ self-employed	395 (1)	67 (0)	737 (3)	631 (2)	0 (0)	0 (0)	1,830 (7)	0 (0)
Rents/Moneylending	0 (0)	0 (0)	0 (0)	0 (0)	0 (0)	0 (0)	0 (0)	0 (0)
Salaried person/s	1,720 (3)	1,702 (3)	732 (1)	0 (0)	0 (0)	0 (0)	4,154 (8)	0 (0)
Remittances/pensions	−308 (−3)	1,332 (13)	3,075 (30)	0 (0)	0 (0)	0 (0)	4,099 (41)	0 (0)
All households	3,019 (9)	557 (2)	6,051 (18)	2,474 (7)	453 (1)	2,223 (7)	14,777 (43)	1,931 (6)

Note: Figures in parentheses represent shares of different sources in per cent.
Source: Survey data

Government salaried jobs	Private salaried jobs	Business and trade earnings	Rental income from machinery	Secondary and tertiary sector	Pensions scholarships and insurance claims	Remittances	Rental income from other assets	Other sources	Total income
0	0	424,250	29,423	453,673	0	0	0	0	566,132
(0)	(0)	(75)	(5)	(80)	(0)	(0)	(0)	(0)	(100)
0	0	3,172	0	3,190	0	339	0	0	29,864
(0)	(0)	(11)	(0)	(11)	(0)	(1)	(0)	(0)	(100)
0	4,278	0	0	7,278	0	0	0	0	23,416
(0)	(18)	(0)	(0)	(31)	(0)	(0)	(0)	(0)	(100)
0	1,086	0	0	1,143	186	0	271	0	19,351
(0)	(6)	(0)	(0)	(6)	(1)	(0)	(1)	(0)	(100)
0	4,800	0	0	8,576	0	0	0	0	41,125
(0)	(12)	(0)	(0)	(21)	(0)	(0)	(0)	(0)	(100)
2,312	2,571	416	0	8,781	156	134	161	118	22,333
(10)	(12)	(2)	(0)	(39)	(1)	(1)	(1)	(1)	(100)
0	12,000	0	0	12,000	0	0	0	12,159	40,704
(0)	(29)	(0)	(0)	(29)	(0)	(0)	(0)	(30)	(100)
0	3,736	18,364	3,135	25,235	0	0	0	0	27,066
(0)	(14)	(68)	(12)	(93)	(0)	(0)	(0)	(0)	(100)
0	0	0	0	0	0	0	0	12,240	12,240
(0)	(0)	(0)	(0)	(0)	(0)	(0)	(0)	(100)	(100)
30,260	13,425	2,441	0	46,126	124	447	0	0	50,851
(60)	(26)	(5)	(0)	(91)	(0)	(1)	(0)	(0)	(100)
0	0	0	0	0	4,072	1,464	456	0	10,091
(0)	(0)	(0)	(0)	(0)	(40)	(15)	(5)	(0)	(100)
4,409	3,676	7,610	626	18,252	312	217	115	313	33,987
(13)	(11)	(22)	(2)	(54)	(1)	(1)	(0)	(1)	(100)

References

Bakshi, Aparajita (2008a), "Social Inequality in Land Ownership in India: A Study with Particular Reference to West Bengal", *Social Scientist,* 39, 9–10, Sept.–Oct., pp. 95–116.

Bakshi, Aparajita (2008b), "A Note on Household Income Surveys in India", paper presented at "Studying Village Economies in India: A Colloquium on Methodology", Chalsa, http://www.agrarianstudies.org/UserFiles/File/S5_Bakshi_A_Note_on_Rural_Household_Incomes_in_India.pdf (accessed on 29 Dec. 2009).

Bhalla, G.S. and Gurmail Singh (2001), *Indian Agriculture: Four Decades of Development,* Sage Publications, New Delhi.

Centre for Economic and Social Studies (CESS) (2008), *Human Development Report 2007: Andhra Pradesh,* for the Government of Andhra Pradesh, Hyderabad.

Chean, Chau-Nan, Tien-Wang Tsaur and Tong-Shieng Rhai (1982), "Gini Coefficient and Negative Income", *Oxford Economic Papers,* 34, 3, pp. 473–78.

Directorate of Economics and Statistics (DES) (2007), *Andhra Pradesh Economy in Brief: 2008,* Government of Andhra Pradesh, Hyderabad.

Duvvury, Nata (1989), "Women in Agriculture: A Review of the Indian Literature", *Economic and Political Weekly,* 24, 43, 28 Oct., pp. WS96–WS112.

Government of Andhra Pradesh (GoAP) (2005), *Report of the Commission on Farmers' Welfare,* Chair: Jayati Ghosh, Hyderabad.

Government of India (GOI) (1996), *Cost of Cultivation of Principal Crops in India,* Directorate of Economics and Statistics, Ministry of Agriculture, New Delhi.

Government of India (GOI) (2007), *Public Distribution System and Other Sources of Household Consumption 2004–05,* 1, NSS 61st Round, July, Ministry of Statistics and Programme Implementation, National Sample Survey Organisation (NSSO).

Government of India (GOI) (2008), Directorate of Economics and Statistics, Department of Agriculture and Cooperation, Ministry of Agriculture, http://dacnet.nic.in/eands/At_Glance_2008/pcrops_new.html (accessed on 29 Dec. 2009).

Government of India (GOI) (2009), *Report of the Commission for Agricultural Costs and Prices: For the Crops Sown during 2008–09 Season,* Department of Agriculture and Cooperation, Ministry of Agriculture, New Delhi.

Government of India (GOI), "Prevailing Minimum Wages and Schedule of Rates (SOR) For Agricultural Labourers (Rs/day)", http://nrega.nic.in/wages.pdf (accessed on 29 Dec. 2009).

International Labour Office (ILO) (1961), "R115 Workers' Housing Recommendation 1961", http://www.ilo.org/ilolex/cgi-lex/convde.pl?R115 (accessed on 29 Dec. 2009).

Kubo, Kensuke (2005), "Cropping Pattern Changes in Andhra Pradesh during the 1990s: Implications for Micro-level Studies", in Ito Seiro (ed.), *Agricultural Production, Household Behavior, and Child Labor in Andhra Pradesh*, Joint Research Programme Series No. 135, Institute of Developing Economies, Chiba, Japan.

Narayana, D. (1988), "A Note on Reliability and Comparability of the Various Rounds of the AIRDIS and AIDIS", unpublished note, Centre For Development Studies, Thiruvananthapuram.

National Sample Survey Organisation (NSSO) (1998), "Note on Household Assets and Liabilities as on 30.06.91: NSS 48th Round (Jan–Dec 1992)", *Sarvekshana*, 22, 2, Oct.–Dec.

National Sample Survey Organisation (NSSO) (2005), *Household Indebtedness in India* (as on 30.06.2002), 59th Round (January to December 2003), Report no. 501.

Nirmala, K. Annie and M. Nalini (2008), "Changing Profiles of Unagatla Village", in G. Niranjan Rao and D. Narasimha Reddy (eds.), *Rural Transformation: Perspectives from Village Studies in Andhra Pradesh,* Daanish Books, Delhi, pp. 293–350.

Palma, Jose Gabriel (2006), "Globalizing Inequality", UN DESA Working Paper no. 35, September, http://secint24.un.org/esa/desa/papers/2006/wp35_2006.pdf (accessed on 29 December 2009).

Planning Commission (2009), "Expert Group on Methodology for Estimation of Poverty (Tendulkar Committee)", Planning Commission, New Delhi, http://planning commission.gov.in/reports/genrep/rep_pov.pdf (accessed on 29 December 2009).

Ramachandran, V.K. (1990), *Wage Labour and Unfreedom in Agriculture: An Indian Case Study,* Clarendon Press, Oxford.

Ramachandran, V.K., Madhura Swaminathan and Vikas Rawal (2002), "Agricultural Workers in Rural Tamil Nadu: A Field Report", in V. K. Ramachandran and M. Swaminathan (eds.), *Agrarian Studies: Essays on Agrarian Relations in Less-Developed Countries*, Tulika Books, New Delhi, pp. 445–72.

Rao, B. Sambasiva (2003), *Agriculture in India: Policy and Performance*, Serials Publications, Delhi.

Rao, C.H. Hanumantha, and S. Mahendra Dev (2003), *Andhra Pradesh Development: Economic Reforms and Challenges Ahead*, Centre for Economic and Social Studies, Hyderabad.

Rao, G. Niranjan and D. Narasimha Reddy (2008), *Rural Transformation: Perspectives from Village Studies in Andhra Pradesh*, Studies in Local-Level Development-6, Daanish Books, Delhi.

Rao, Y.V. Krishna, and S. Subrahmanyam (2002), *Development of Andhra Pradesh: 1956–2001: A Study of Regional Disparities*, N.R.R. Research Centre, Hyderabad.

Rawal, Vikas (2008), "Estimates of Rural Household Incomes in India: Selected Methodological Issues", paper presented at "Studying Village Economies in India: A

Colloquium on Methodology", Chalsa, http://www.agrarianstudies.org/UserFiles/Files/S5_Rawal_Estimation_of_Rural_Household_Incomes_in_India.pdf

Rawal, Vikas, Madhura Swaminathan and Niladri Sekhar Dhar (2008), "On Diversification of Rural Incomes: A View from Three Villages of Andhra Pradesh," *The Indian Journal of Labour Economics*, 51, 2, pp. 237–56.

Reddy, A. Ranga (2003), *The State of Rayalaseema,* Mittal Publications, New Delhi.

Reddy, M. Atchi (2008), "Changing Land and Tenancy Relations: A Study of Annareddy-palem in Nellore District, 1960–2000", in G. Niranjan Rao and D. Narasimha Reddy (eds.), *Rural Transformation: Perspectives from Village Studies in Andhra Pradesh*, Daanish Books, Delhi, pp. 403–36.

Revathi, E. (2008), "Woman's Work and Technology: Irrigation Induced Dynamics in Timmapur of Karimnagar District", in G. Niranjan Rao and D. Narasimha Reddy (eds.), *Rural Transformation: Perspectives from Village Studies in Andhra Pradesh*, Daanish Books, Delhi, pp. 153–90.

Sen, Abhijit, and M.S. Bhatia (2004), *State of Indian Farmers: A Millennium Study: Cost of Cultivation and Farm Income*, Volume 14, Academic Publishers, New Delhi.

Shah, Ghanshyam, Harsh Mander, Sukhadeo Thorat, Satish Deshpande and Amita Baviskar (2006), *Untouchability in Rural India*, Sage Publications, New Delhi.

Sharma, H.R. (1994), "Distribution of Landholdings in Rural India, 1953–54 to 1981–82: Implications for Land Reforms", *Economic and Political Weekly*, 29, 13, 26 March, pp. A12–A25.

Sundarayya, P. (1976), *The Land Question*, All India Kisan Sabha, New Delhi.

Sundarayya, P. (1977), "Class Differentiation of the Peasantry: Results of Rural Surveys in Andhra Pradesh" (Part I), *Social Scientist*, 5, 56, March, pp. 432–65, and (Part II), *Social Scientist*, 5, 57, April, pp. 45–60.

Sundarayya, P. (2006), *Telangana People's Struggle and Its Lessons*, Foundation Books, on behalf of Sundarayya Vignana Kendram, Hyderabad.

Surjit, V. (2008), "Farm Business Incomes in India: A Study of Two Rice Growing Villages of Thanjavur Region, Tamil Nadu", Thesis submitted to the University of Calcutta for the degree of Doctor of Philosophy (Science).

Swaminathan, Madhura and Vikas Rawal (2009), "Is India Really a Low Inequality Country? A Village View of Household Incomes", UNU–WIDER, Helsinki.

Thorat, Sukhadeo (2009), *Dalits in India: Search for a Common Destiny*, Sage Publications, New Delhi.

Unni, Jeemol (1989), "Changes in Women's Employment in Rural Areas, 1961–83," *Economic and Political Weekly*, 24, 17, 29 April, pp. WS23–WS31.

Vaidyanathan, A. (2006), "Agrarian Crisis: Nature, Causes and Remedies," *The Hindu*, 8 Nov.

World Bank (1996), "India's Public Distribution System: A National and International Perspective", Poverty and Social Policy Department, Nov.; reprinted as Radhakrishna, R. and K. Subbarao (1997), World Bank Discussion Paper No. 380, Washington D.C.